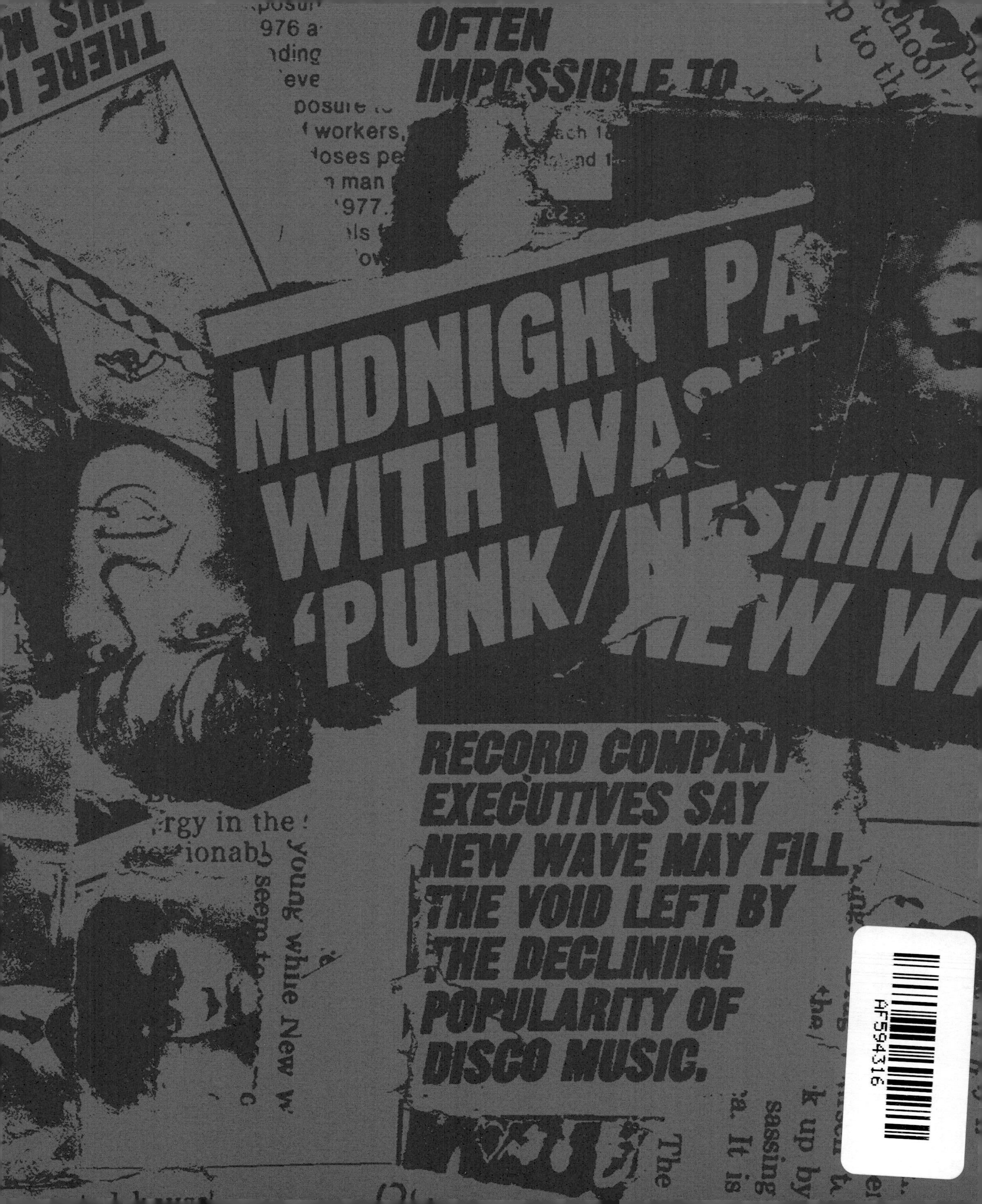

OFTEN IMPOSSIBLE TO
RECORD COMPANY EXECUTIVES SAY NEW WAVE MAY FILL THE VOID LEFT BY THE DECLINING POPULARITY OF DISCO MUSIC.
young white New w

Published by Akashic Books

ISBN-13: 978-1-61775-167-7
Library of Congress Control Number: 2012954413
Second printing
Printed in China

Akashic Books | Instagram: @AkashicBooks | Twitter: @AkashicBooks
Facebook: AkashicBooks | Email: info@akashicbooks.com | Website: www.akashicbooks.com

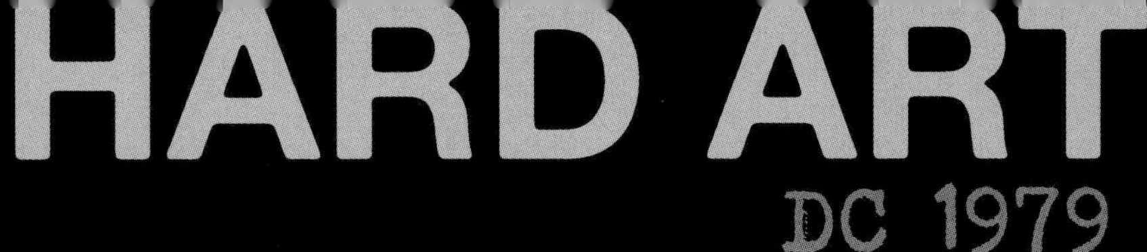

HARD ART DC 1979

PHOTOGRAPHY: LUCIAN PERKINS

Narrative: Alec MacKaye

Essay: Henry Rollins

EDITOR:
Lely Constantinople

PROJECT MANAGER:
Jayme McLellan

Design by Nick Pimentel and Lisa Hill

03

The Washington Post

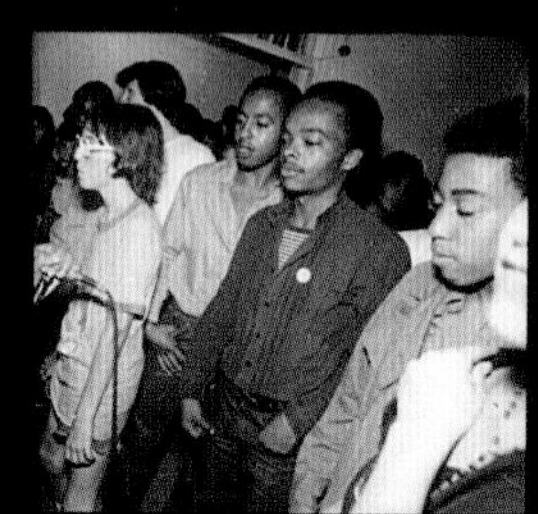
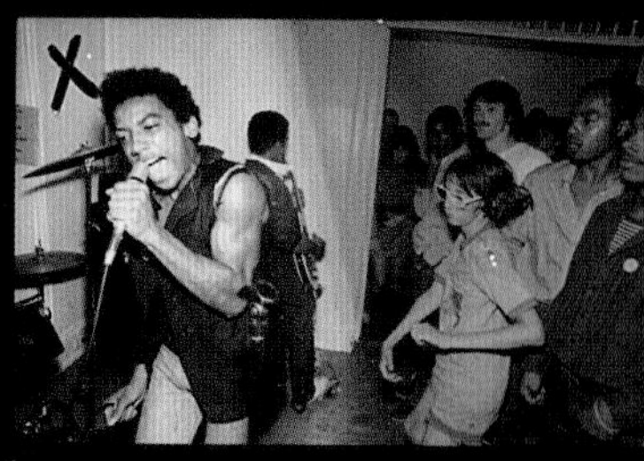
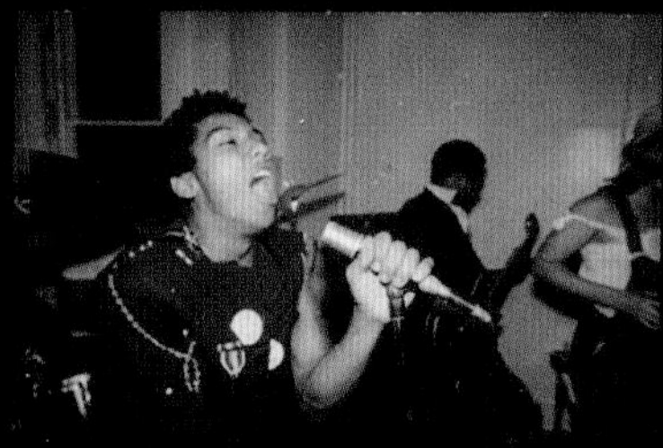
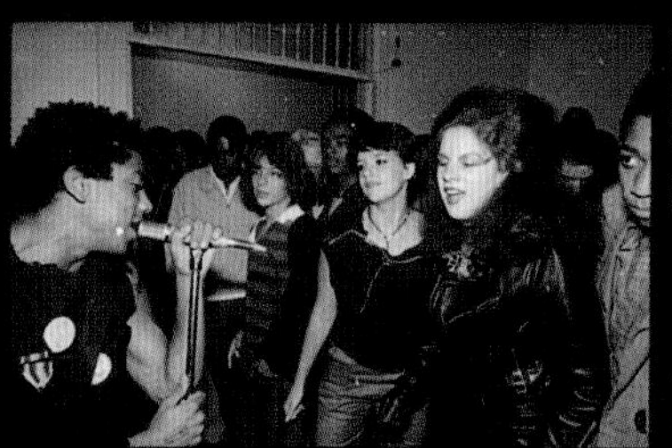
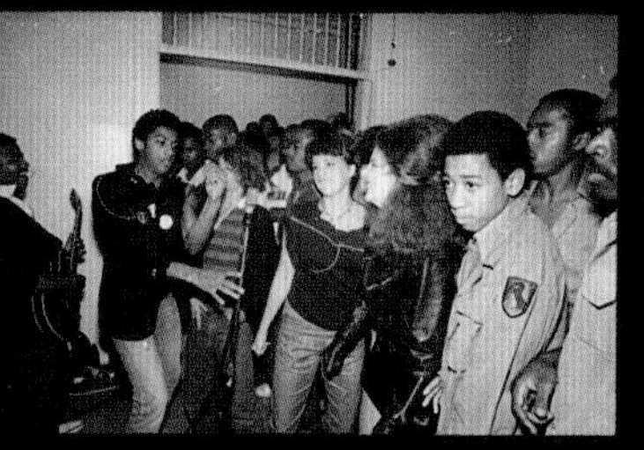
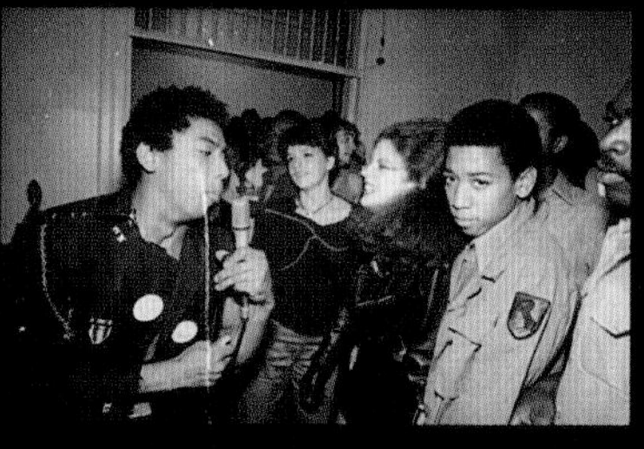
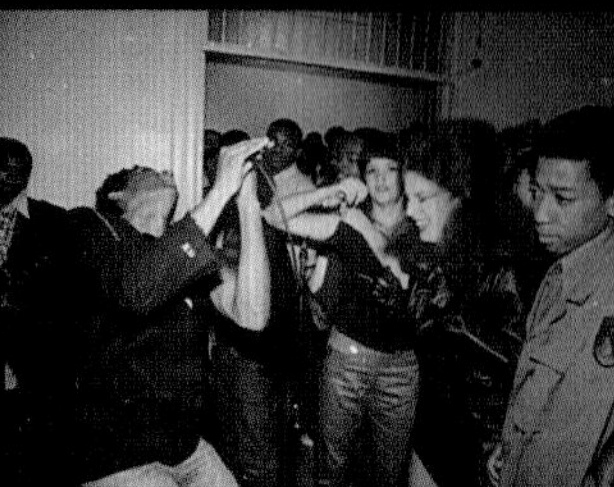
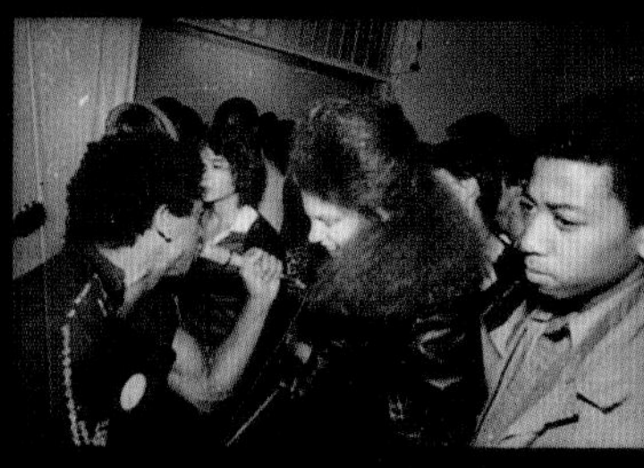
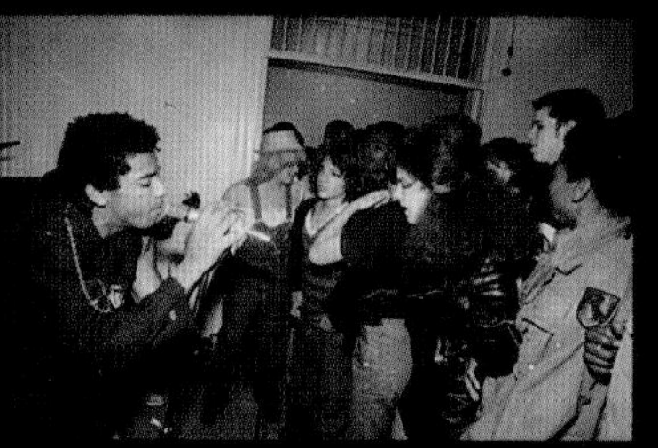
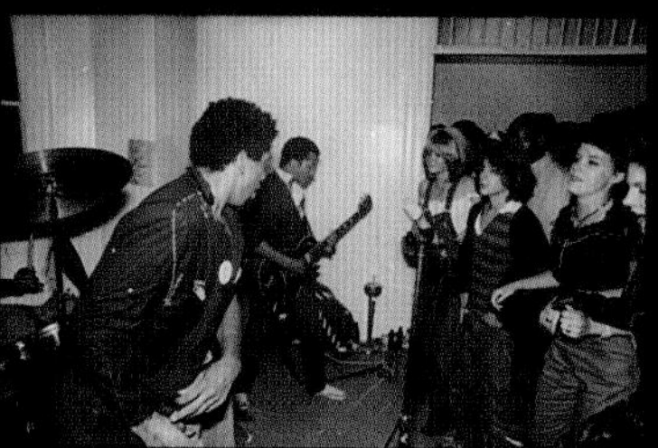
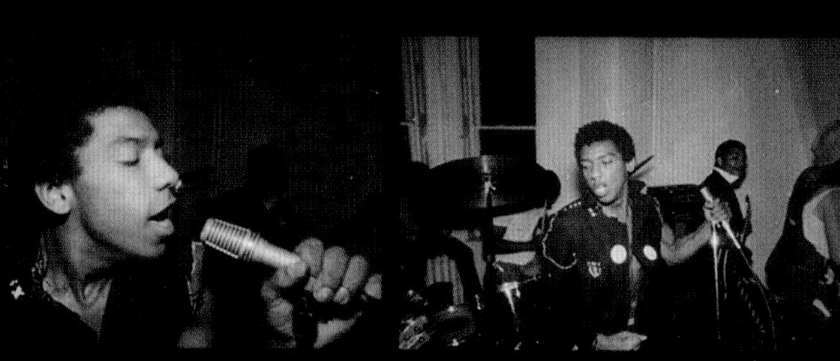
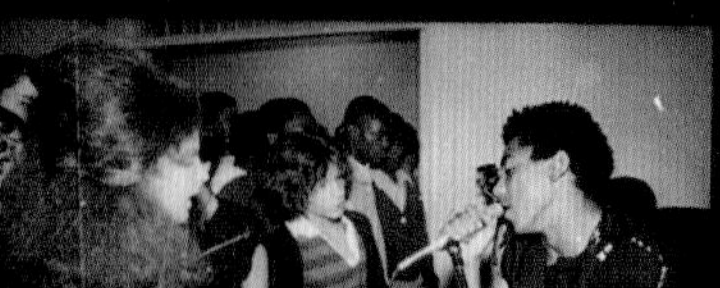
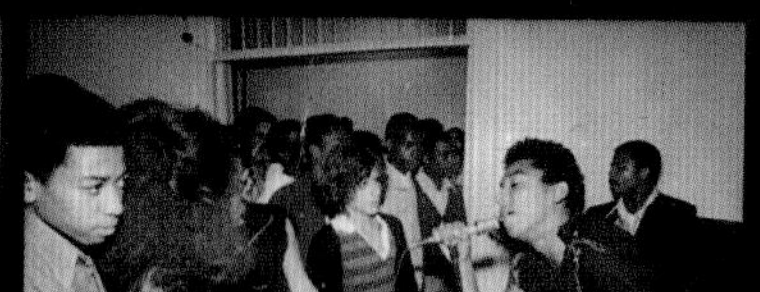
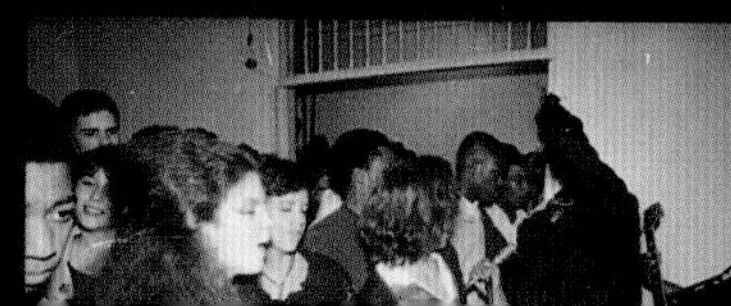
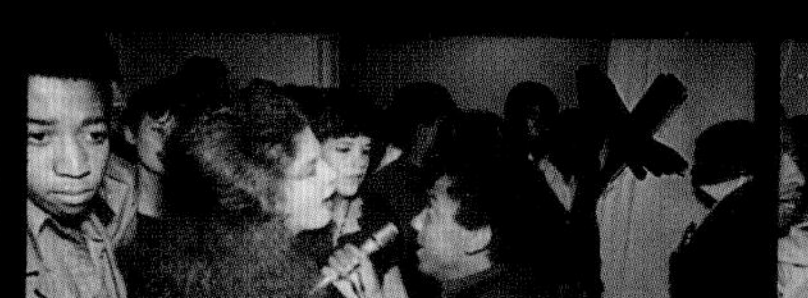
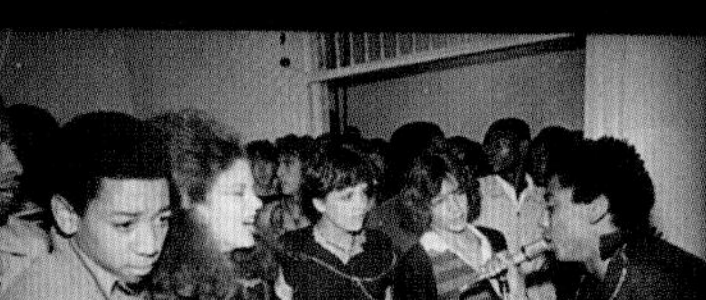

IN THE BASEMENT

Lely Constantinople

In 1995, *Washington Post* photographer Lucian Perkins hired me to organize his extensive photographic collection, negative by negative. His wide-ranging career included some of the most searing images of war in Russia, Bosnia, Palestine, and Iraq; perennial visits to the New York runway shows; and a mass of local stories around the DC area. I was excited by the work in large part because I was hired to look, on my own and more or less at my own pace, at an eclectic mound of photographs and figure out how best to organize and catalog them. Among tens of thousands of images, spanning a then twenty-five-year career at the *Post*, were these photographs.

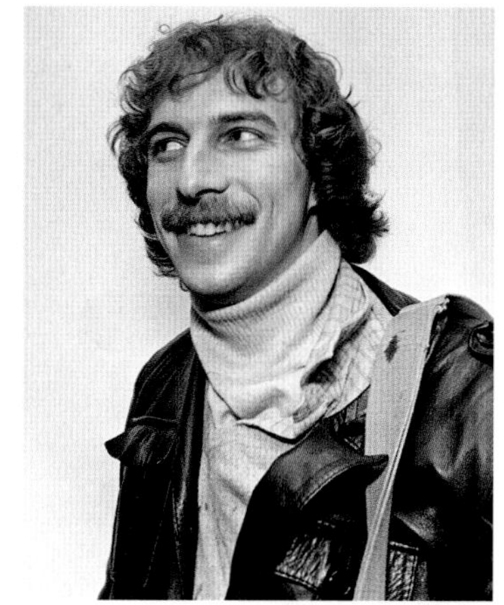

Lucian Perkins, 1979, Hard Art Gallery

After going through some material of Russia, I came across a pile of unmarked negatives of punk shows. They were compositionally bold—frames packed tight yet loose and impulsive—showing chaotic, unselfconscious scenes. With few exceptions, the people being photographed didn't look like they were being observed or inspected; they were uninhibited. Particularly striking were photographs that appeared to be

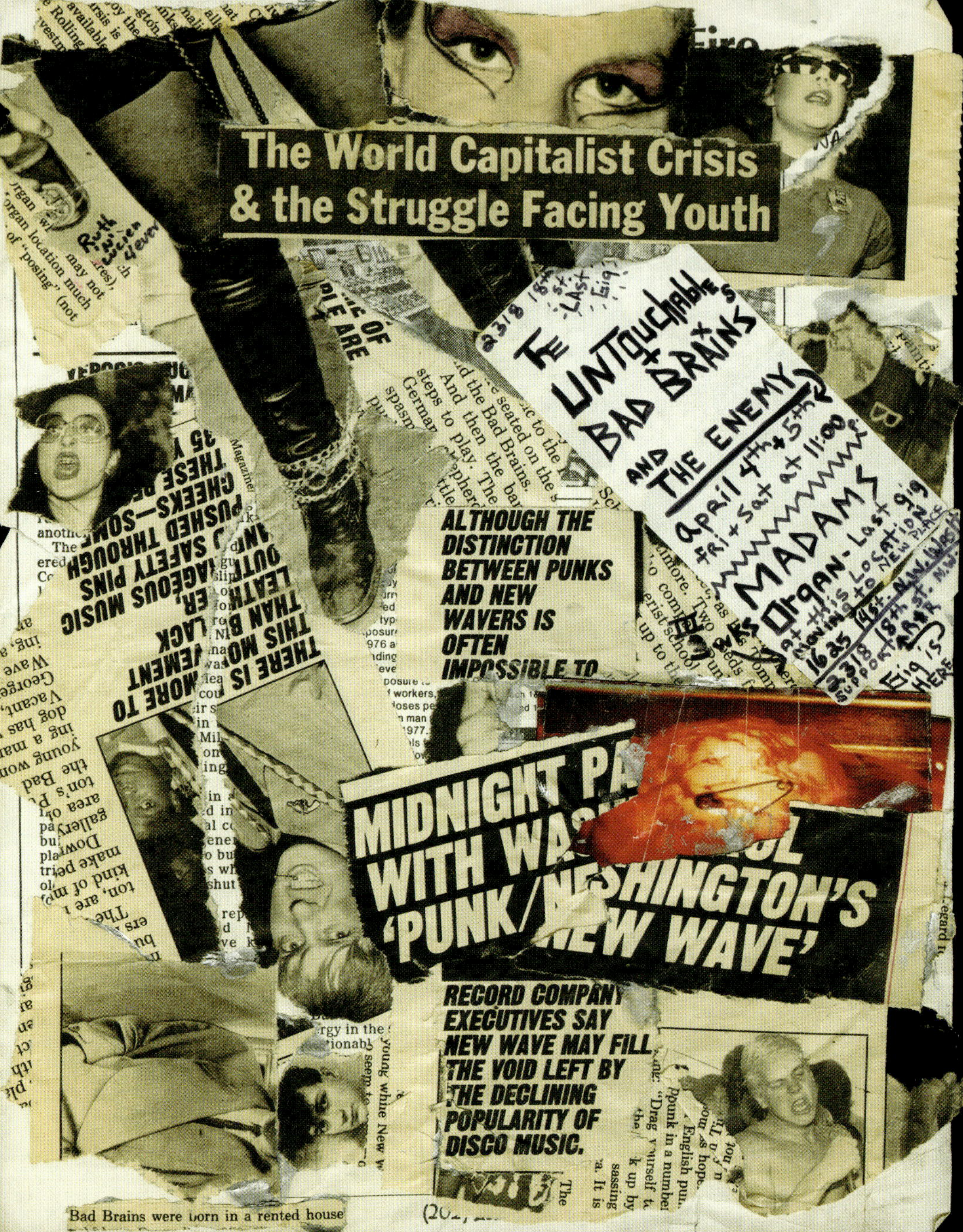

The World Capitalist Crisis
& the Struggle Facing Youth
The Untouchables
Bad Brains
and
The Enemy
April 4th + 5th
Fri + Sat at 11:00
Madams Organ - Last gig at this location
ALTHOUGH THE DISTINCTION BETWEEN PUNKS AND NEW WAVERS IS OFTEN IMPOSSIBLE TO
MIDNIGHT PA
WITH WA
'PUNK/
SHINGTON'S
EW WAVE'
RECORD COMPANY EXECUTIVES SAY NEW WAVE MAY FILL THE VOID LEFT BY THE DECLINING POPULARITY OF DISCO MUSIC.
Bad Brains were born in a rented house

taken outside. Punks, white and black, played to an entirely black and truly all-ages crowd, who were at times baffled, excited, and irreverent. The shots at the Valley Green show, with Bad Brains and Trenchmouth playing, remain some of the strangest and most remarkable photographs of Perkins' work, regardless of subject.

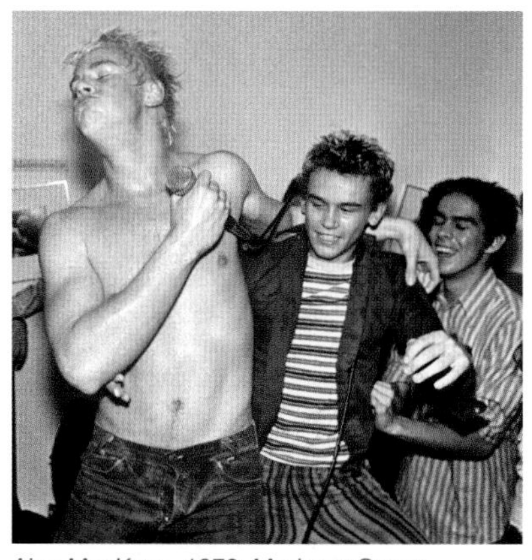
Alec MacKaye, 1979, Madams Organ

It was after looking at hundreds of images of what appeared to be several different shows that I recognized my then boyfriend (now husband) Alec MacKaye, in an instant, dancing with someone nearly twice his size. He was fourteen at the time. I asked Lucian if I could take the negatives to my darkroom to make contact sheets to surprise Alec and his brother Ian. They were amazed by the discovery. Only a few of the images had ever surfaced (a handful appeared in a 1980 *Washington Post Magazine* cover story as well as in *Banned in DC* and *Dance of Days*, two books documenting the early DC punk scene), and the brothers had always wondered whether more shots existed from these pivotal shows. Not many people took photographs of shows back then, so Lucian's presence was noticed.

In 2007, Jayme McLellan, the director of Civilian Art Projects in DC, approached me to see if Lucian might be interested in doing an exhibition of his punk work. I no longer worked for him but he had allowed me to retain the punk images in the hopes of possibly publishing or exhibiting them at some point. *HARD ART, DC 1979* grew from her invitation.

These photographs resonate because they are an unfettered look at something open. Lucian was unsure of what he was looking at, let alone documenting. The uncertainty, and his raw talent, make the resulting photographs vital. Lucian's disconnection from the scene allowed him to be stimulated by all of it, not just by the bands playing. So he often turned his attention away from the bands and spent time looking at how the audience and musicians interacted, the stairwells, the walls, the flyers, the detritus under the stage—the whole scene. The same can be said for the people being photographed: they were not aware of what they were doing because they were in the throes of it. Something was being created.

DC SPACES

Jayme McLellan

In the mid-1990s I saw my first Lucian Perkins photograph. It was an image on the front page of *The Washington Post* of a US soldier holding his rifle in front of a bombed-out landscape. He was facing a young Croatian boy. Even now, when I think back to this image, I remember the energy between the two. There was a palpable camaraderie in a desolate and desperate landscape, a sharing of the hope of interaction and engagement with another. Experiencing this image, I felt something indefinable—a sense of larger purpose maybe. I dropped everything and moved headfirst into making art, specifically black-and-white photography, and soon began to organize the art exhibitions of my friends. The only other time I felt something so powerful, that moved me into immediate action, was through music.

From my perspective, the HARD ART project tipped off when Lucian delivered a framed black-and-white photograph of HR to my then gallery for an art auction. In the photo, HR's eyes are closed, a microphone in his left hand, *B.B.* written on his right. The lapel of his jacket displays a button with the handwritten message, *Think for yourself, Schmuck!* The image reminded me of that first Perkins photograph that started everything. Now I realize that we often do not recognize the very real forces at play pushing us forward. They may be beyond our rational perception, but we feel the energy. The war photo and the HR photo tapped into the same realm.

At first the team—Lely, Lucian, Alec, and yours truly—had no clue the initial spark would result in this book and a traveling exhibition. We definitely did not expect the first edition to sell out. We knew the images captured intensity and the power of photography to tell a story. It was the addition of Alec MacKaye's writing, based on his interviews with and stories from the characters involved, and the thousands of hours that we poured into the project that brought it to fruition. This book was born in the fray of living and pushing creative things into being; we've come out with joint history.

In the first edition, my words paid homage to the art spaces that hosted these shows. The punk scene owes much to spaces like Madams Organ, d.c. space, and the Hard Art Gallery. Like my gallery, Civilian Art Projects, these were cash-strapped spaces existing on the backs of a few for the sake of many. I've found myself alone, or with beloved interns, cleaning up debris, including piss and holes in the wall, after the best nights of music. These images convey a deeply creative scene and the full vigor exploding forth because a tight legion of the like-minded made it so.

From the unwavering supporters and exhibition viewers to the bands and artists who continue to inspire us, we have been awed by the precious nature of what this book harnesses—the power of community. We thank those who against all odds ran those spaces. This book is proof of their unique importance, and that great things can happen in community-driven art spaces. Your sweat matters! This is a true collaboration among friends to make something enduring and larger than any individual. I am humbled and grateful to be a part of this. Many thanks to all involved in manifesting this book into being and carrying it forward. This is what art does at its best.

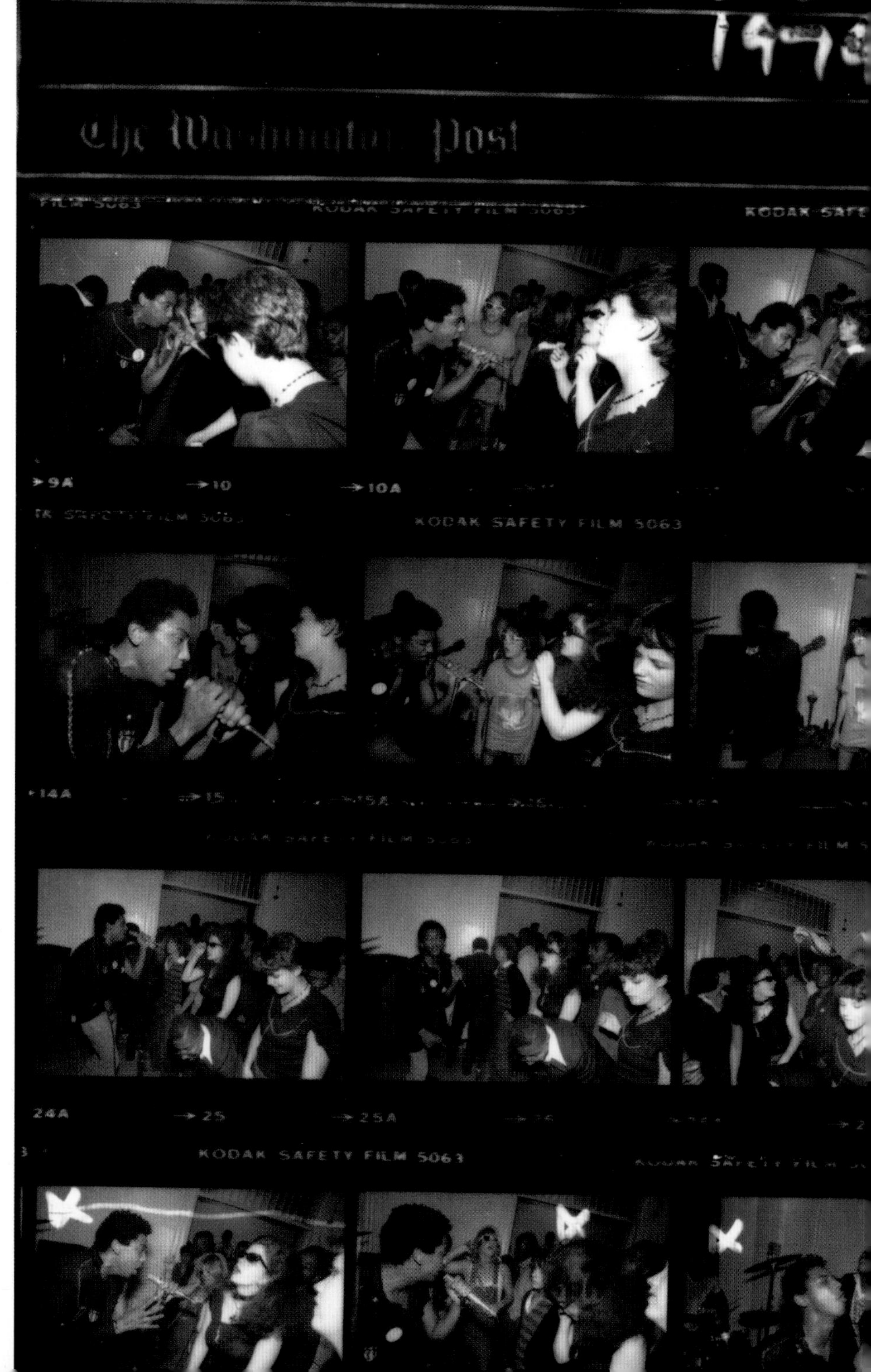

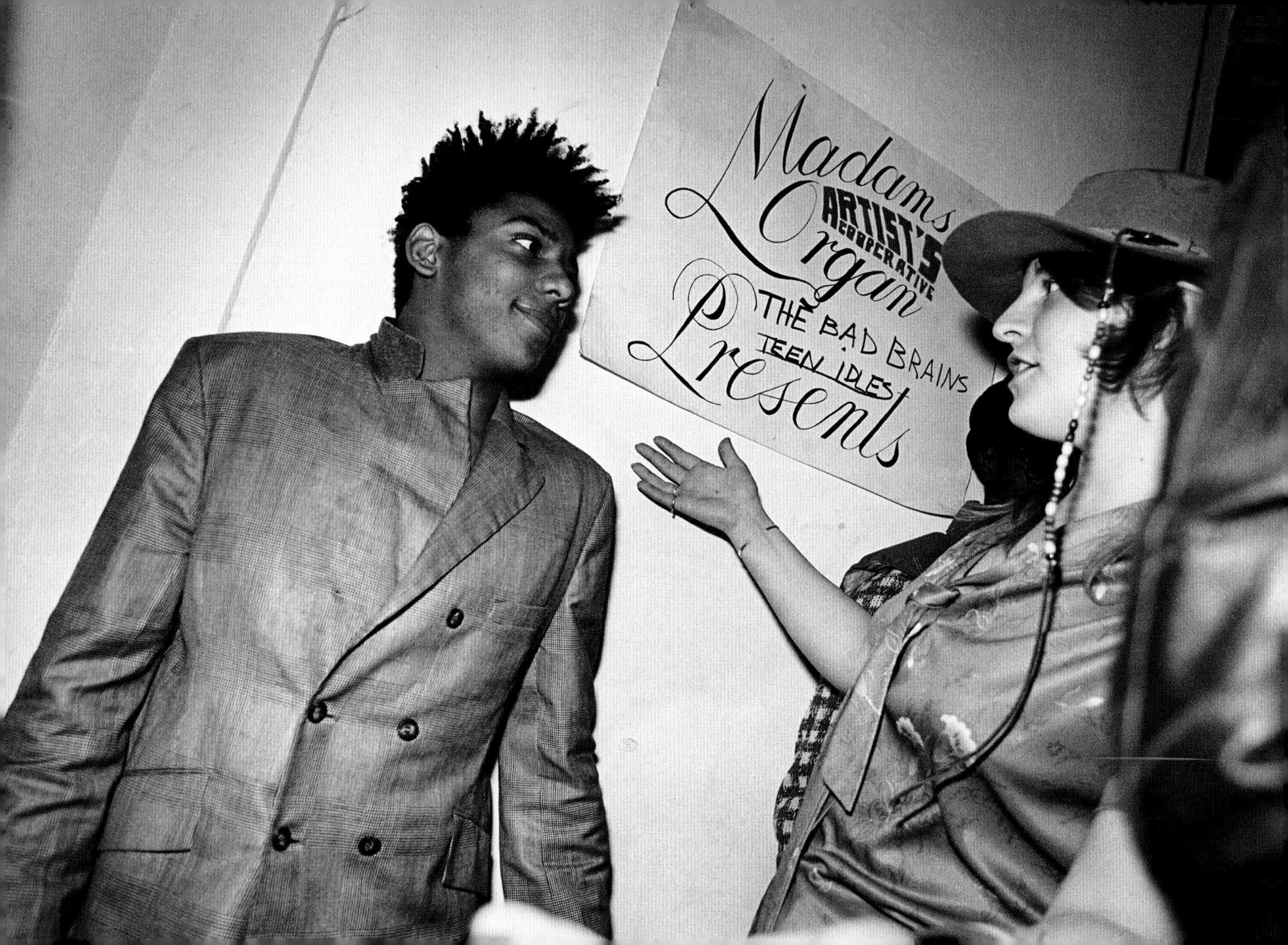
Madams Organ
ARTIST'S COOPERATIVE
THE BAD BRAINS
TEEN IDLES
Presents

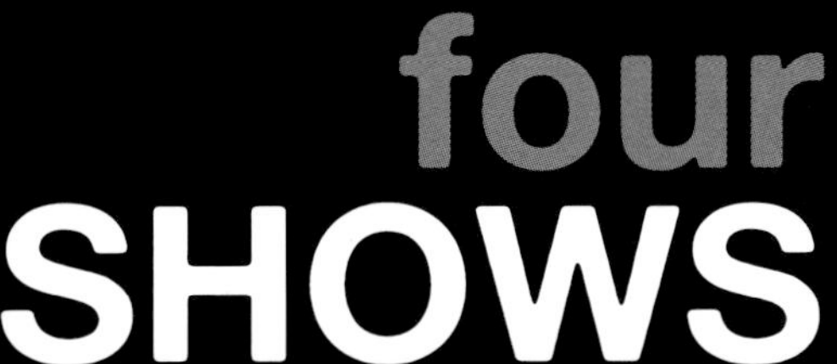

VALLEY GREEN HOUSING COMPLEX

1 3920 Wheeler Road, SE
September 9, 1979

HARD ART GALLERY

2 1407 15th Street, NW
September 15, 1979

MADAMS ORGAN ARTIST'S COOPERATIVE 1

3 2318 18th Street, NW
November 11, 1979

MADAMS ORGAN ARTIST'S COOPERATIVE 2

4 2318 18th Street, NW
January 25/26, 1980

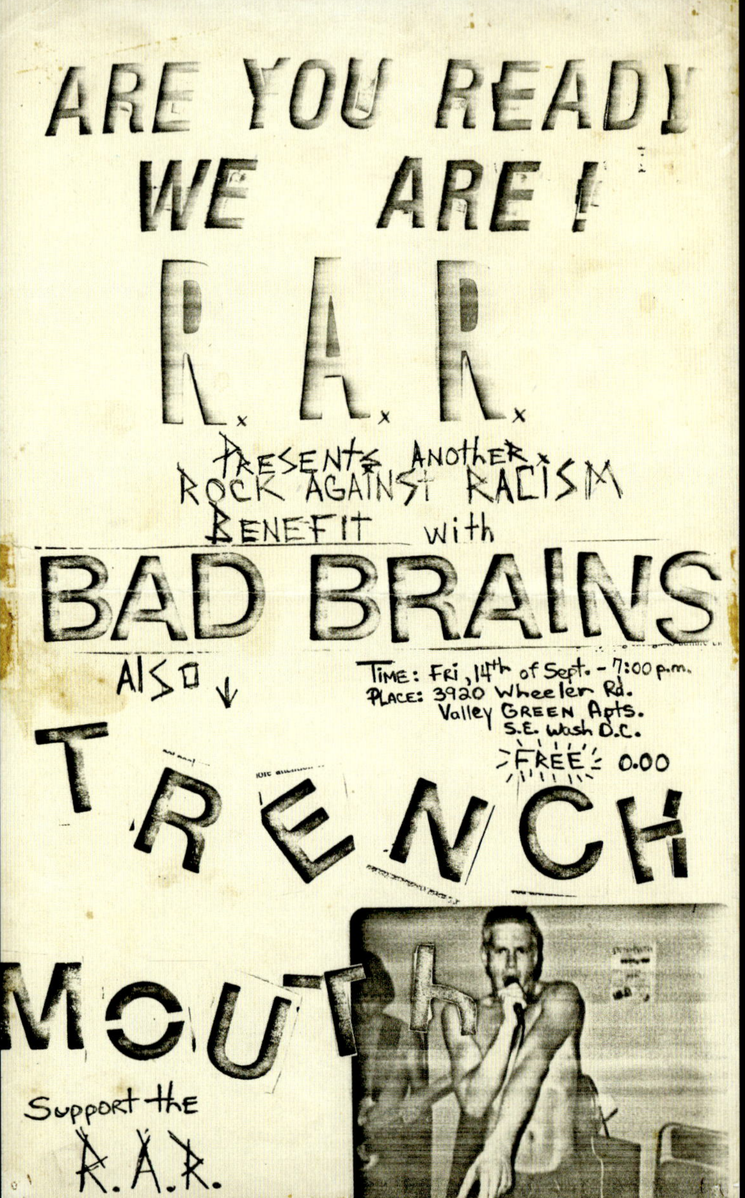

Valley Green Housing Complex

3920 Wheeler Road, SE
September 9, 1979

Rock Against Racism

Bad Brains
Trenchmouth

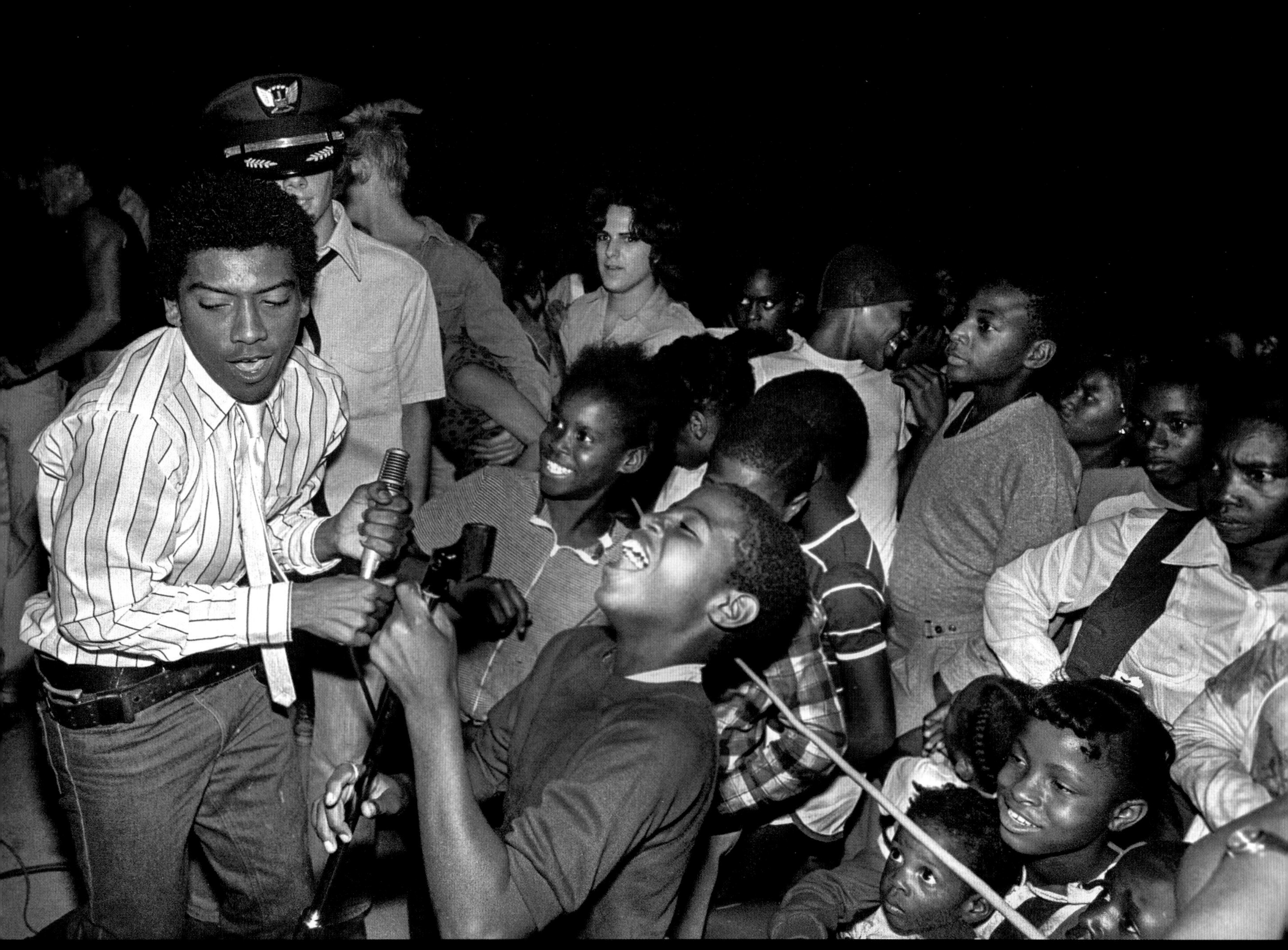

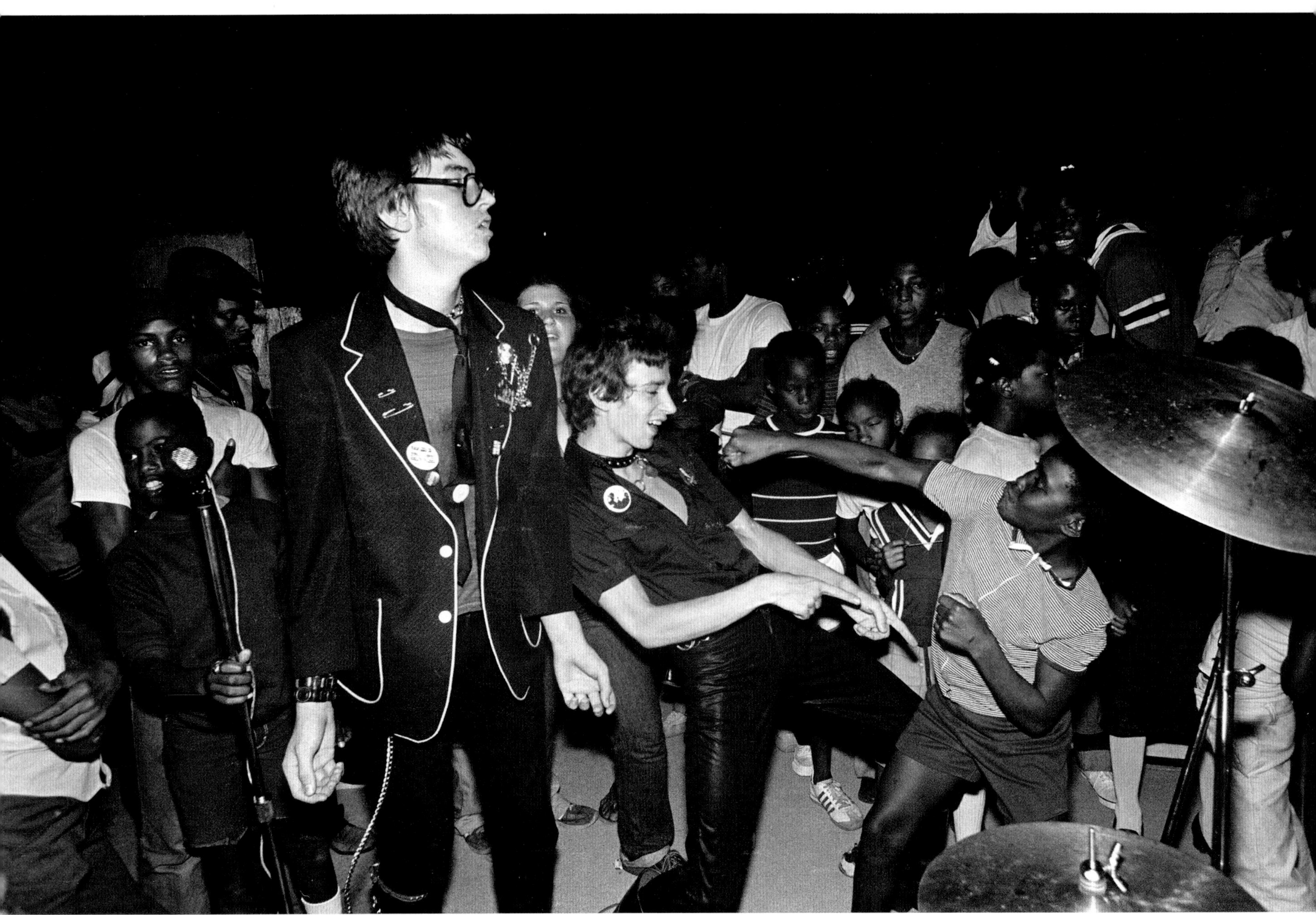

VALLEY GREEN

Narrative by Alec MacKaye

Valley Green was an unlikely name for the urban compound that greeted us. It was in a valley, I suppose. Actually, on a hill overlooking Oxon Run—but the name was a hopeful whitewash on a tough spot. Conceived by local city council members to be a solution to poverty, it was instead a hothouse of social ills for the people who had to live there.

Notorious even when it was new, it had transgressed to mythic status by the time we found our teenaged selves driving along Wheeler Road, trying to locate the place. Washington Heights was already one of the roughest neighborhoods during a time when crime statistics were reaching epic levels in DC.

I don't know if the initial aim made its mark, but a further purpose was definitely served.

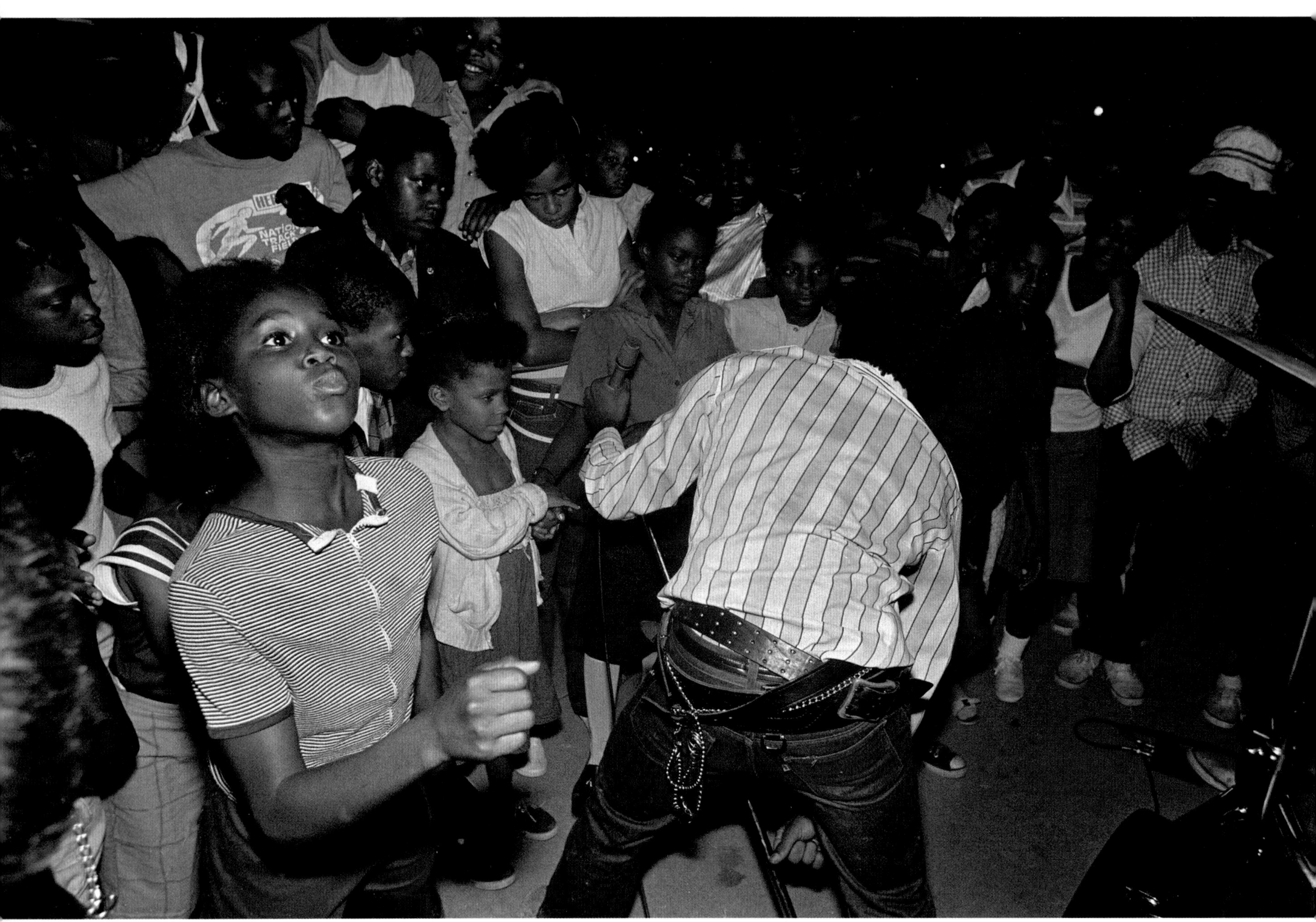

It was Bad Brains singer HR's idea to put on shows at Valley Green. He met some people who lived there while working as a parking lot guard at Greater Southeast Community Hospital. Inspired by some free outdoor "Rock Against Racism" gigs in London, HR thought something should be done in DC. The London festivals were massively attended, well-produced operations featuring rosters of known bands like The Clash, X-Ray Spex, Sham 69, and Steel Pulse. In contrast, the Bad Brains gigs in DC were unheralded, unproduced, DIY pop-ups, witnessed mostly by neighbors who had never heard of the entire genre of music, much less particular bands.

It is evident in the pictures that an impact was made, arguably something more street-level direct than if hordes of same-thinking music consumers descended on a place and transformed it into a green-zone party for their own entertainment. I don't know if the initial aim made its mark, but a further purpose was definitely served.

Part of HR's plan was to get punk rockers to step out of the embrace of the downtown art scene and take it to the streets. It was as much a testament to our desperation to play and see our music as it was confidence that the idea would stand on its own and do some good. But the very fact that these shows happened at all changed the memories, and in some small and large ways the lives, of some of the people who witnessed them. A small seed can grow strong in the heart of a young person.

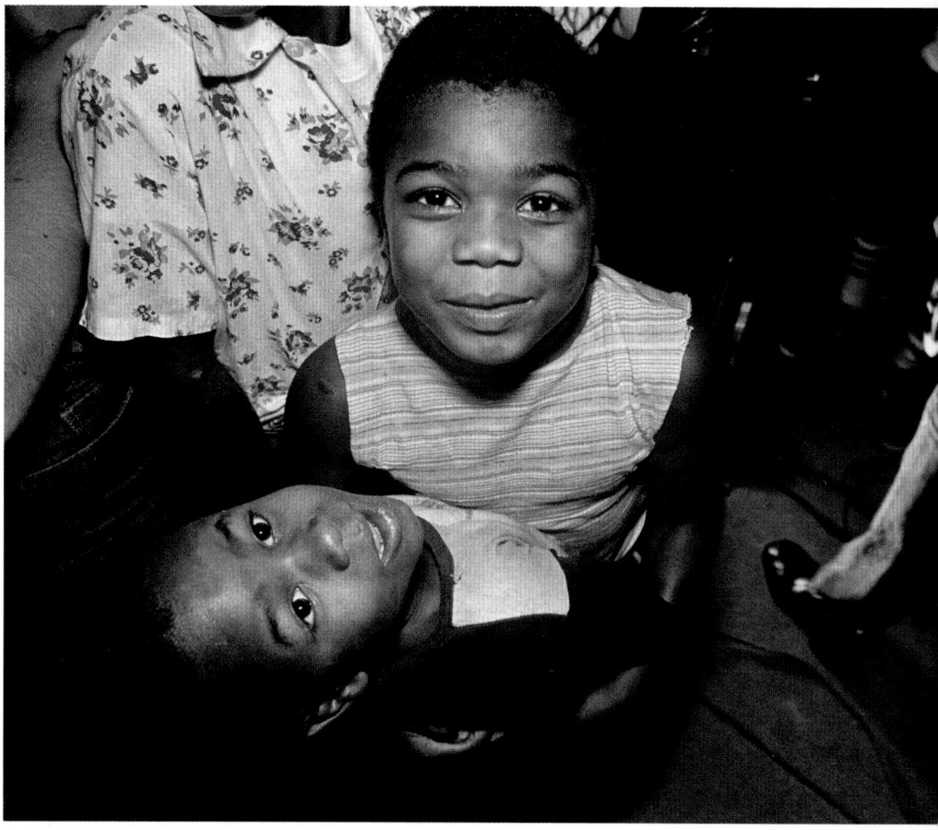

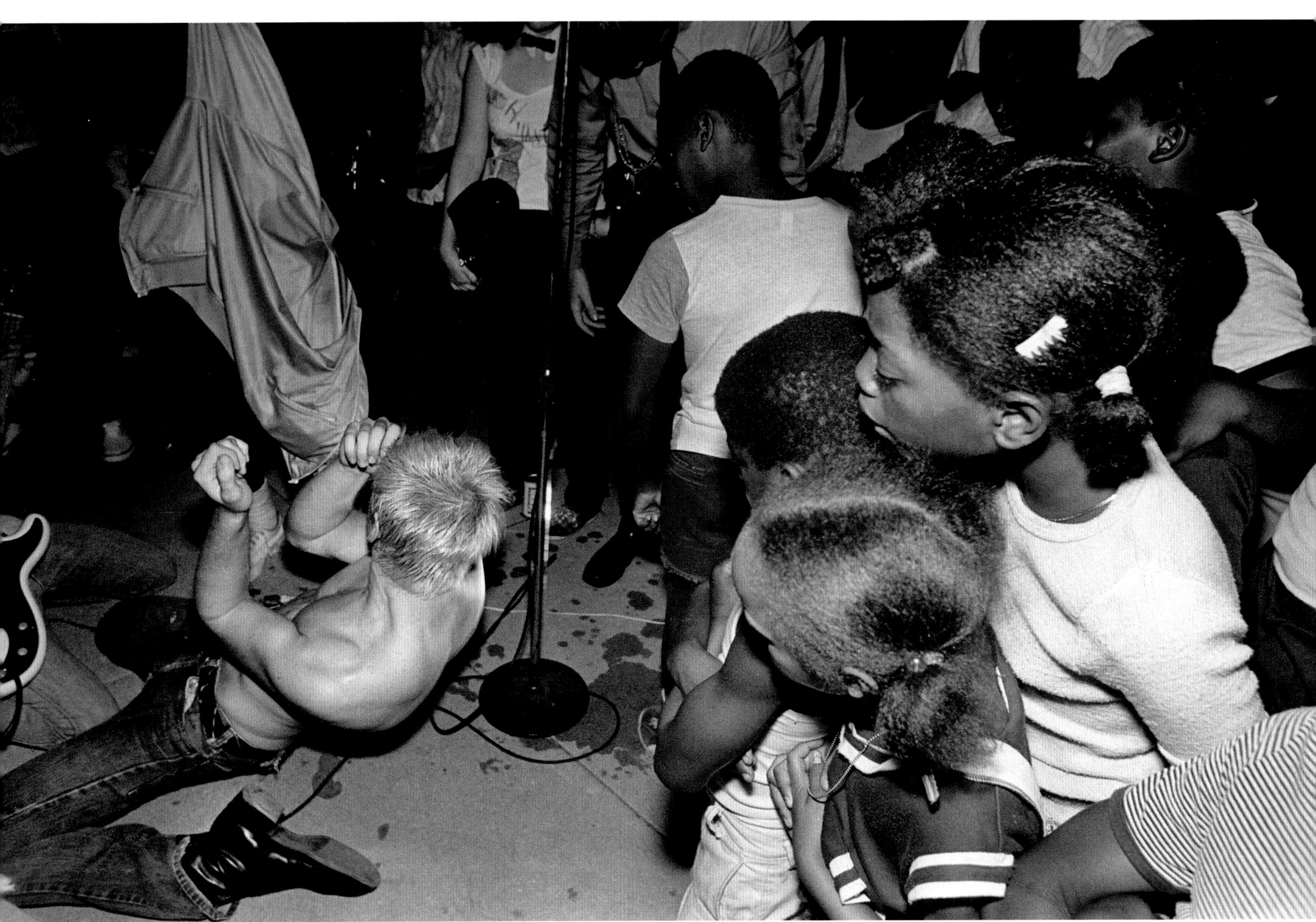

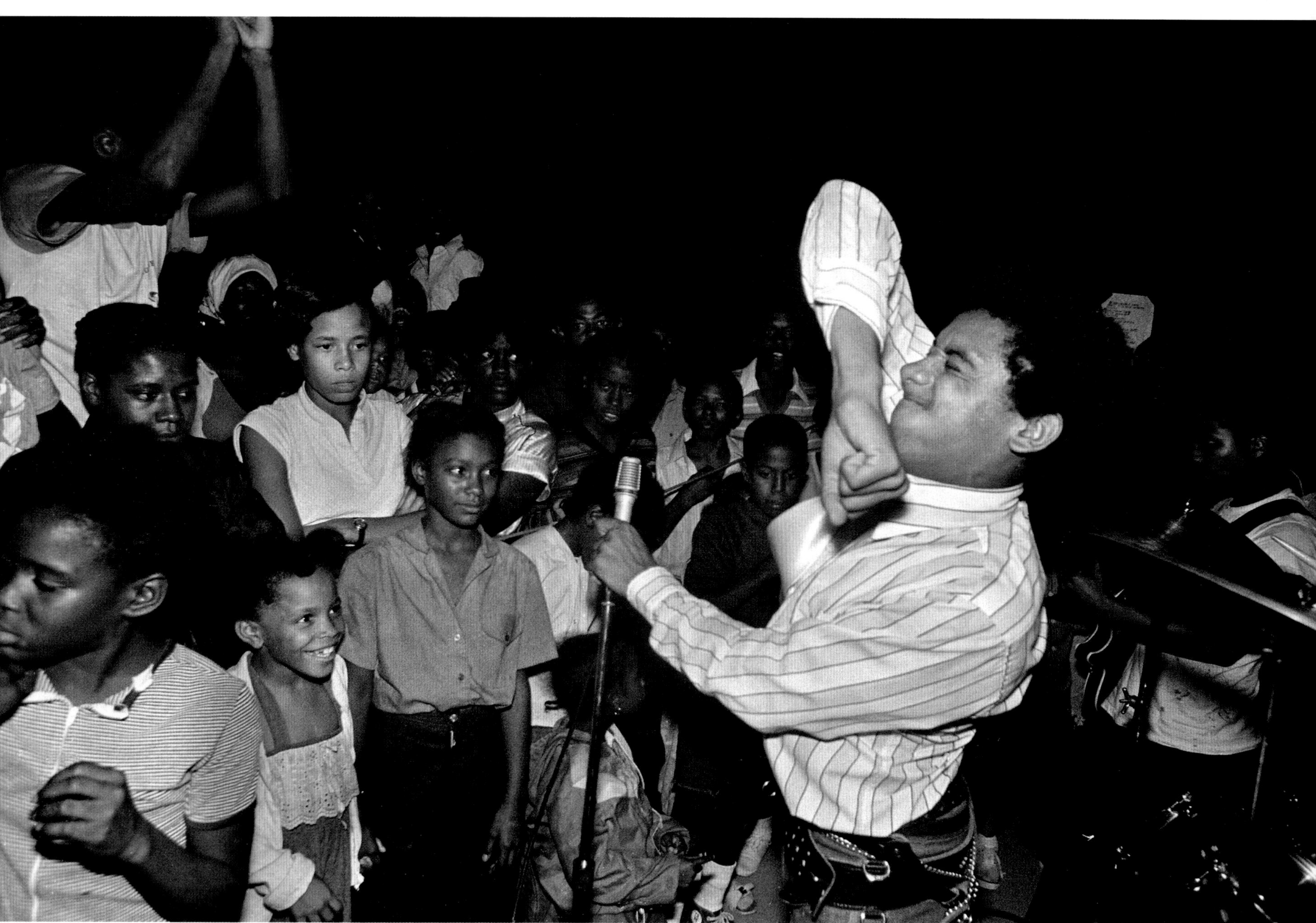

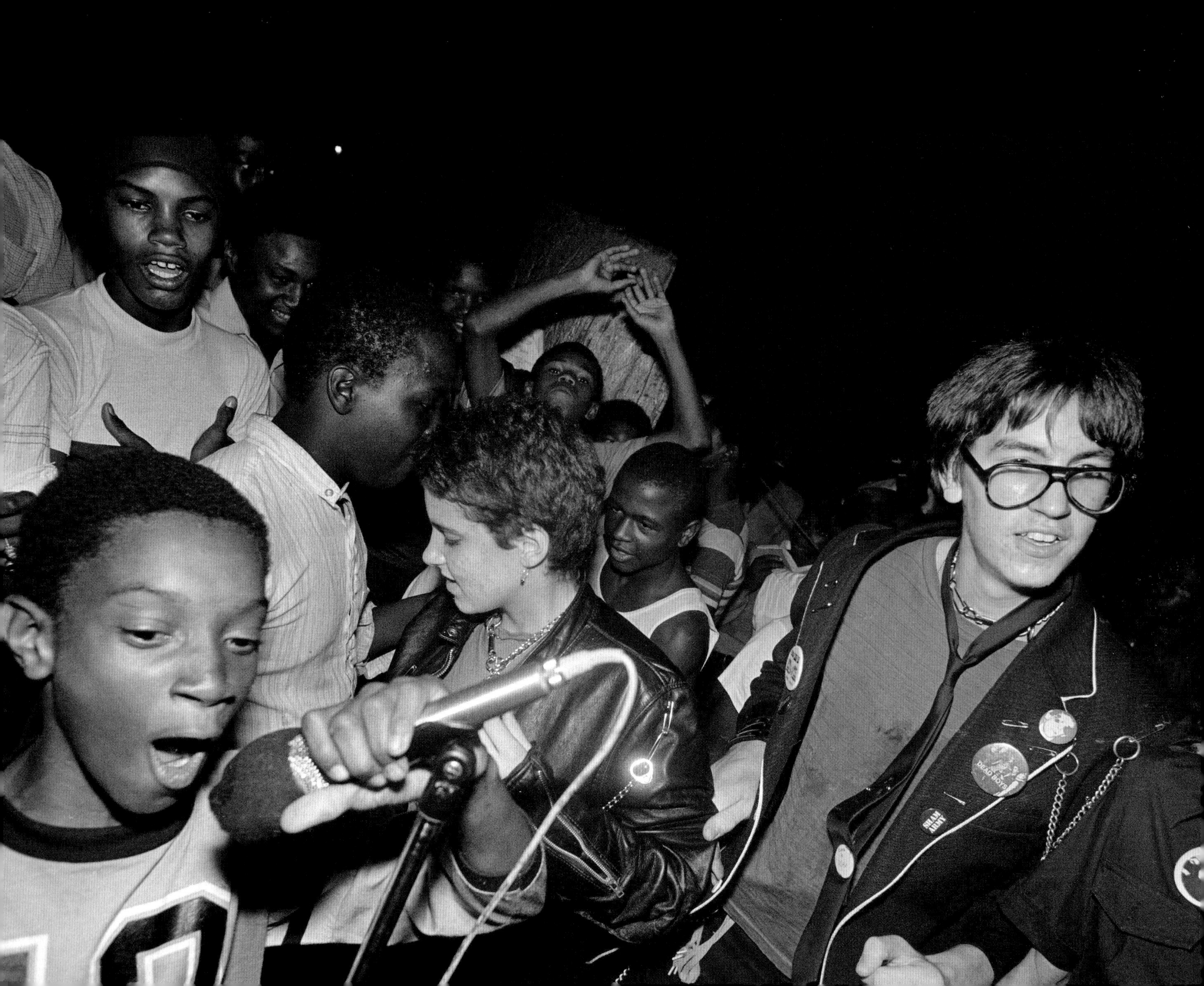
DEAD BOYS
SHAM ARMY

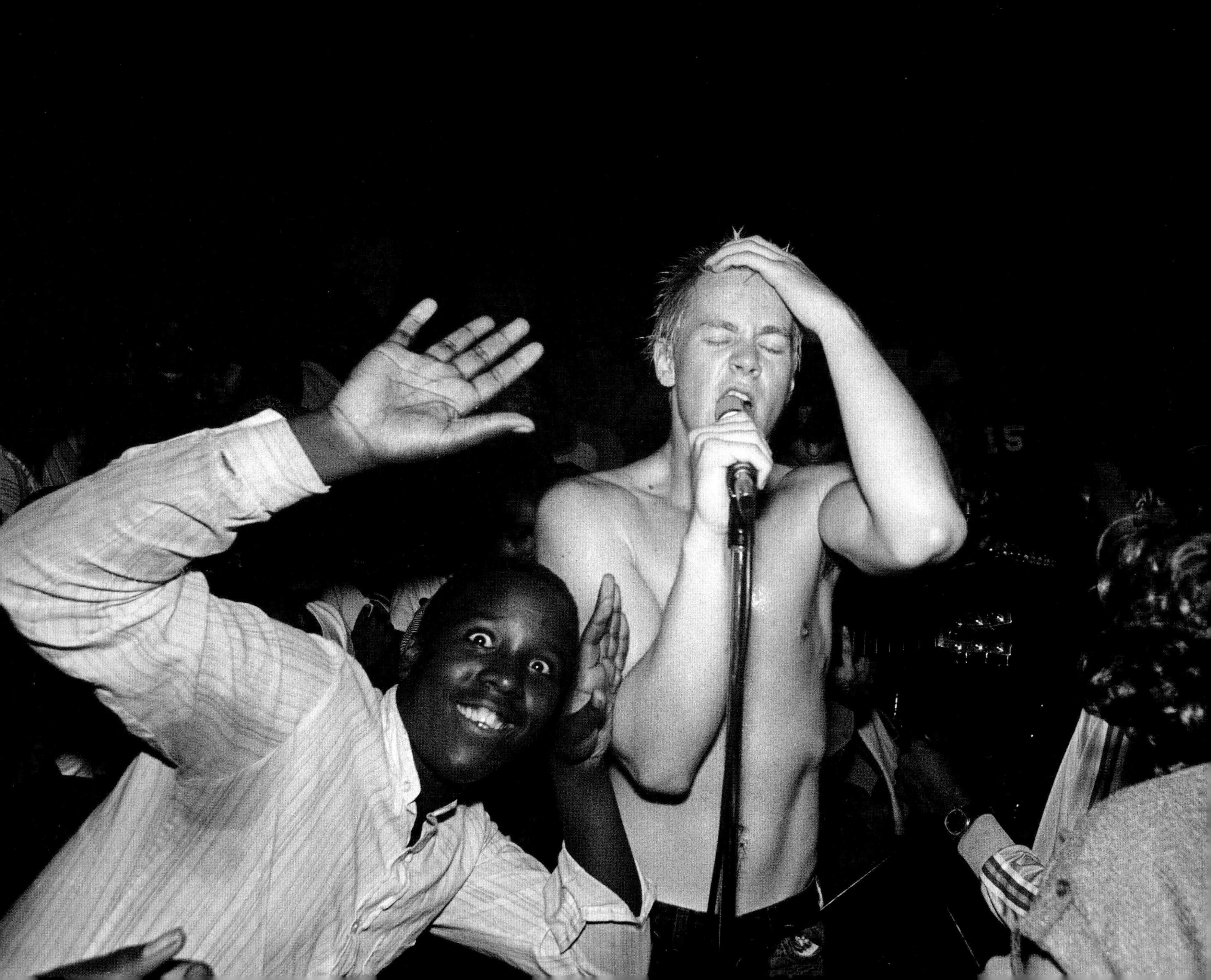
15

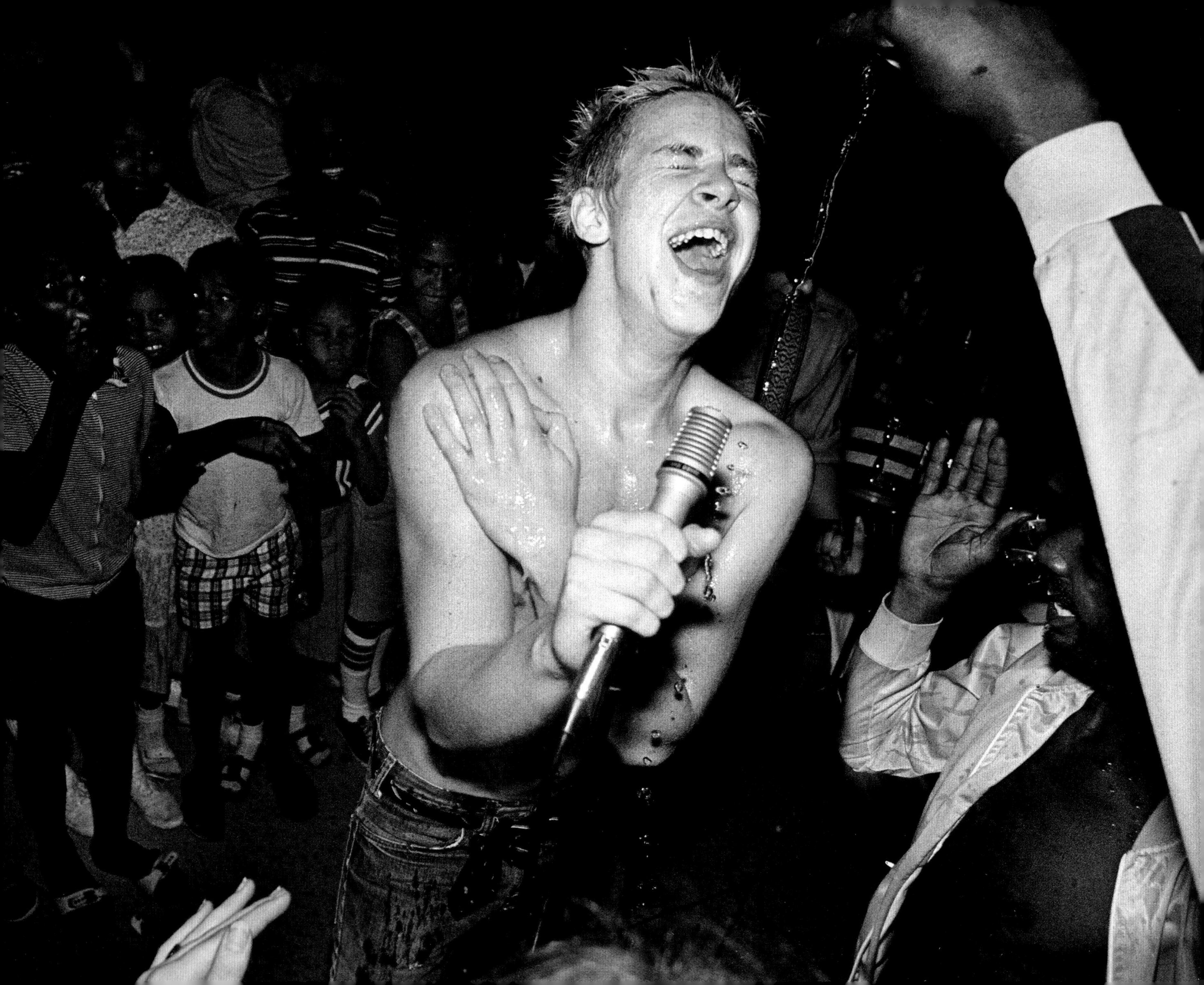

Part of HR's plan was to get punk rockers to step out of the embrace of the downtown art scene and take it to the streets.

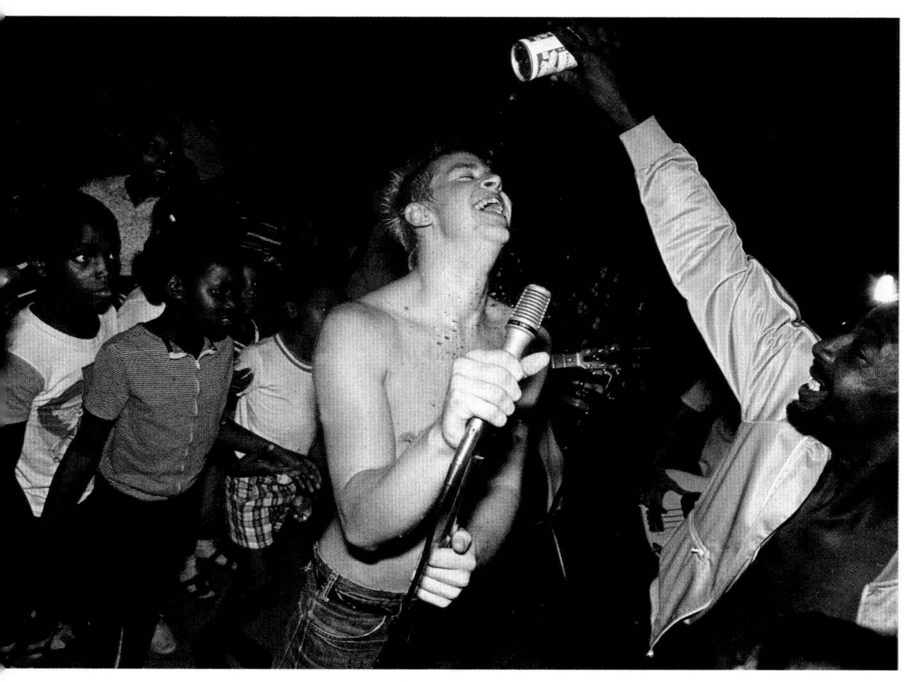

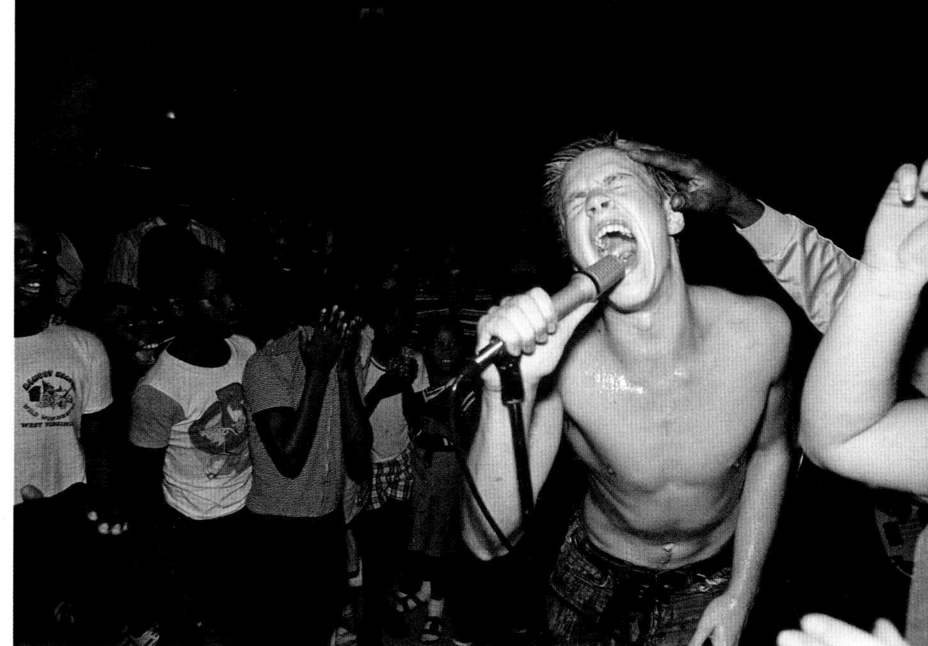

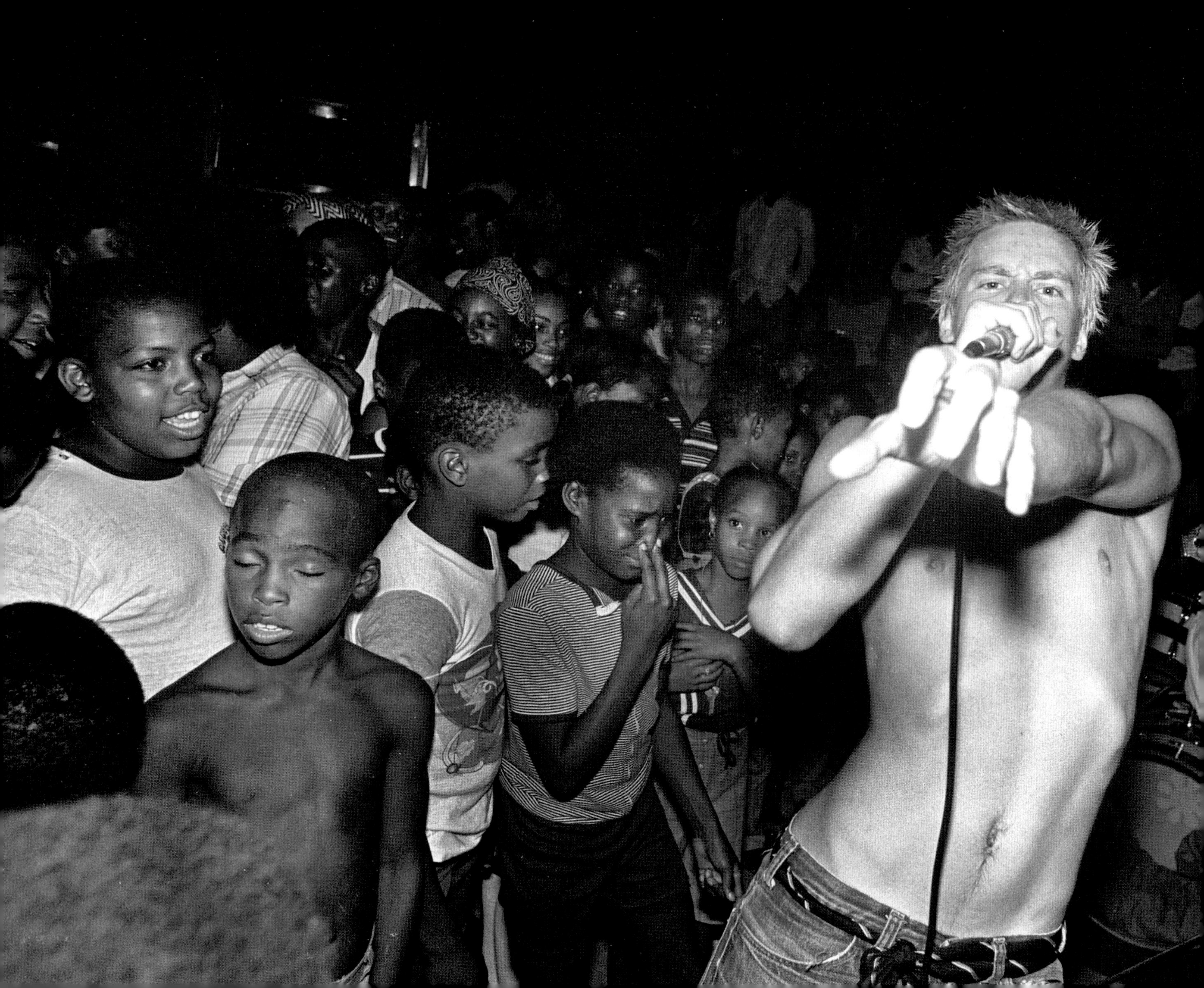

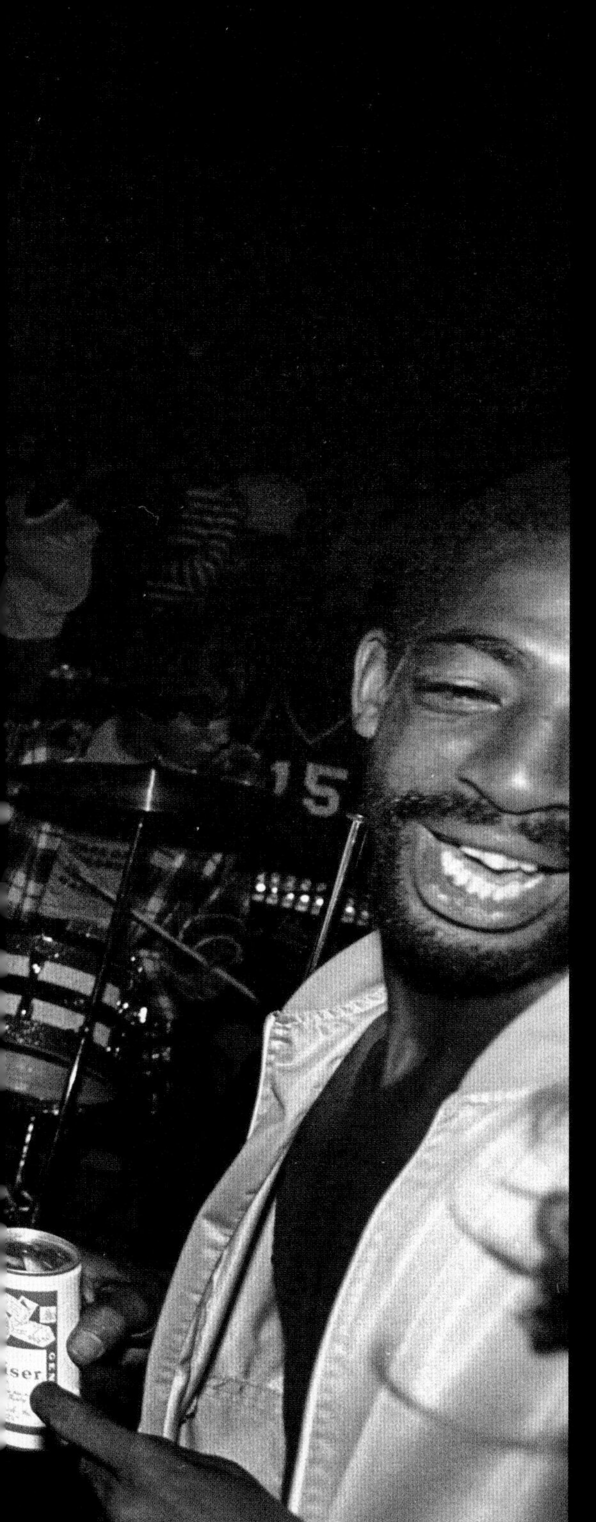
15

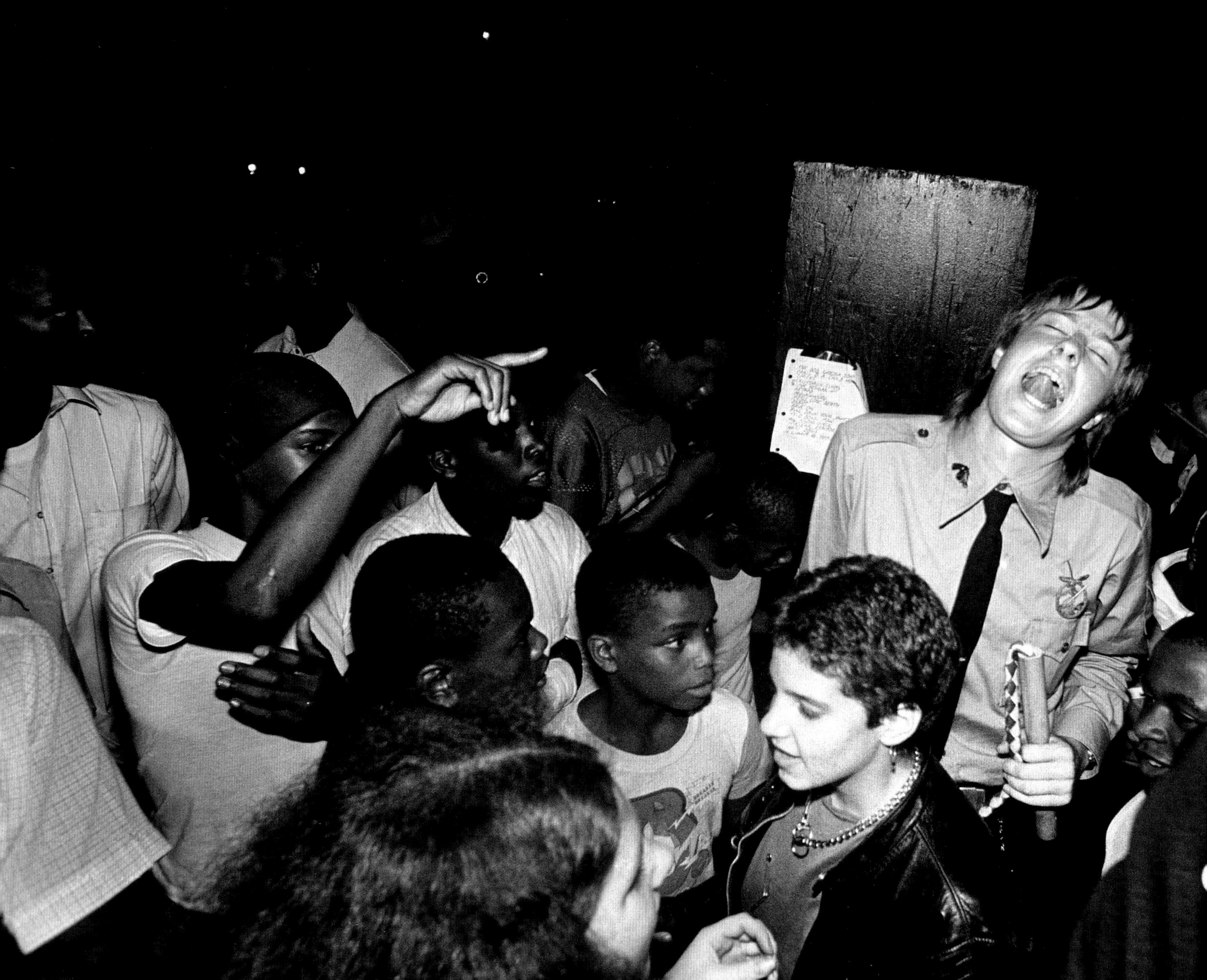

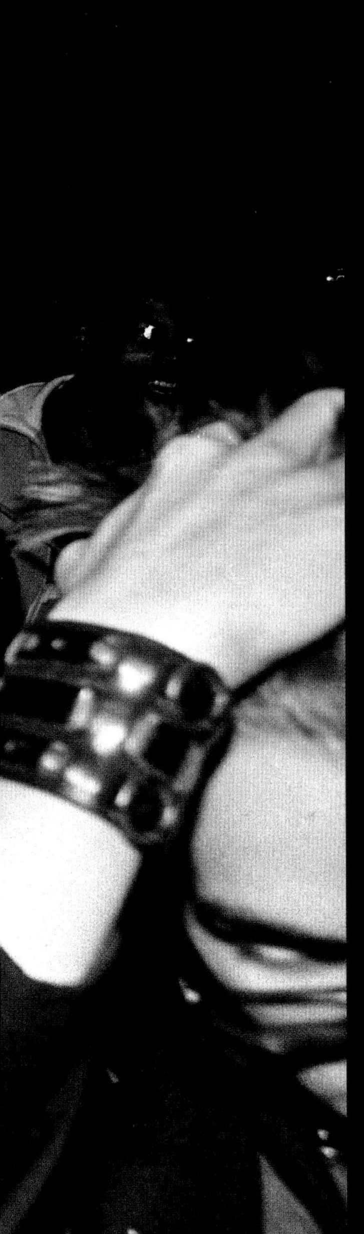

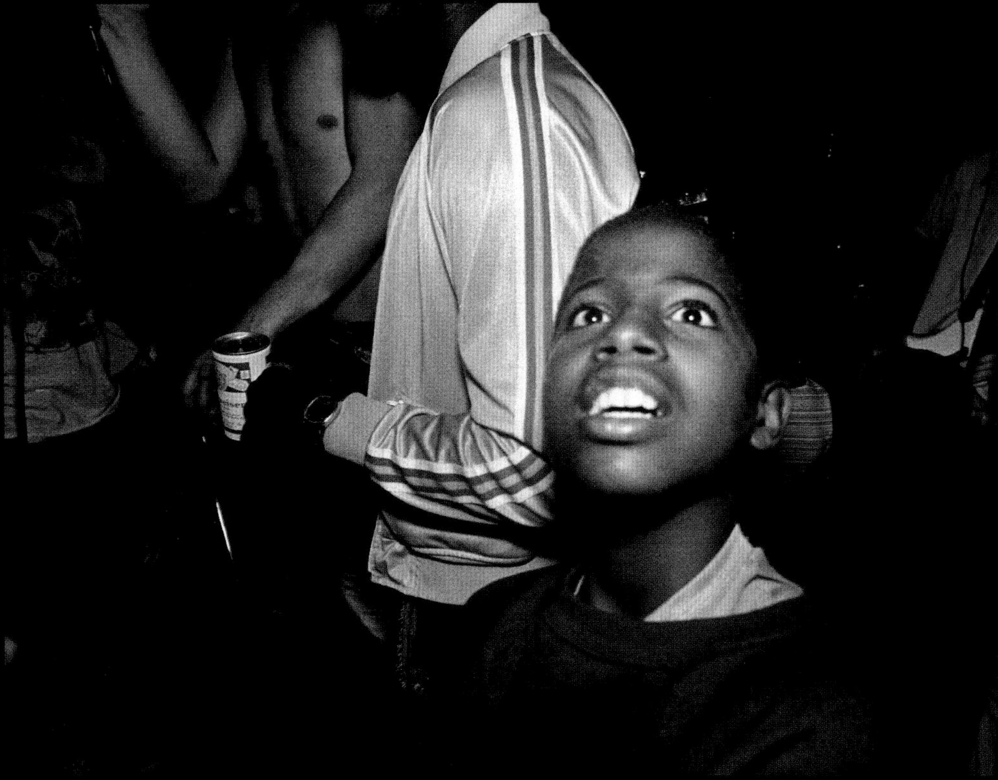

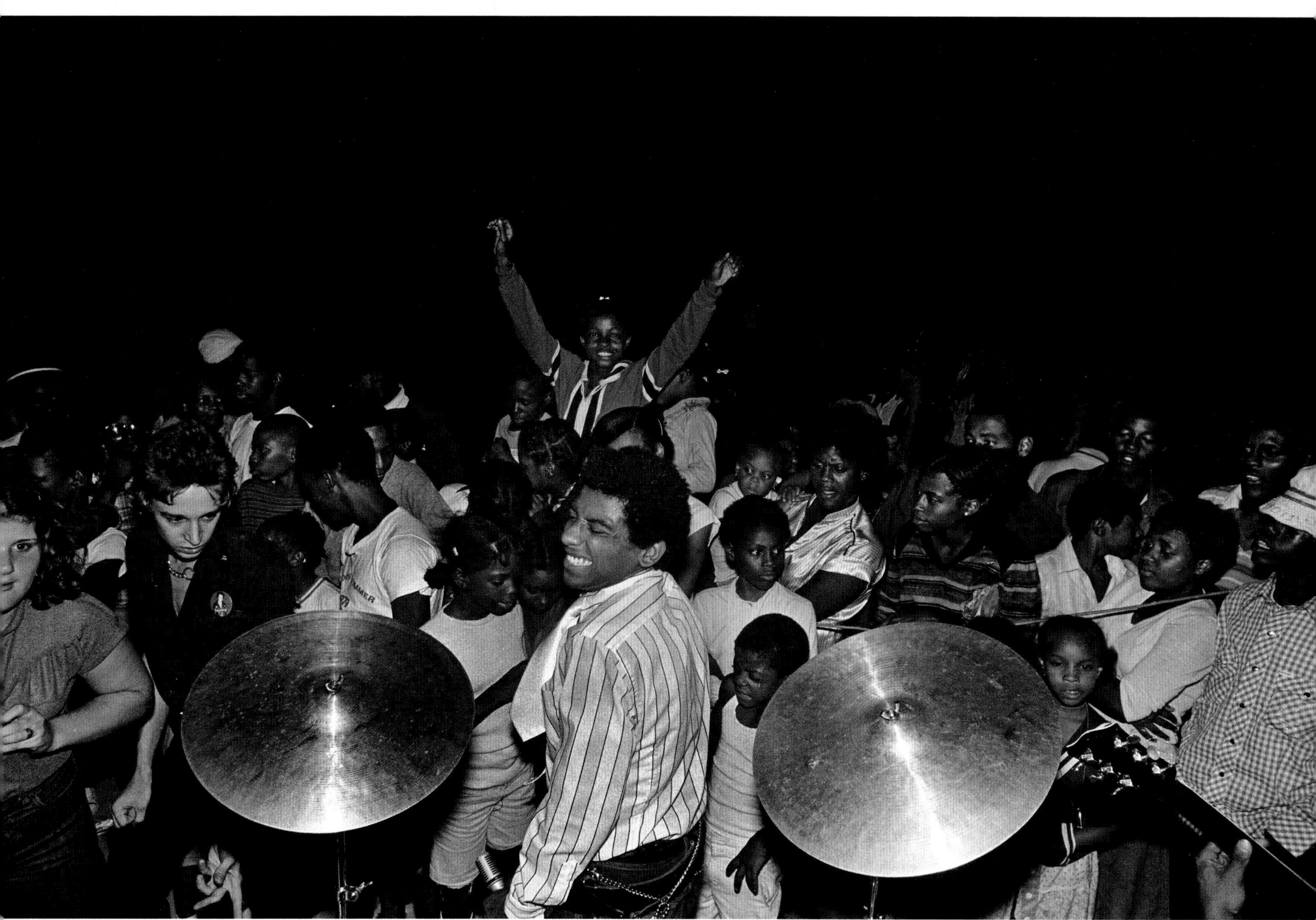

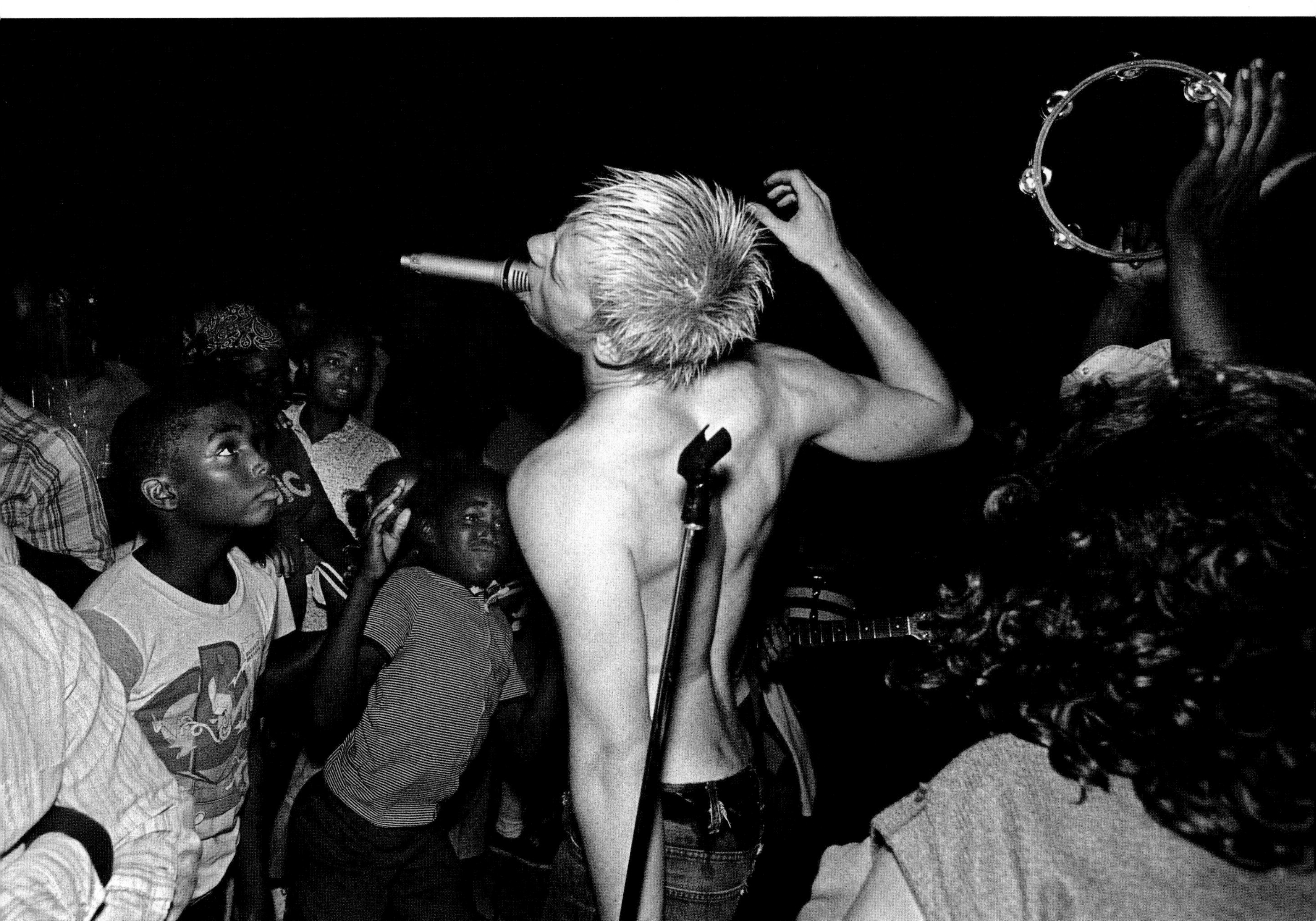

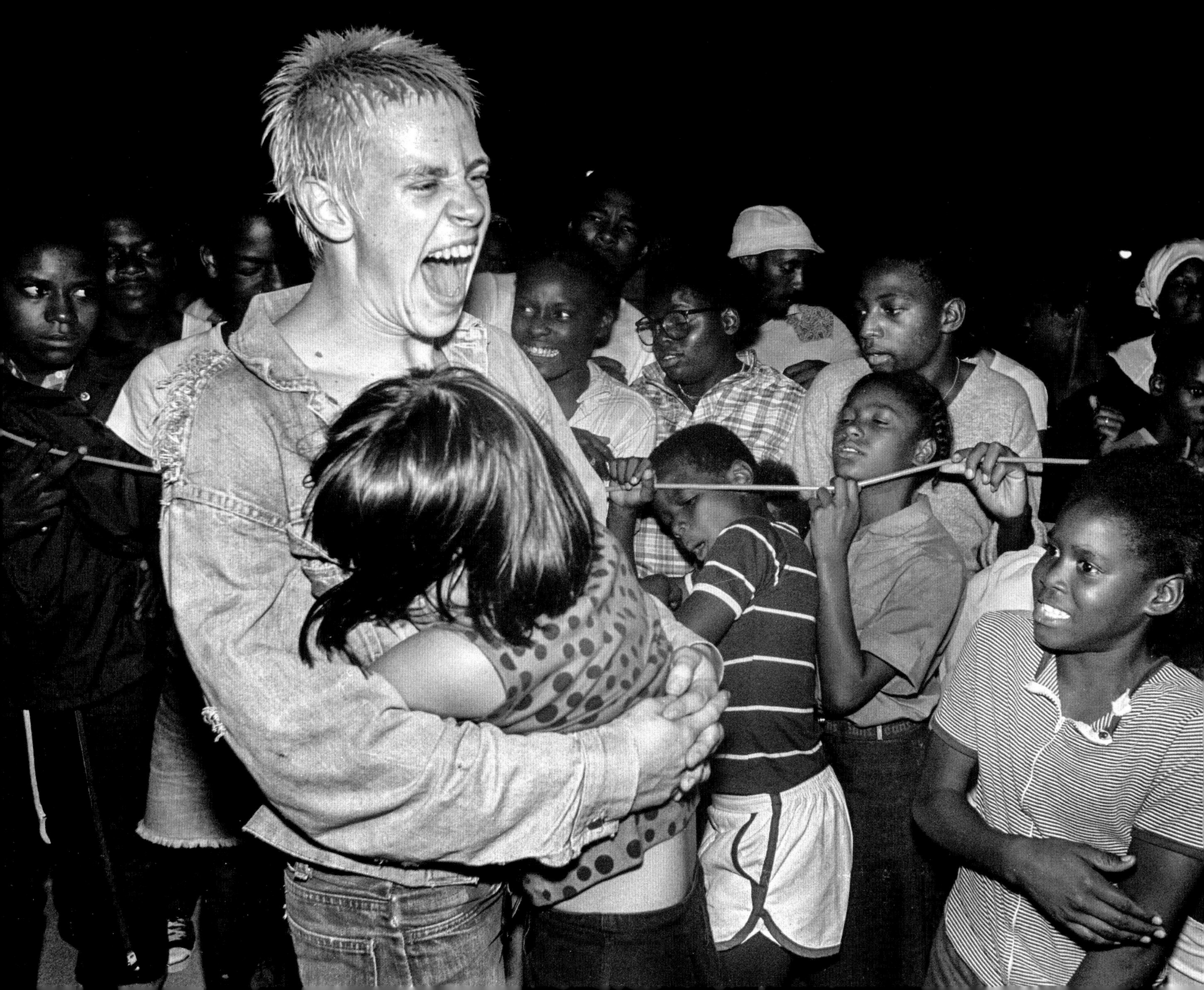

Inspired by some free outdoor "Rock Against Racism" gigs in London, HR thought something should be done in DC.

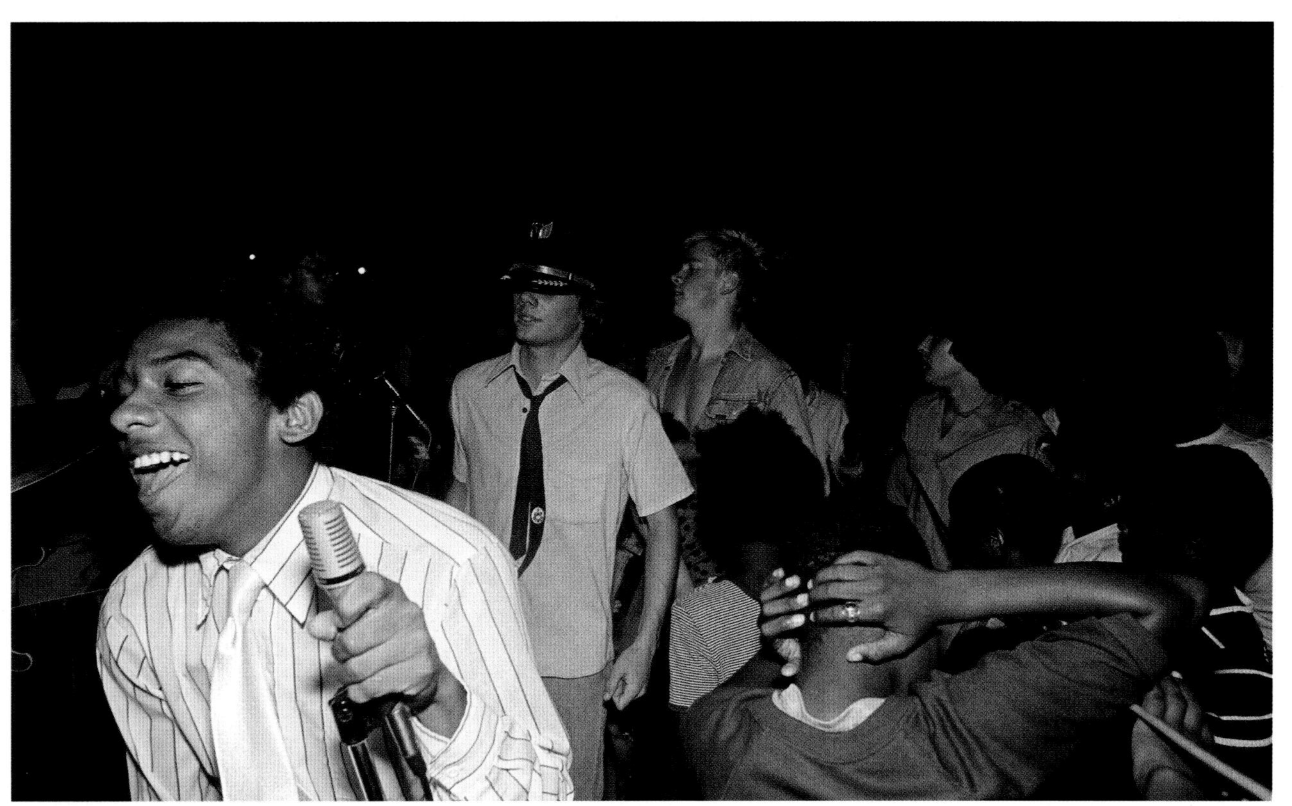

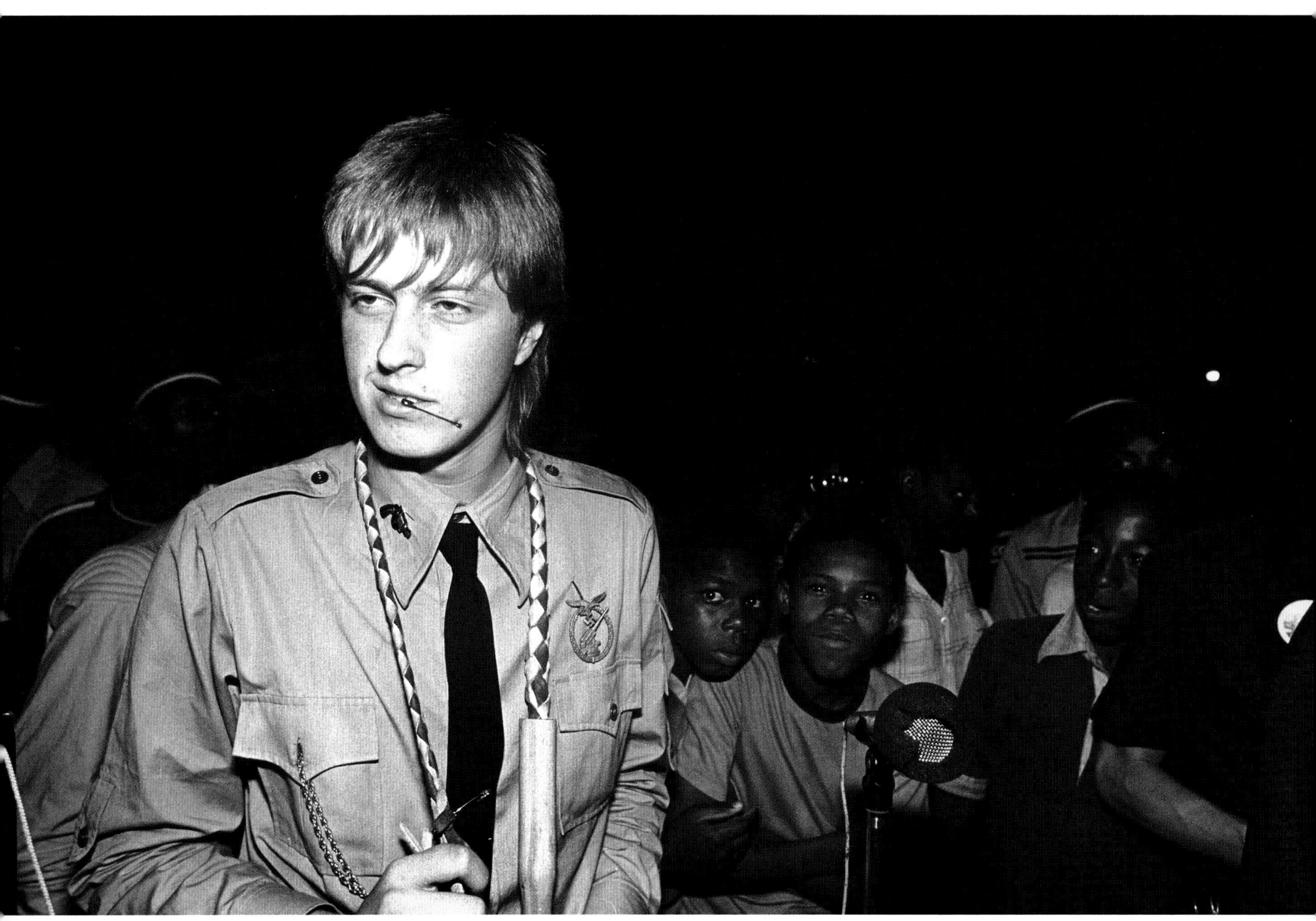

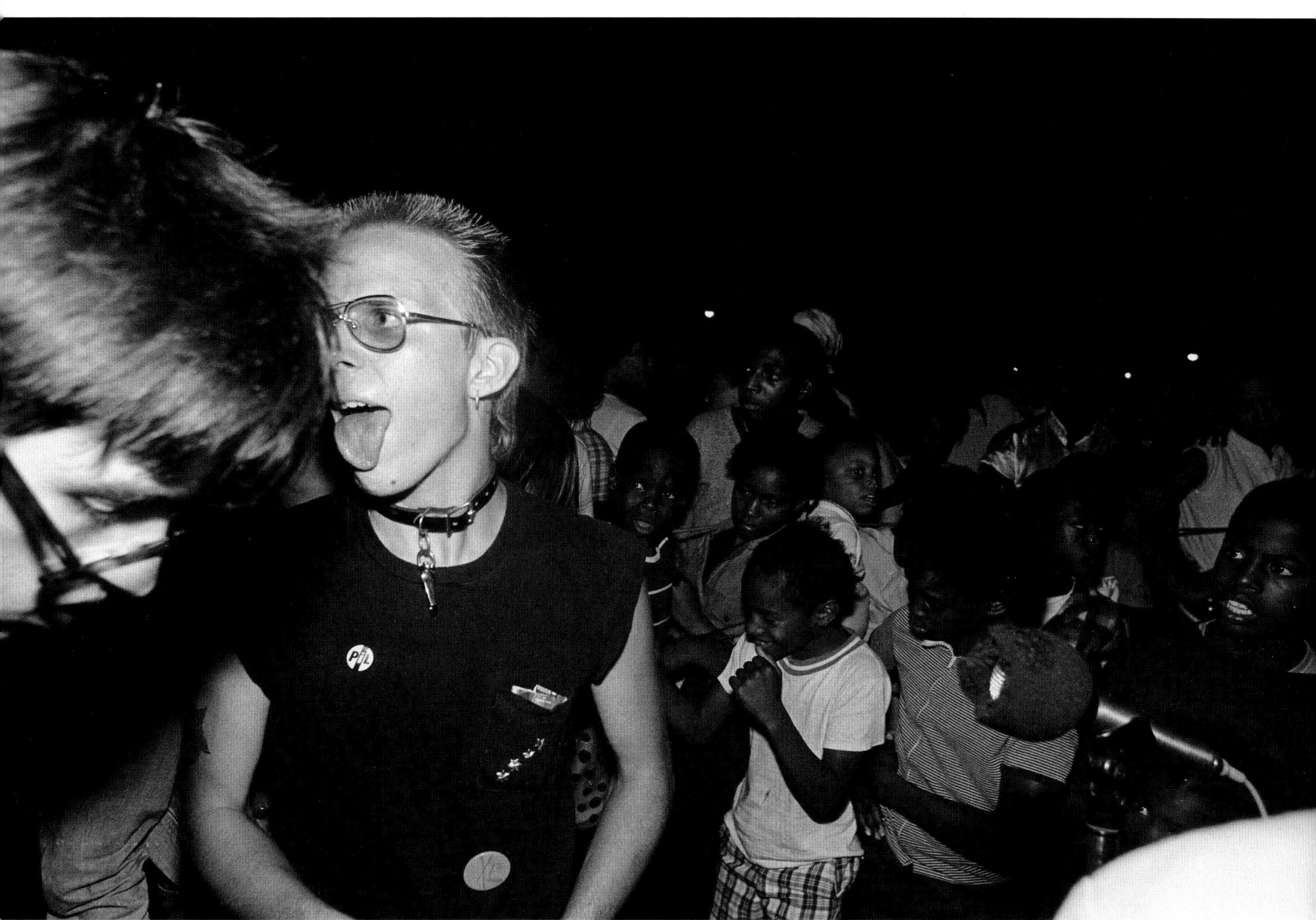

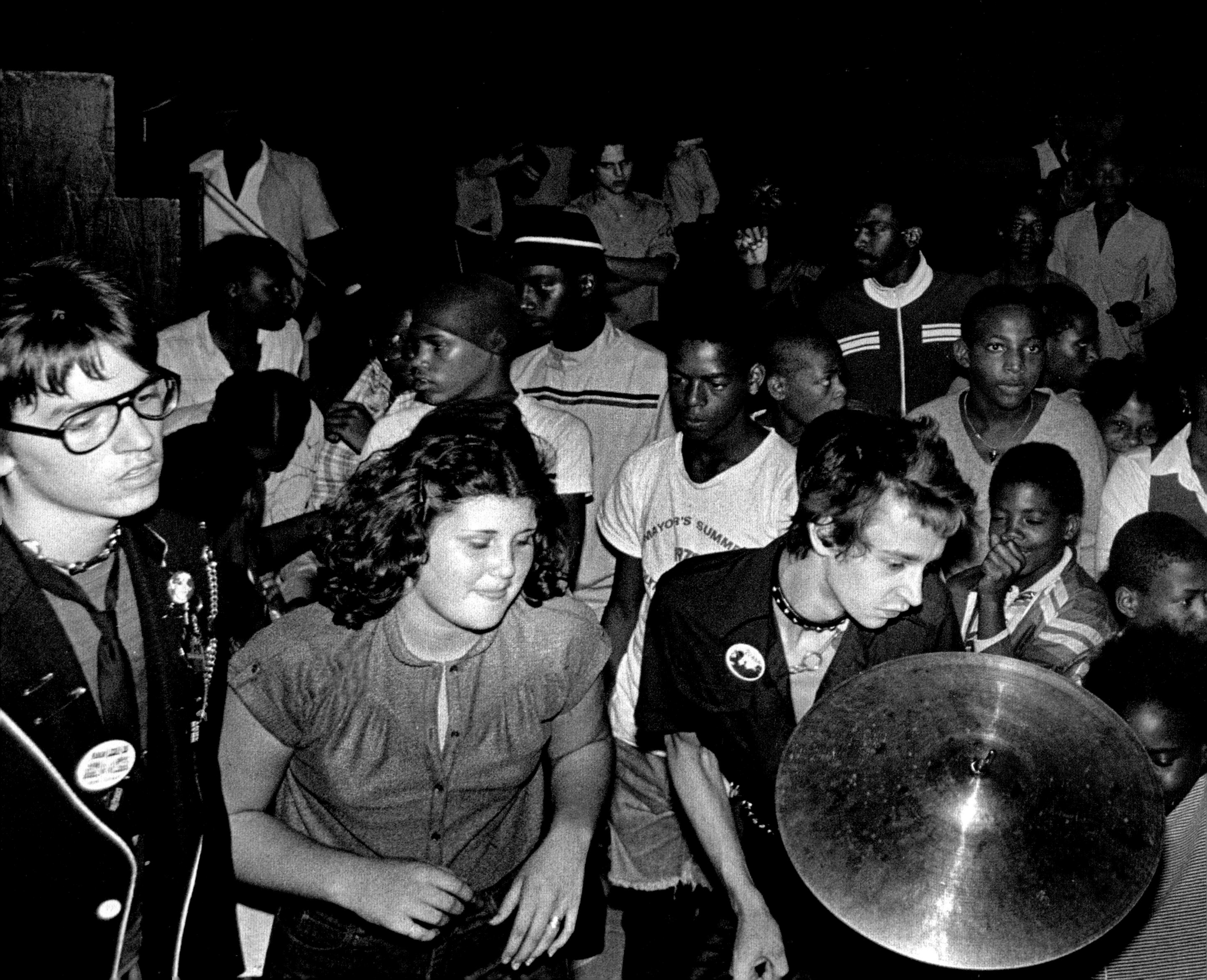

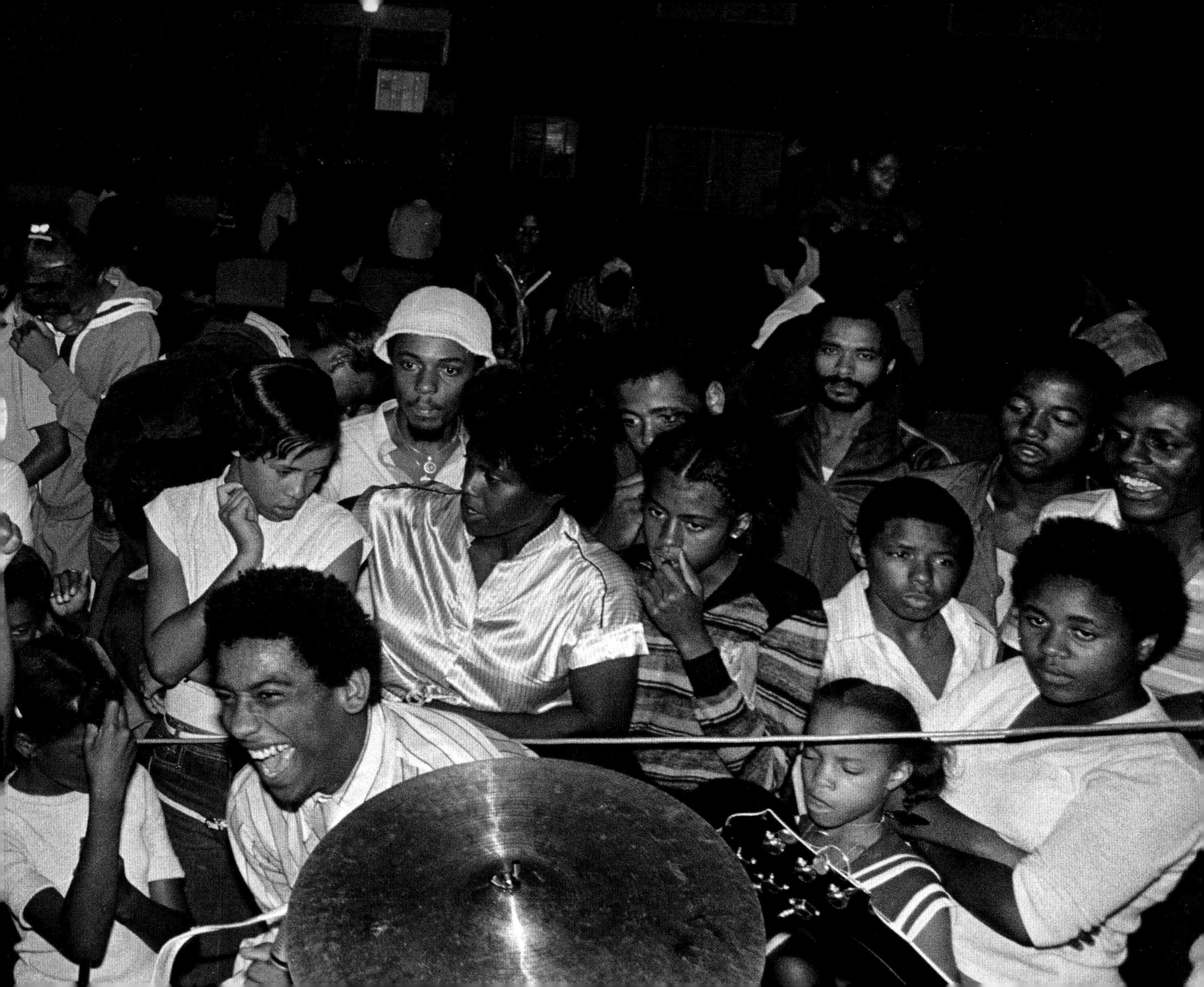

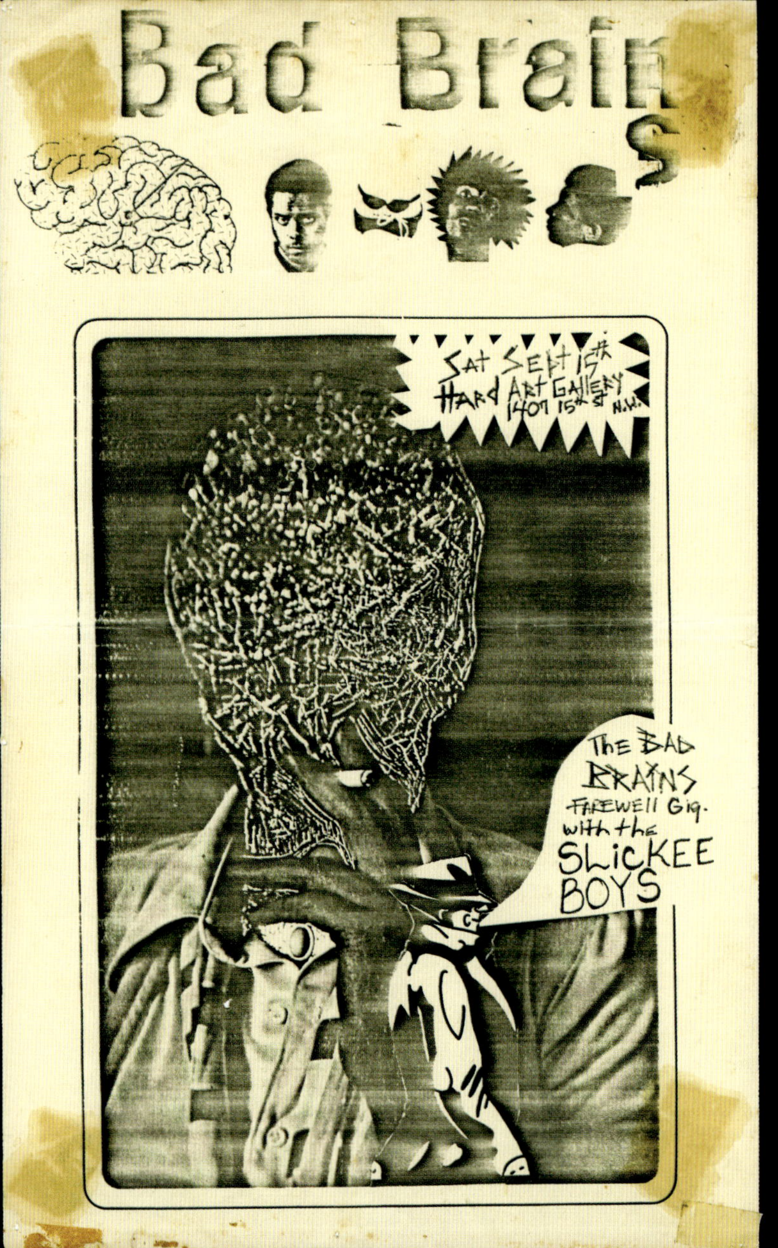

Hard Art Gallery

1407 15th Street, NW
September 15, 1979

Bad Brains
The Slickee Boys

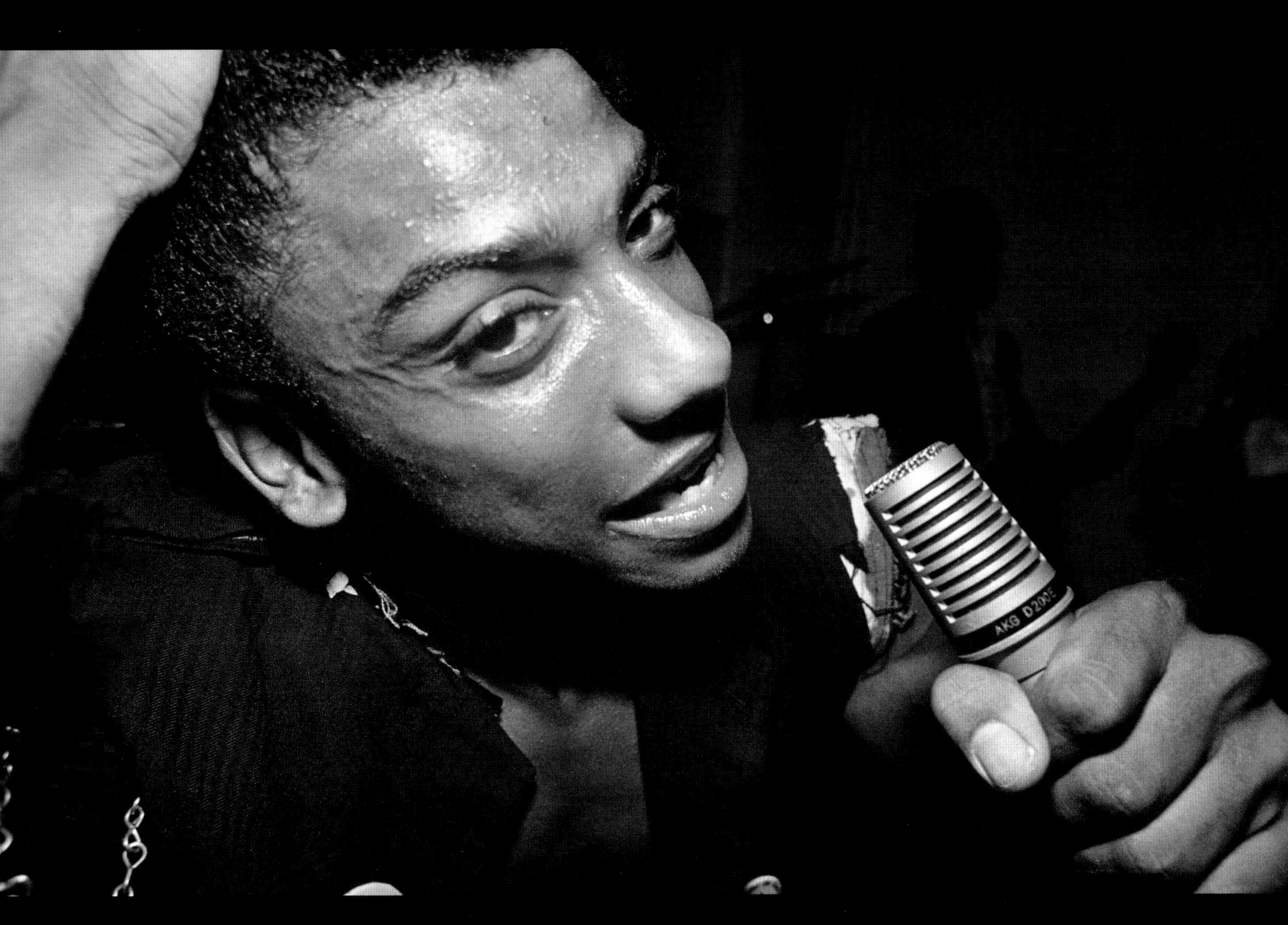
AKG D200E

Getting there meant walking along a dark, mostly deserted 15th Street with a number of abandoned buildings.

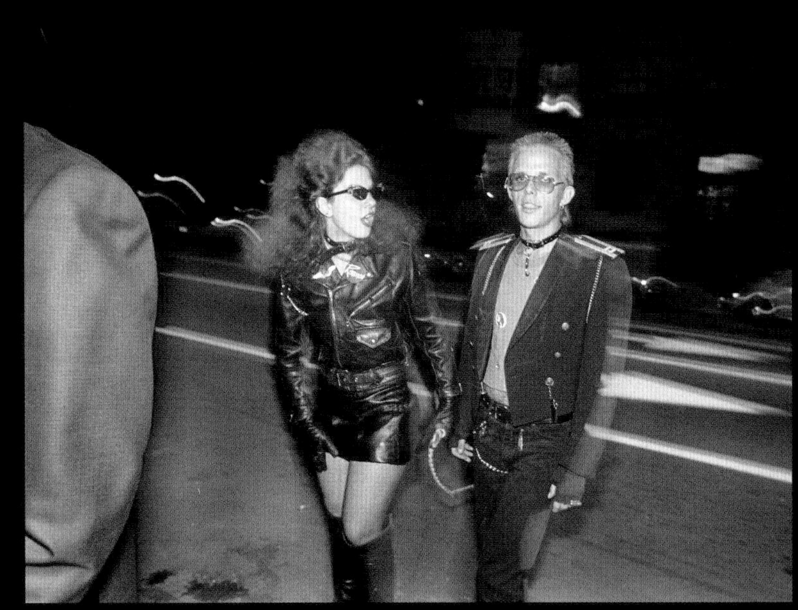

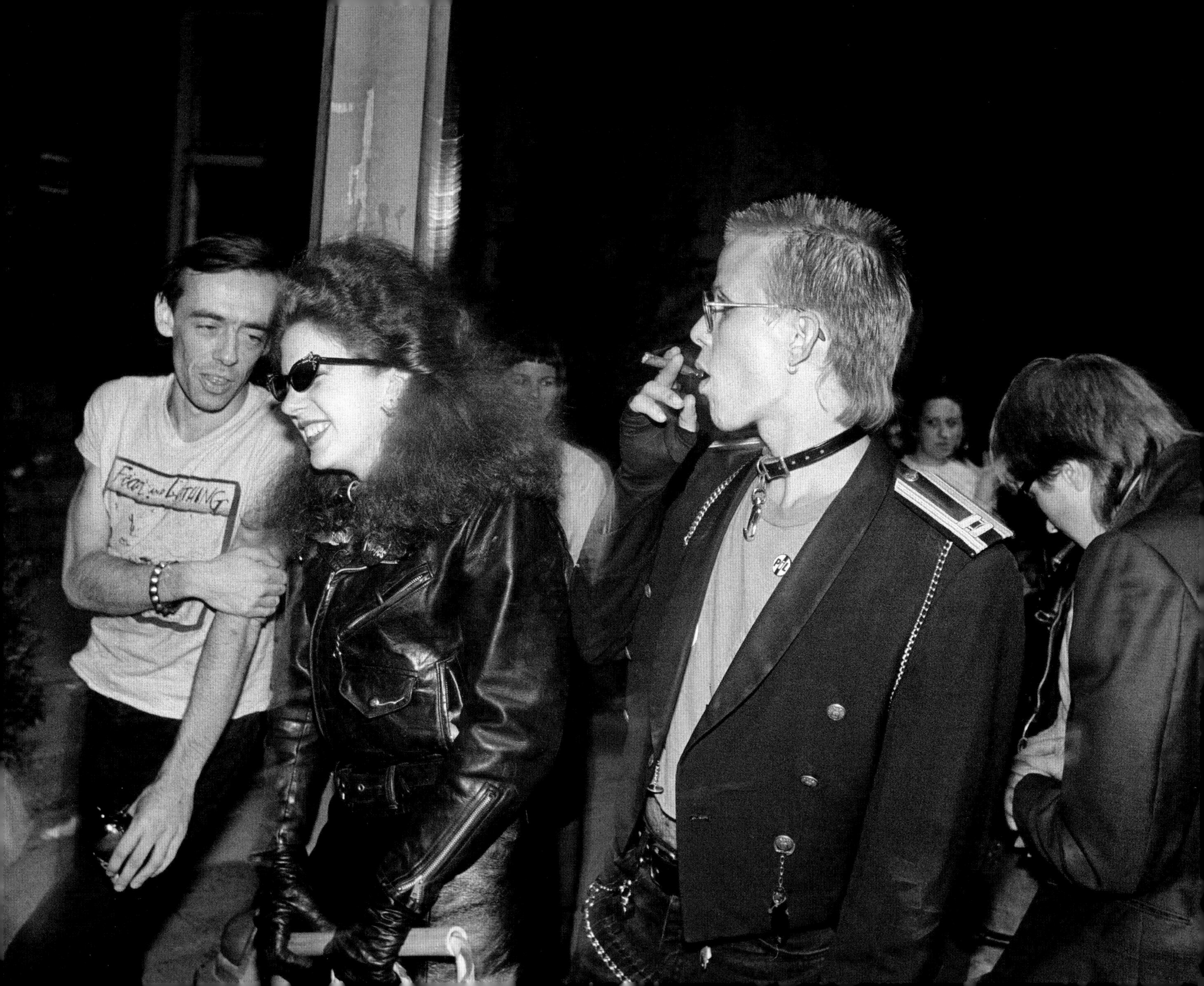

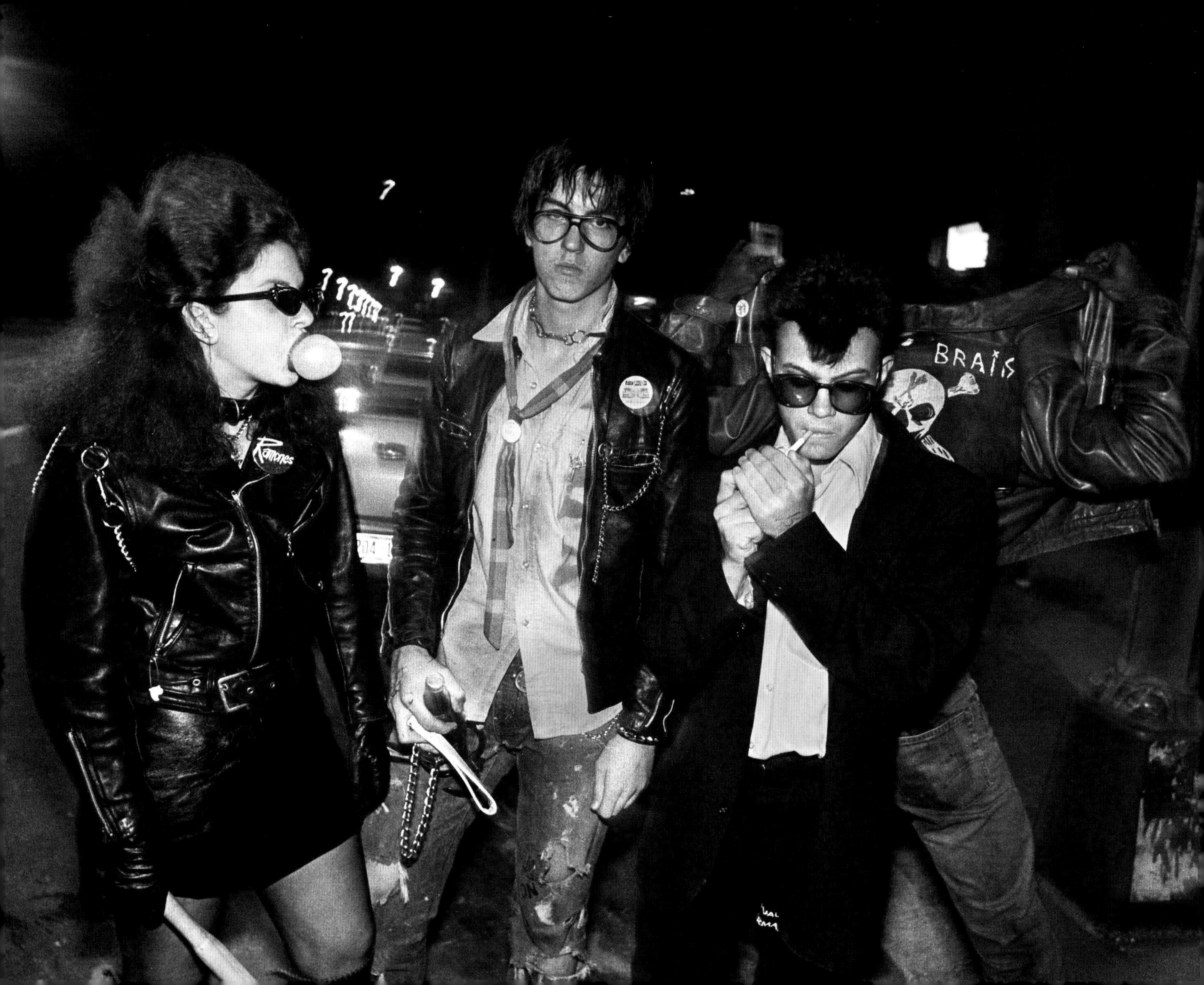

Ramones
BRAIS

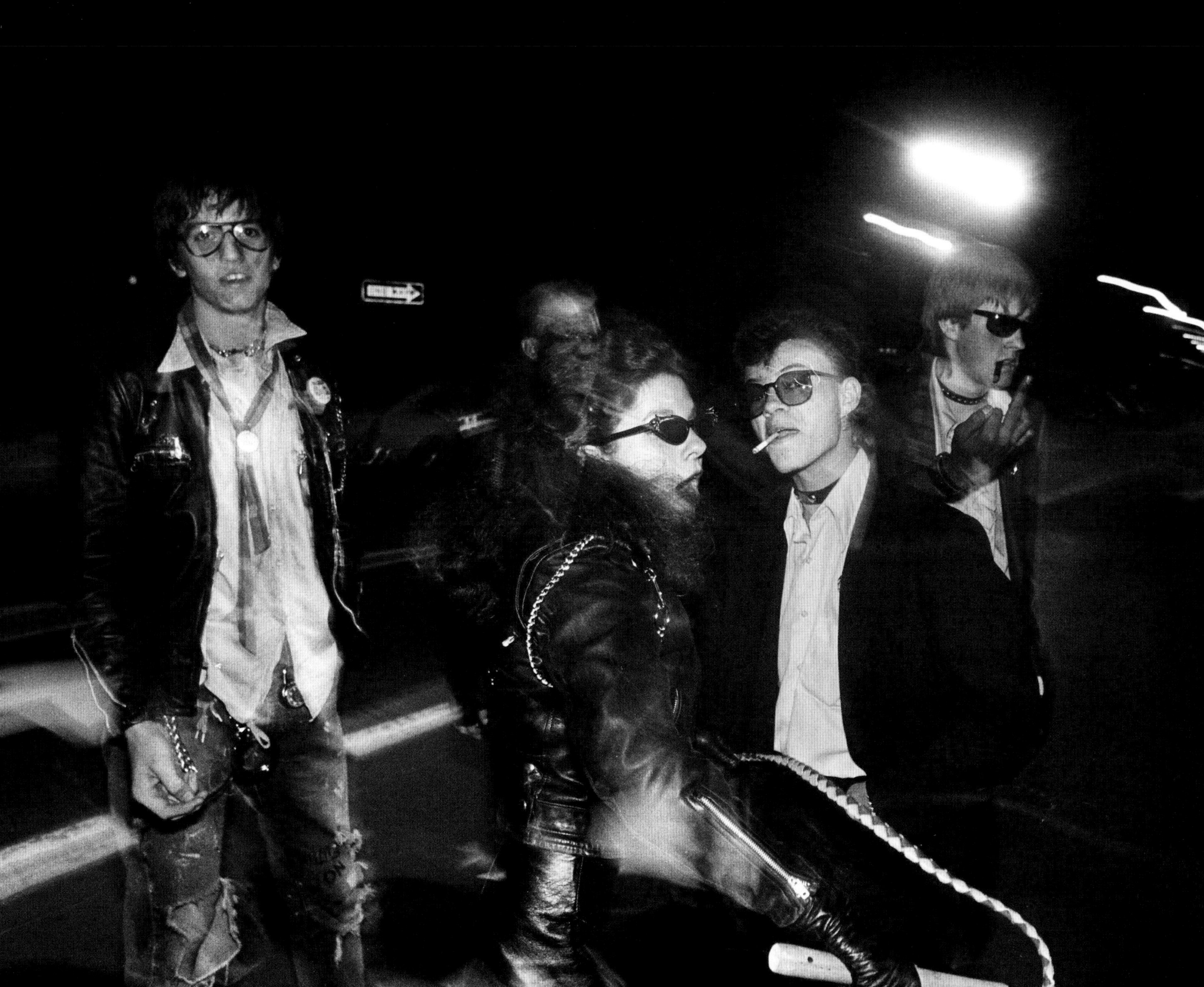

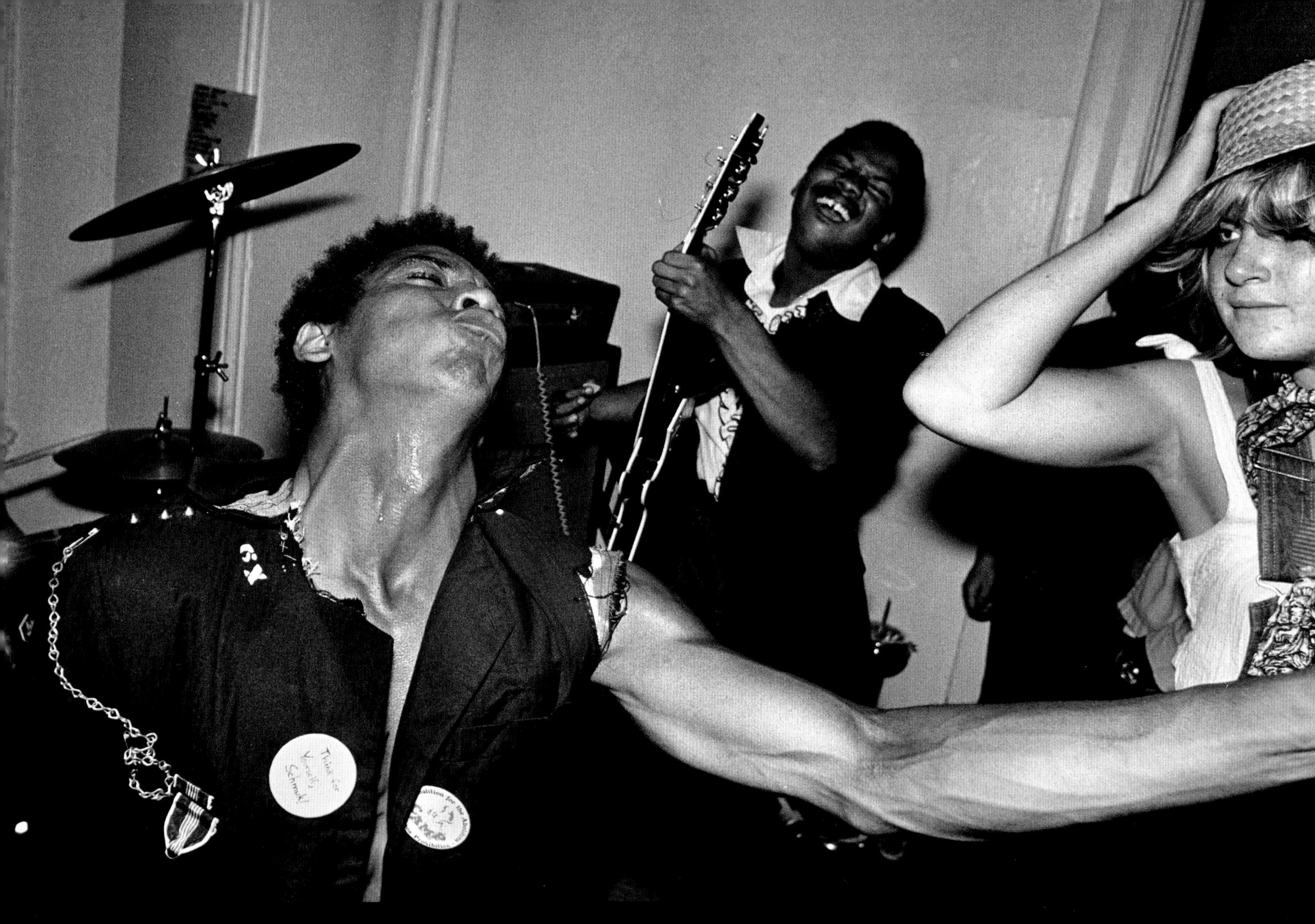
Think for Yourself, Schmuck!

HARD ART GALLERY

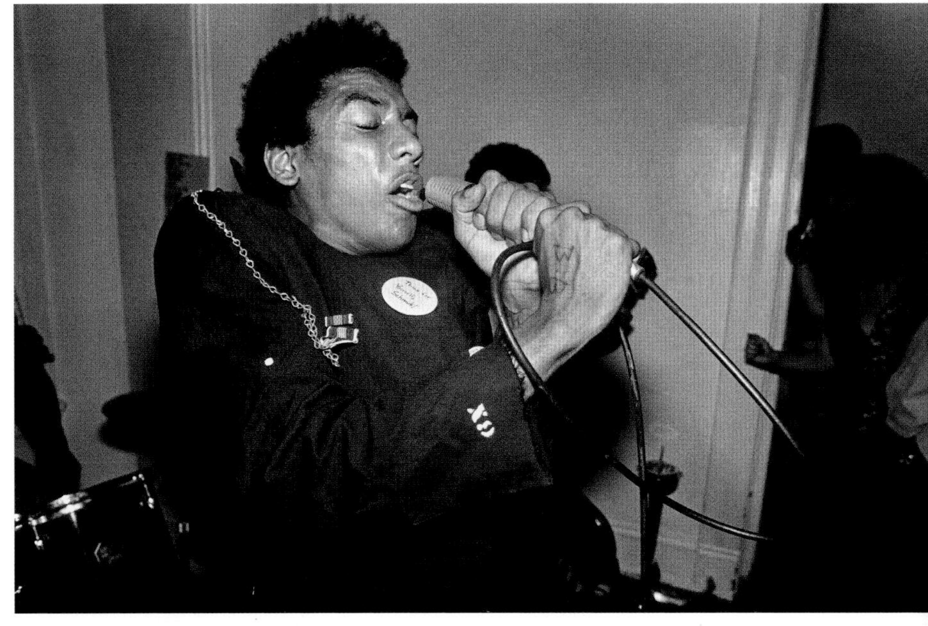

In a way, Rogelio Maxwell literally *found* Hard Art Gallery. It had been active during the early '70s but mysteriously shut down sometime around 1976, when he came across it empty, with the sign still out front. He negotiated with the landlord, reignited the gallery, and moved upstairs with various other young artists. Hard Art was relatively fresh, and committed to showing visual art in a nontrashed environment. It was not the free-for-all that Madams Organ offered; less risky or dangerous in some respects, Hard Art only hosted a handful of punk shows. I think the first music I saw there was The Enzymes with Rhoda and the Bad Seeds.

The neighborhood was still marginal, having not yet recovered from the 1968 riots and the tough times that followed. Hard Art was tidy, spare, and the walls were painted all white. Even the floors got a new coat of paint on a regular basis. Instead of a lawn in the front yard, it had towering, heavy-headed sunflowers.

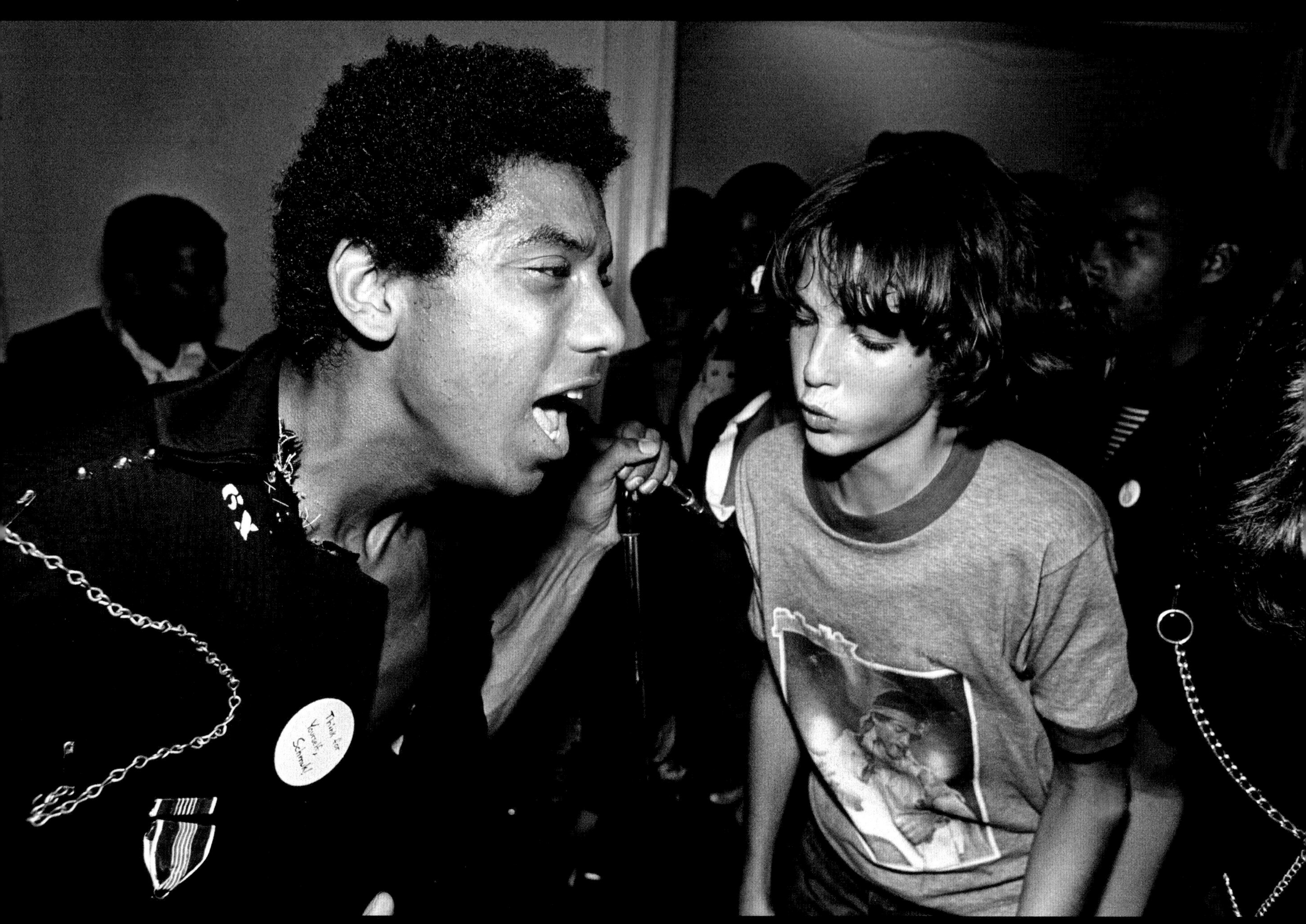
Think for
Yourself,
Schmuck!

The image has stuck with me for decades. Getting there meant walking along a dark, mostly deserted 15th Street with a number of abandoned buildings. Then there was the gauntlet of sunflowers that may have looked joyful in the daylight, but rustled and loomed after dark.

The Slickee Boys guitarist Kim Kane put his foot all the way up on a shelf during a couple of songs—the shelf was at least chest-high and he had a rubber pork chop taped to his leg. Kim generally seemed more than human to me, in his cartoony appearance, his all-out showmanship, and in his encouraging, generous nature when talking to him. I was floored to see him just hanging out at an Untouchables gig one time. The Slickee Boys were like that—confident in what they were doing and interested in what others were doing.

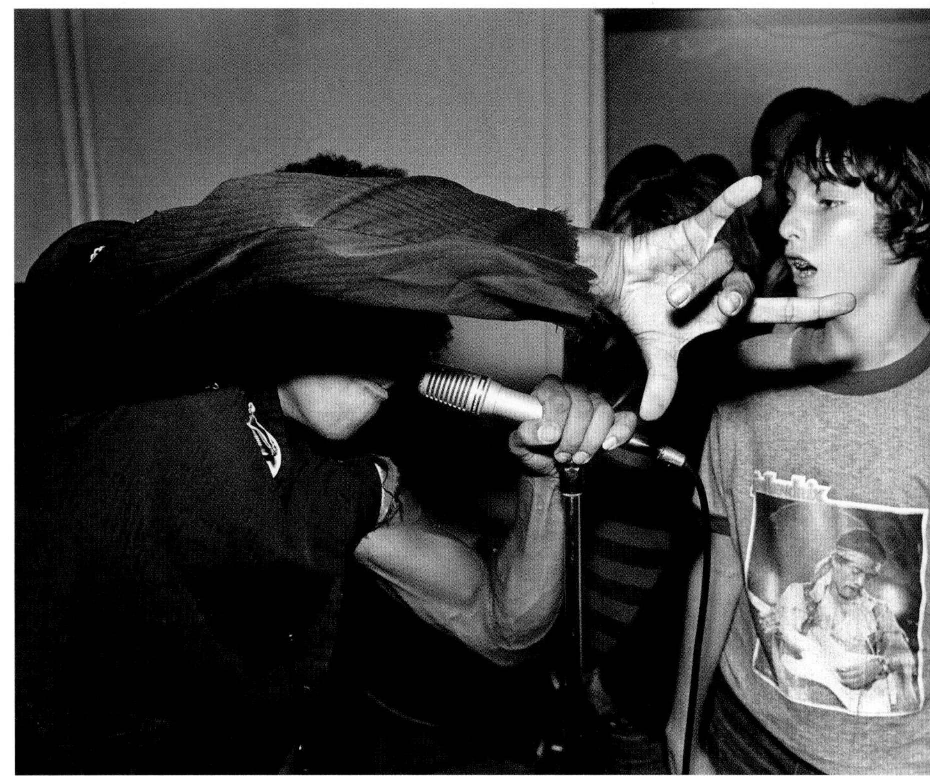

Bad Brains were running out of places to play when HR called Rogelio to ask if they could do a show at Hard Art. It was the last gig for Bad Brains before their first attempt at moving to New York. By then they had become our friends, as well as being an amazing band, so no one wanted to see them go. As the pictures indicate, they crushed it that night. It was the biggest show Hard Art ever did and with it came some damage.

It was the last gig for Bad Brains before their first attempt at moving to New York.

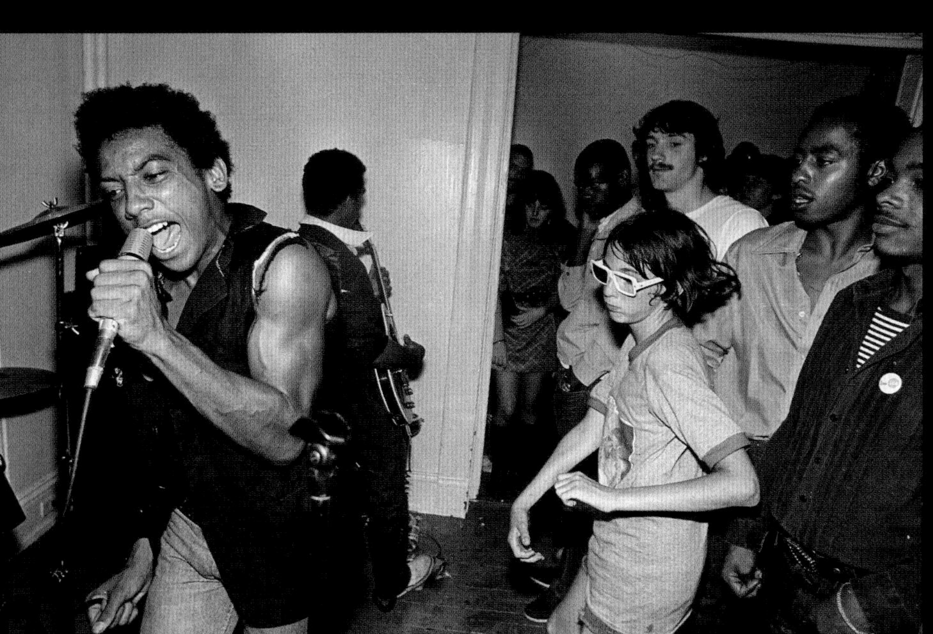

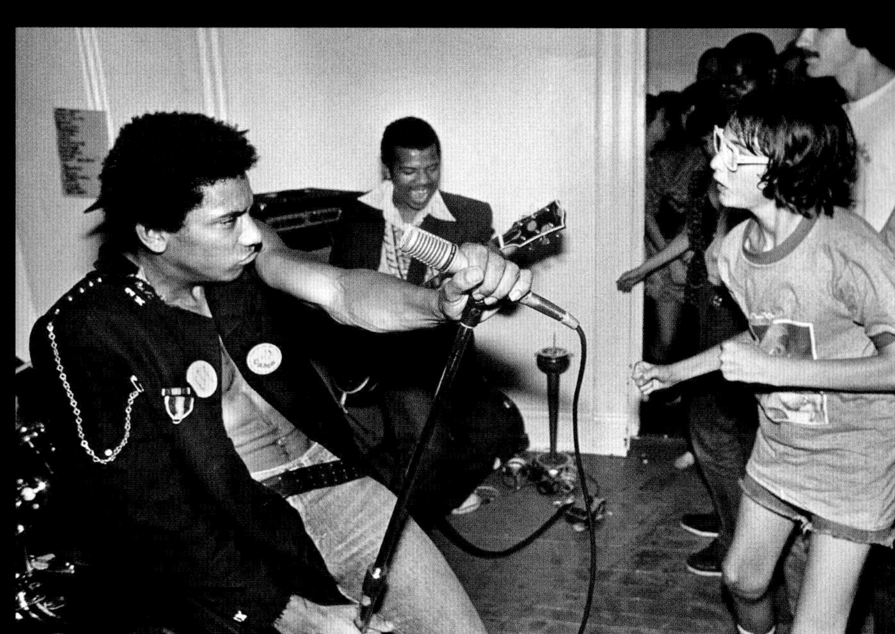

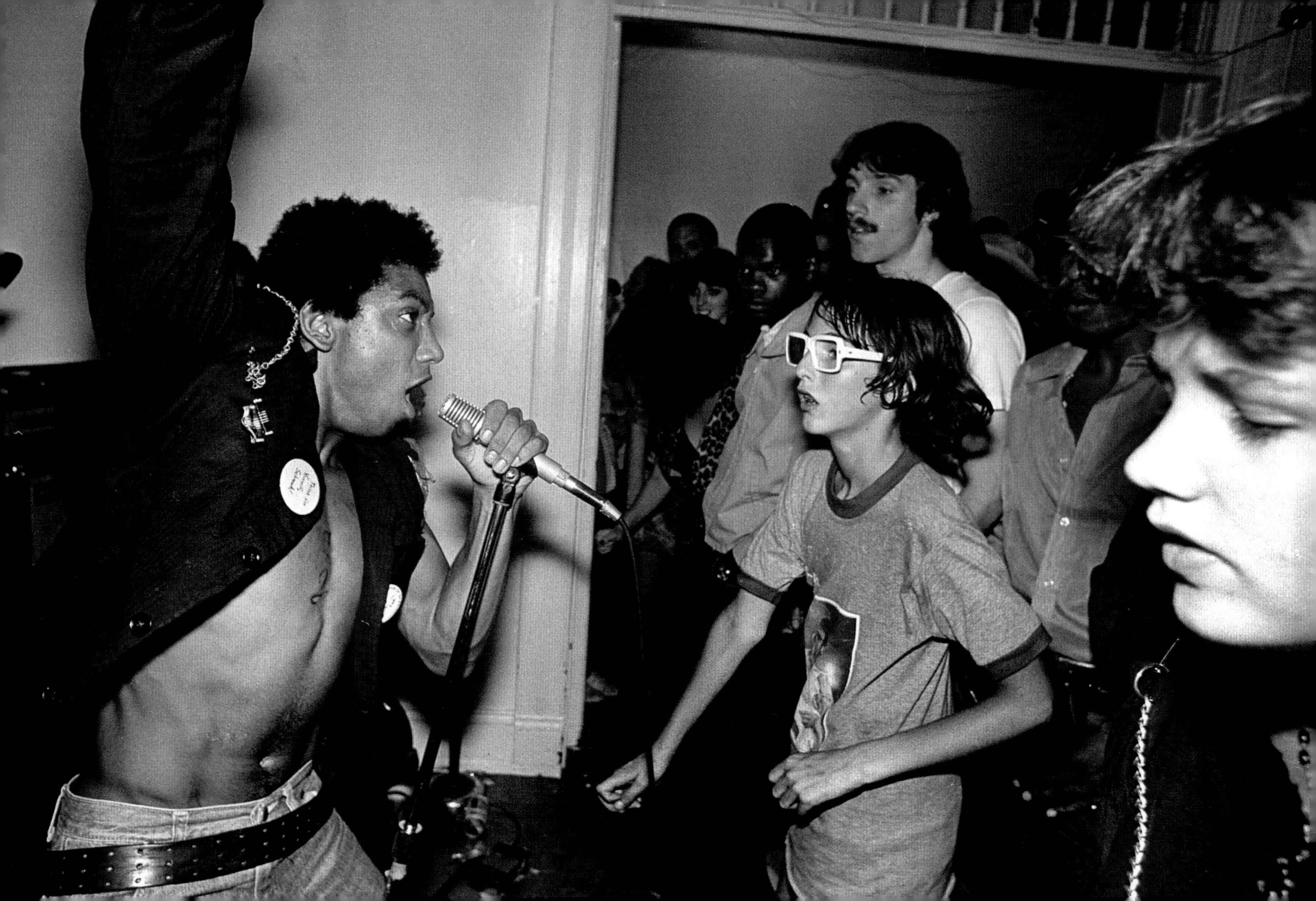

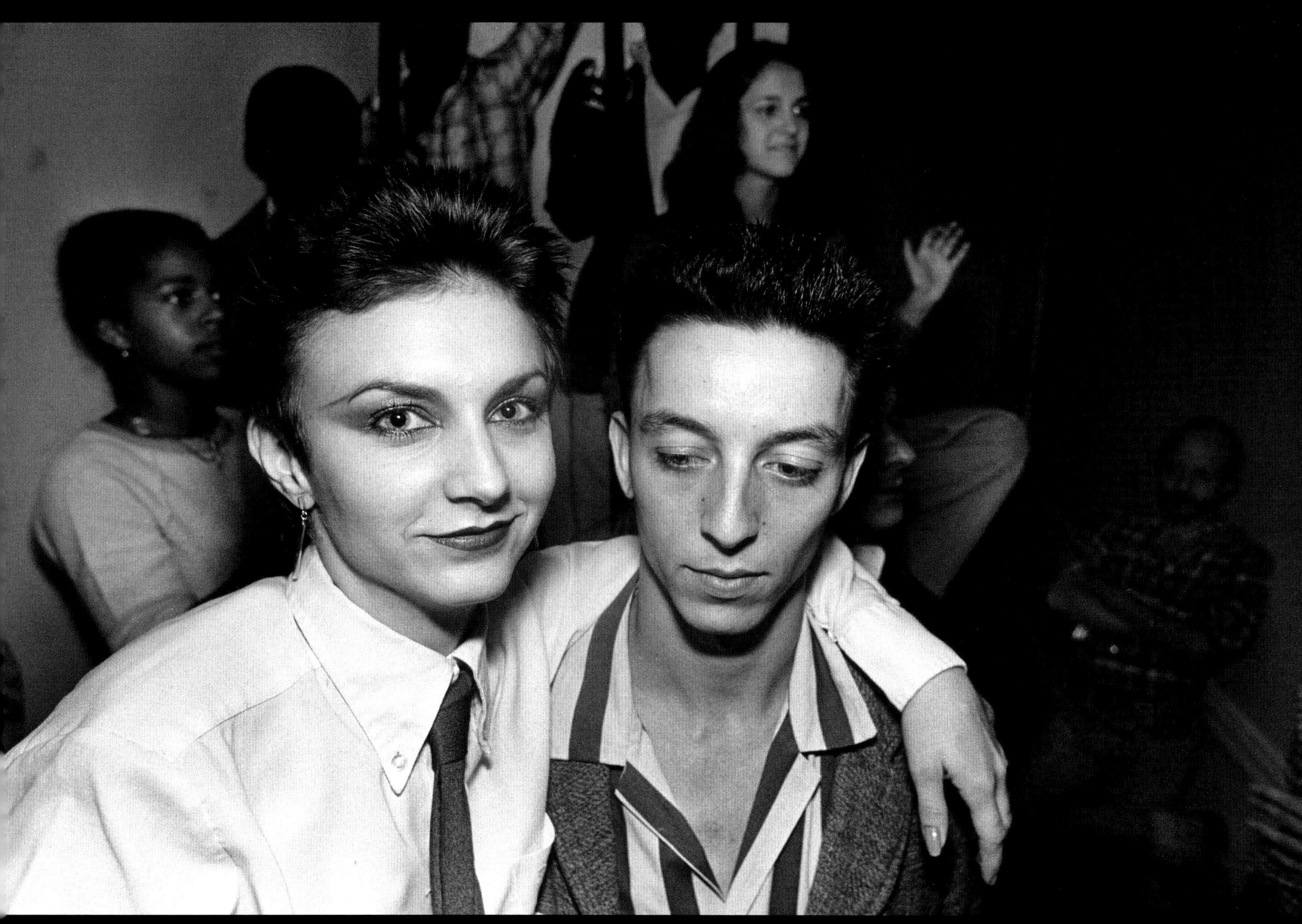

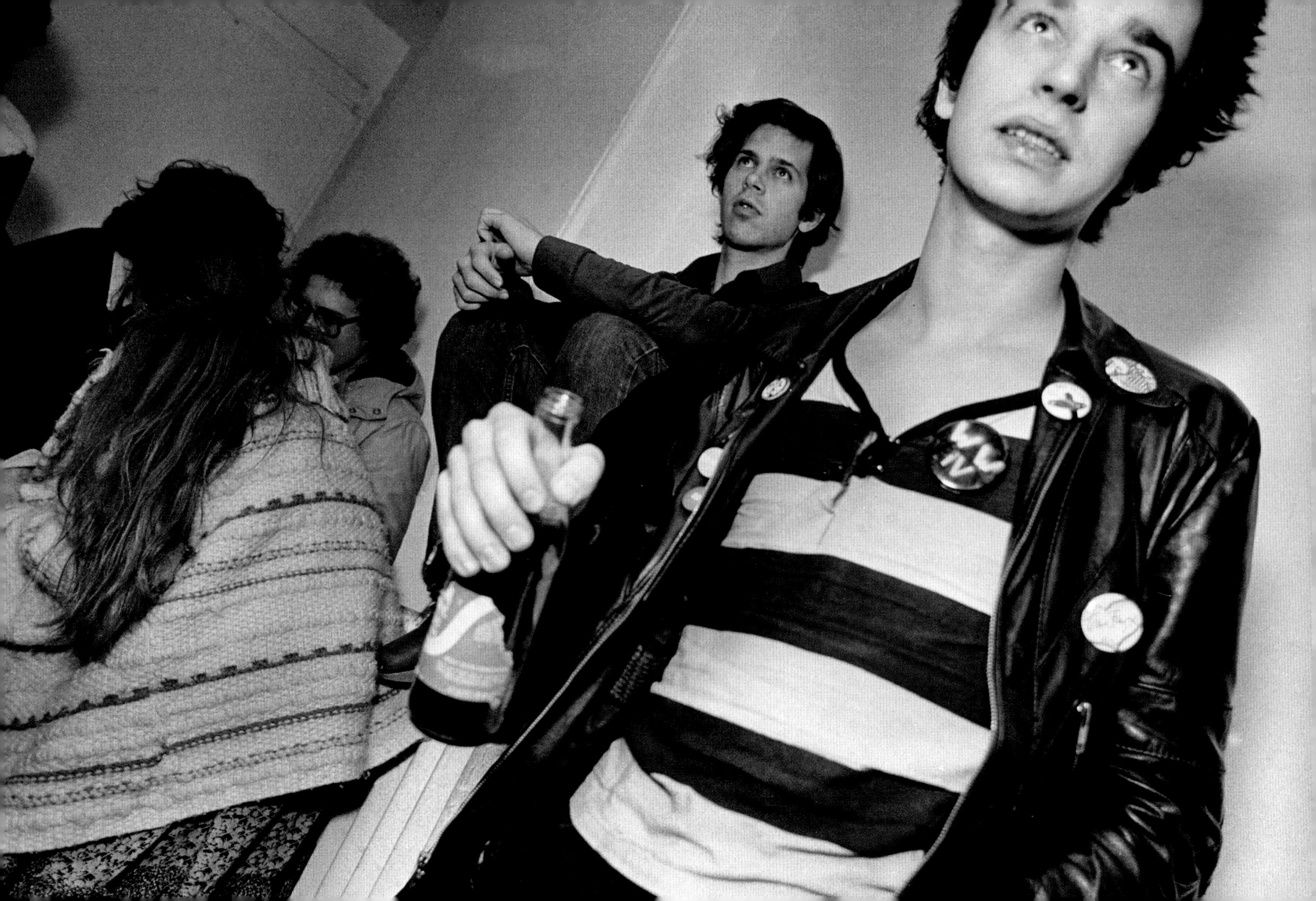

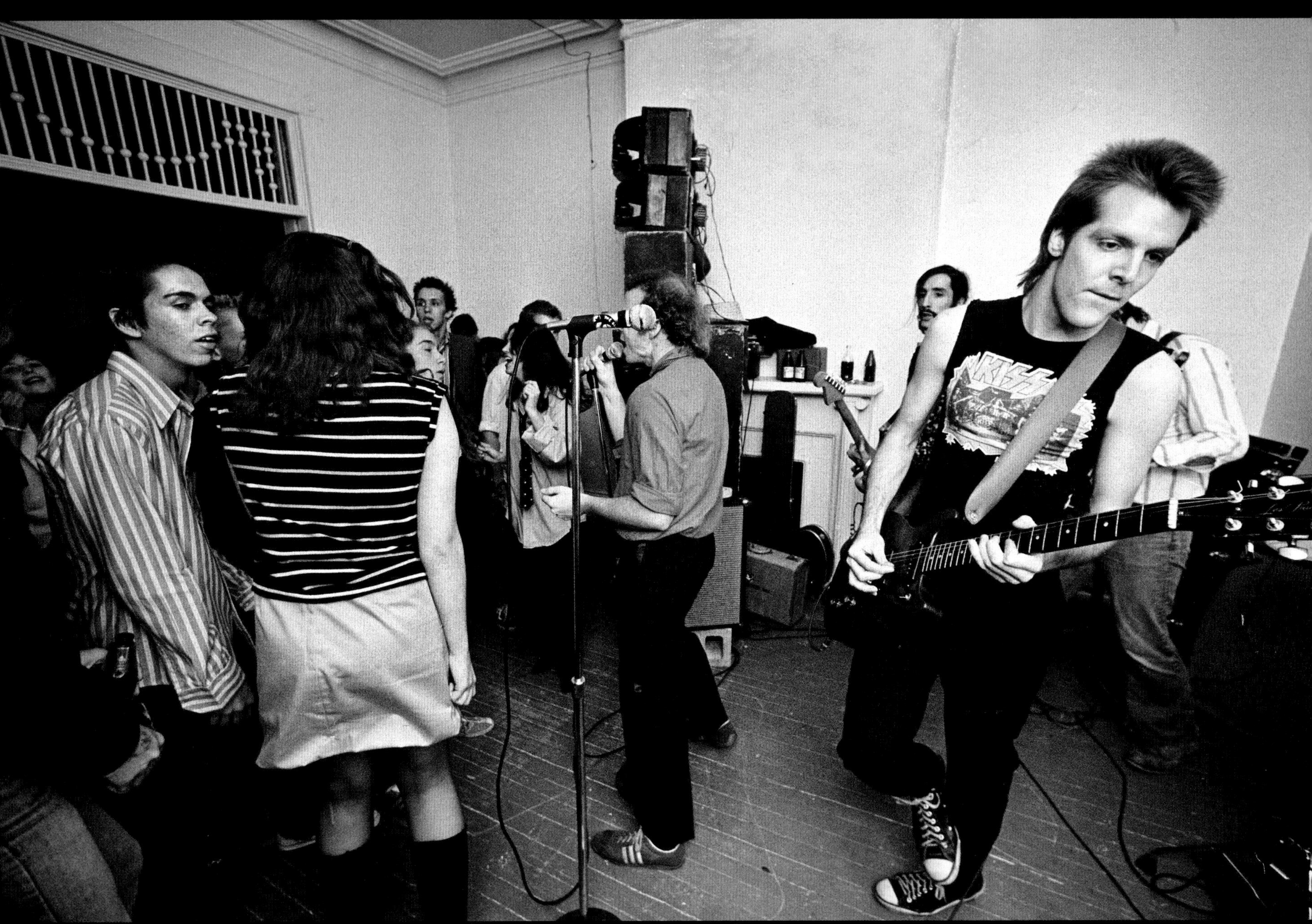
KISS

The Slickee Boys were like that—confident in what they were doing and interested in what others were doing.

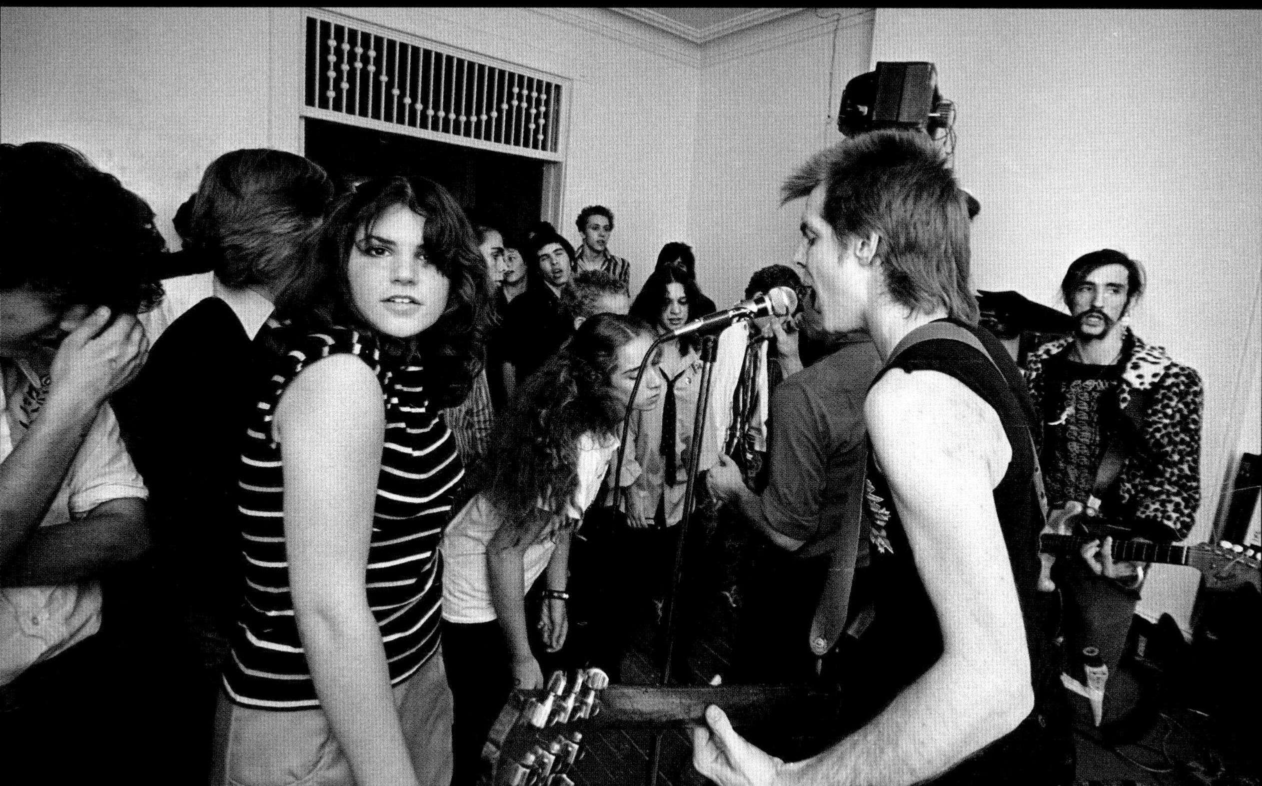

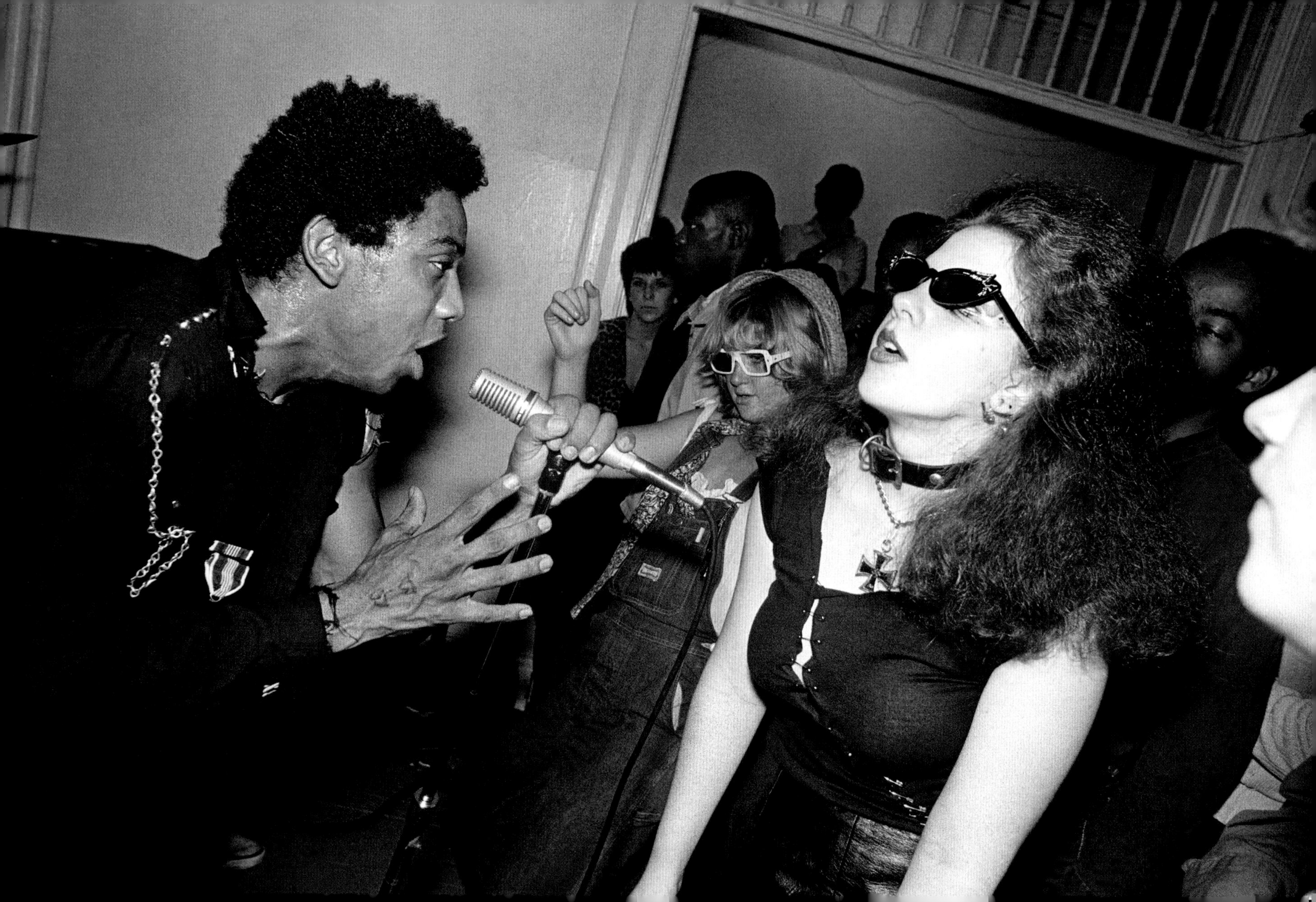

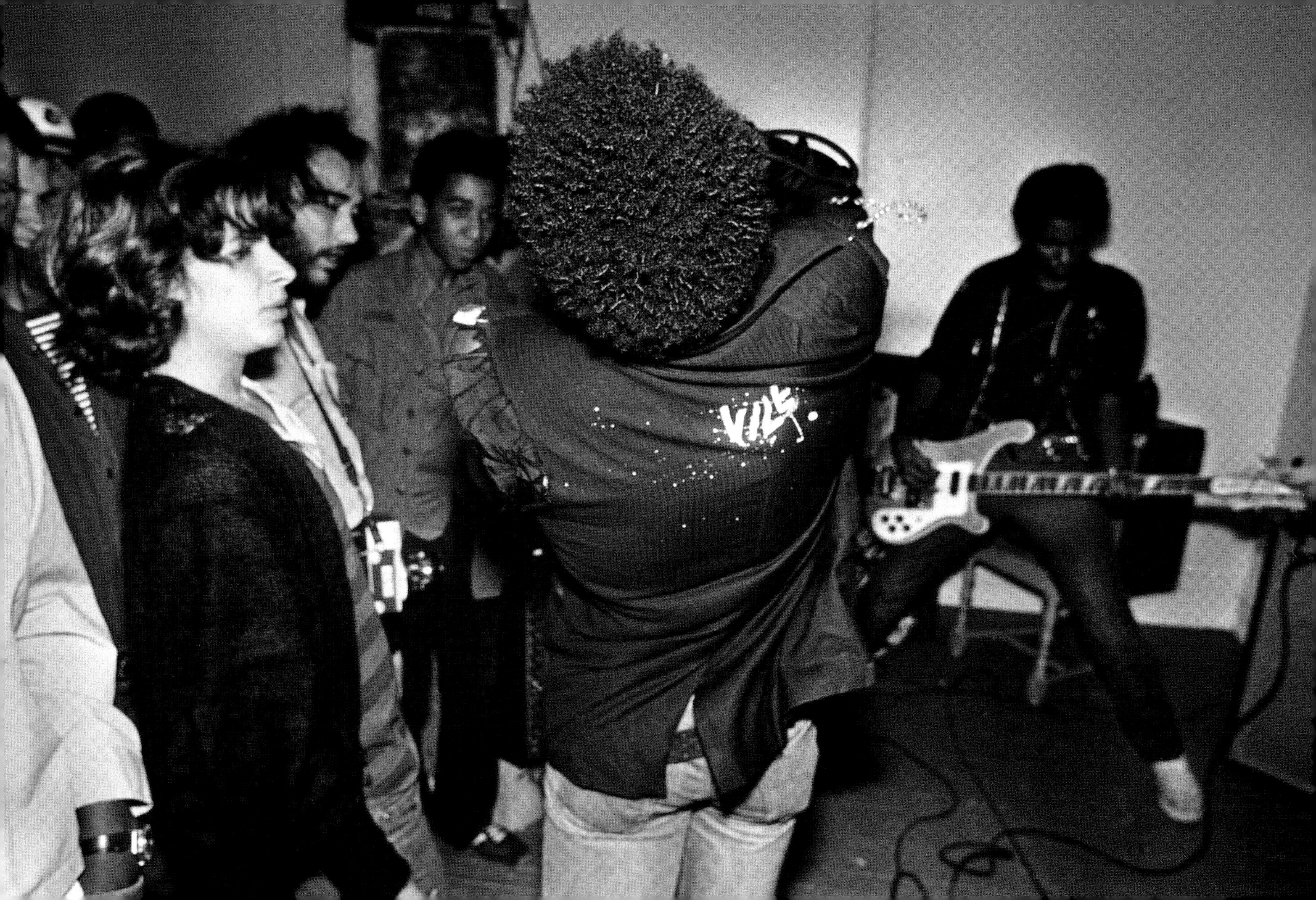

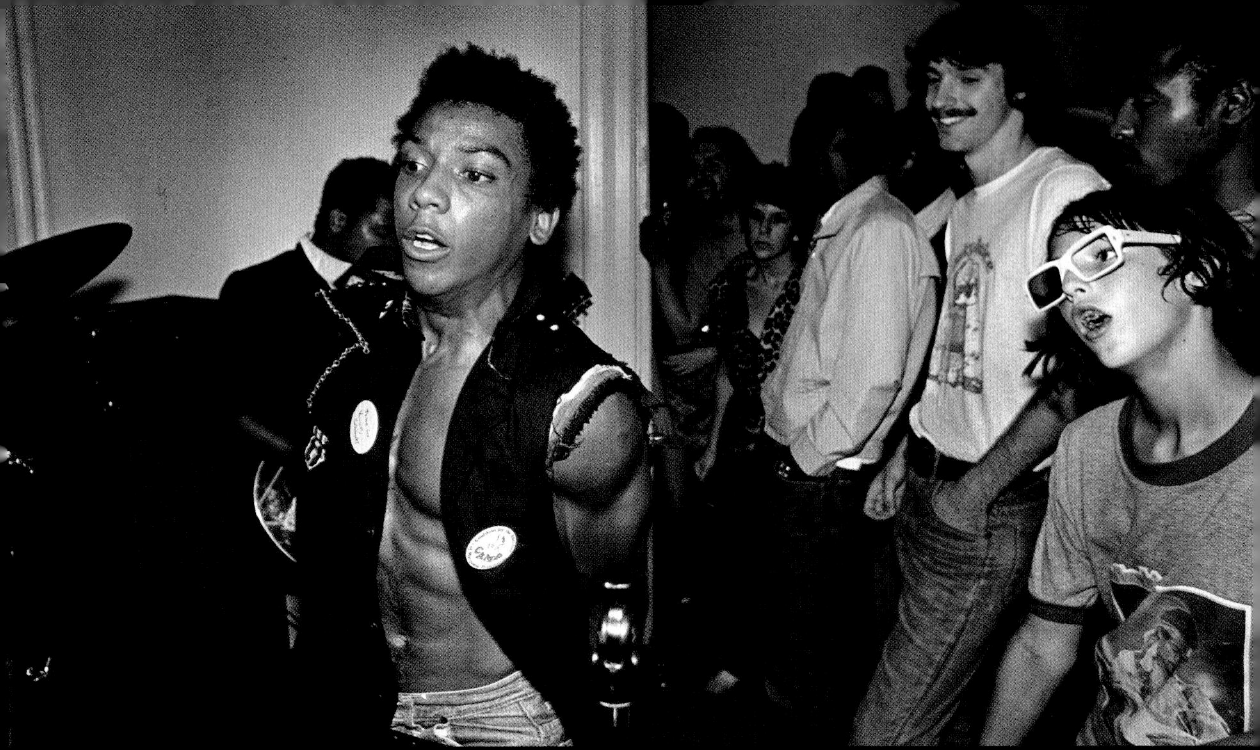

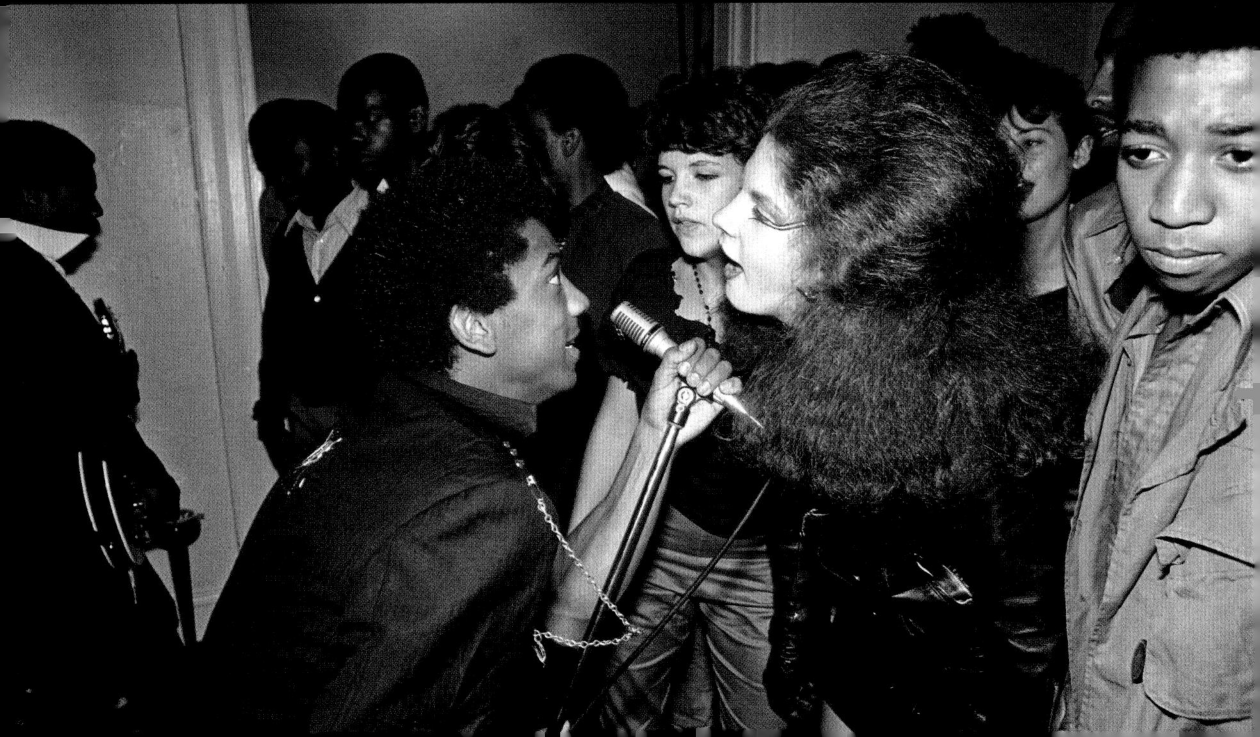

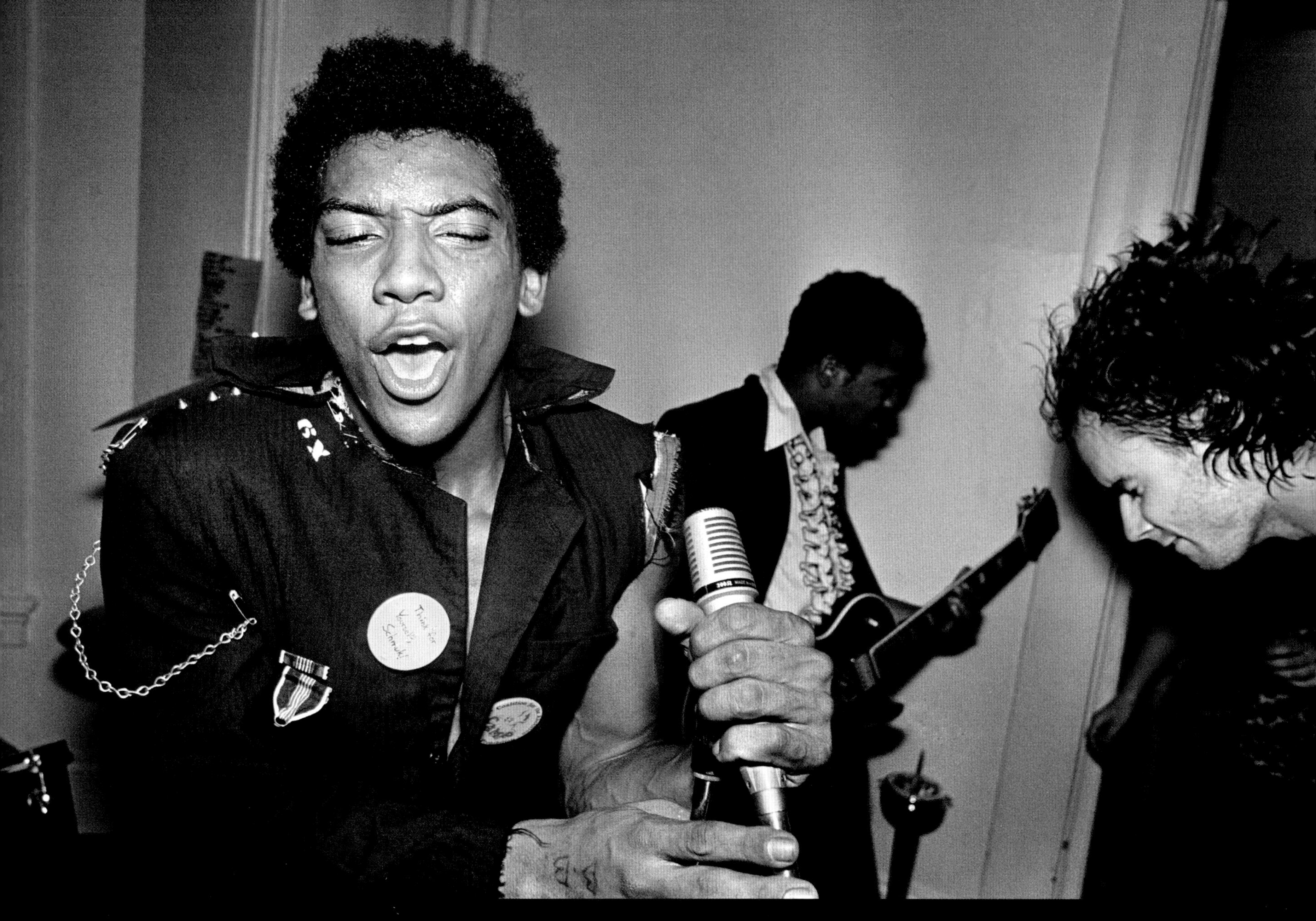

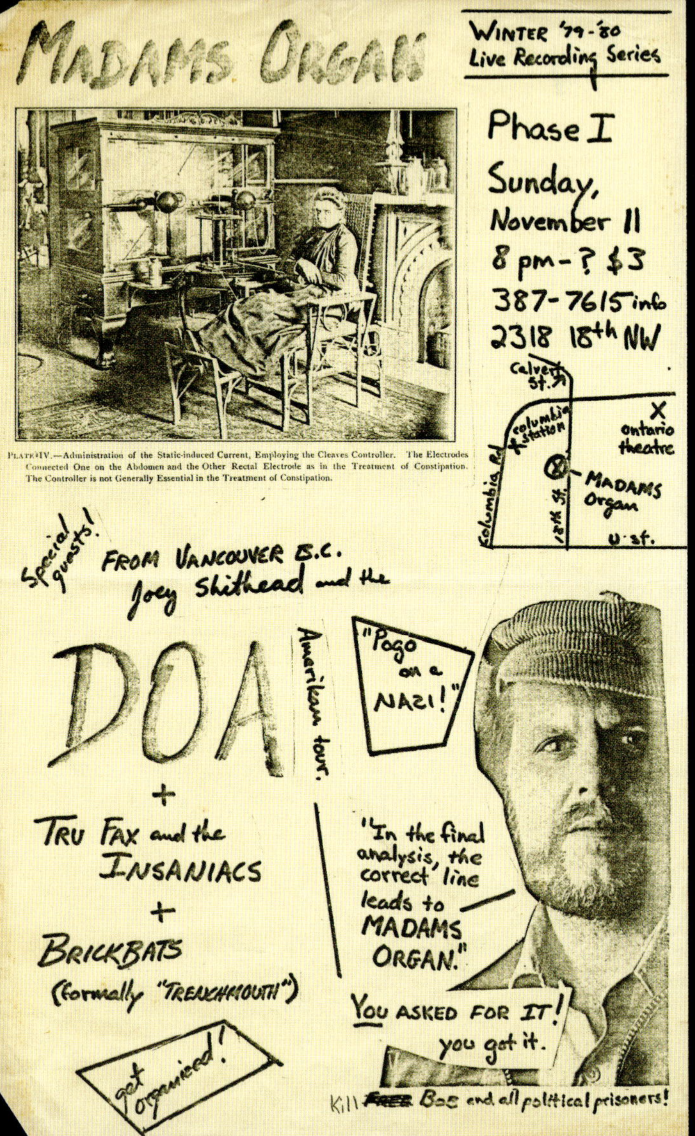

Madams Organ Artist's Cooperativ

2318 18th Street, NW
November 11, 1979

D.O.A.
Tru Fax & the Insaniacs
Brick Bats (Trenchmouth)

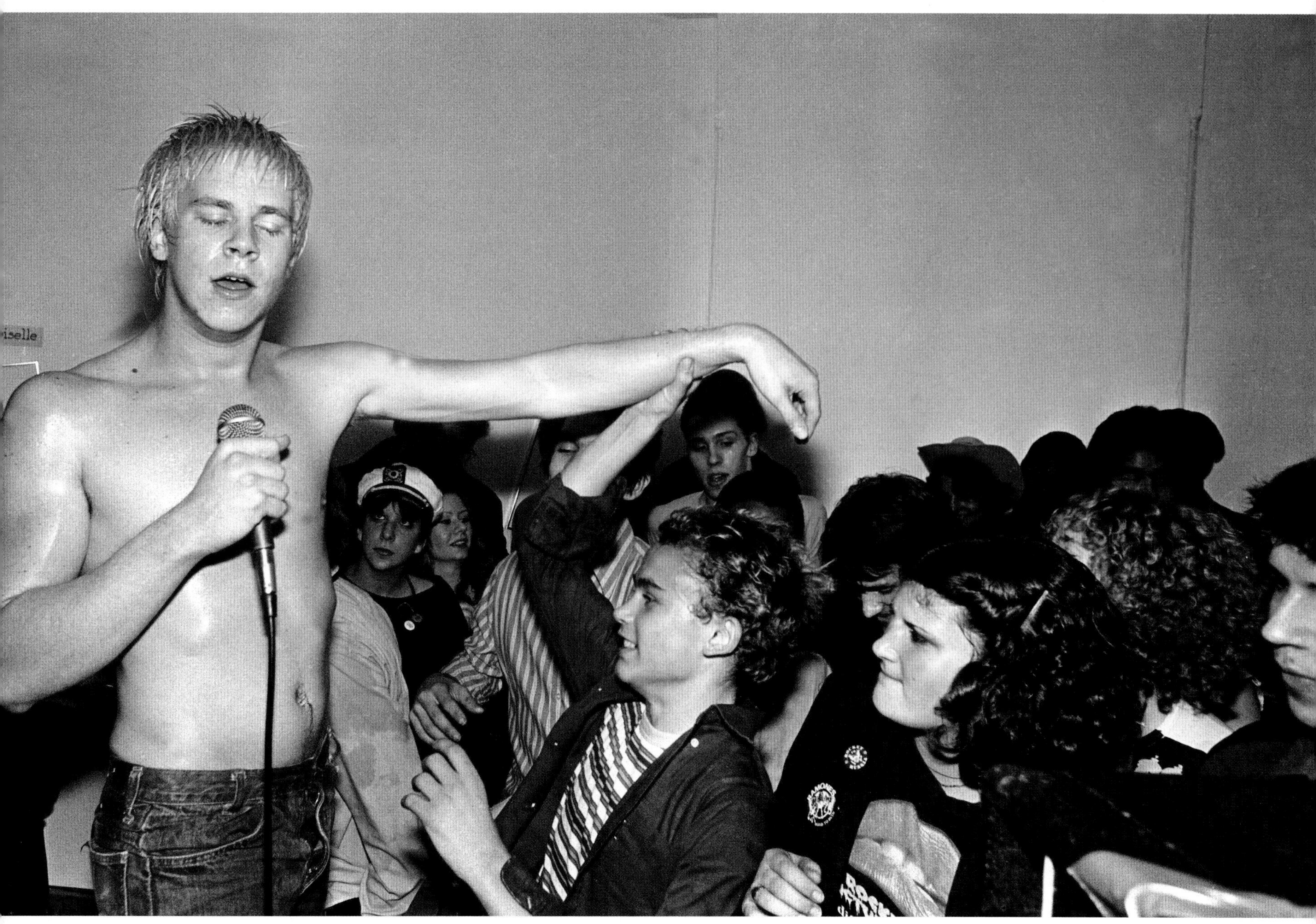

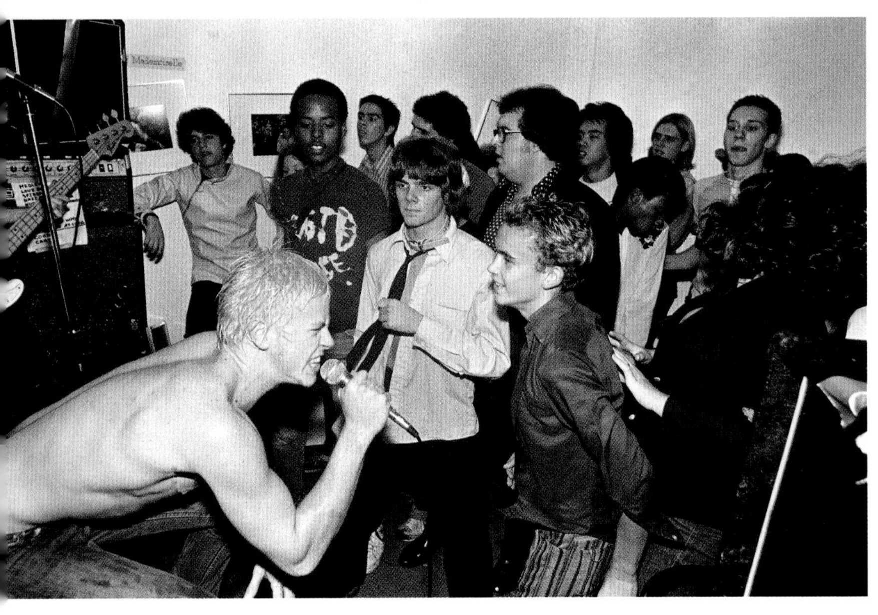

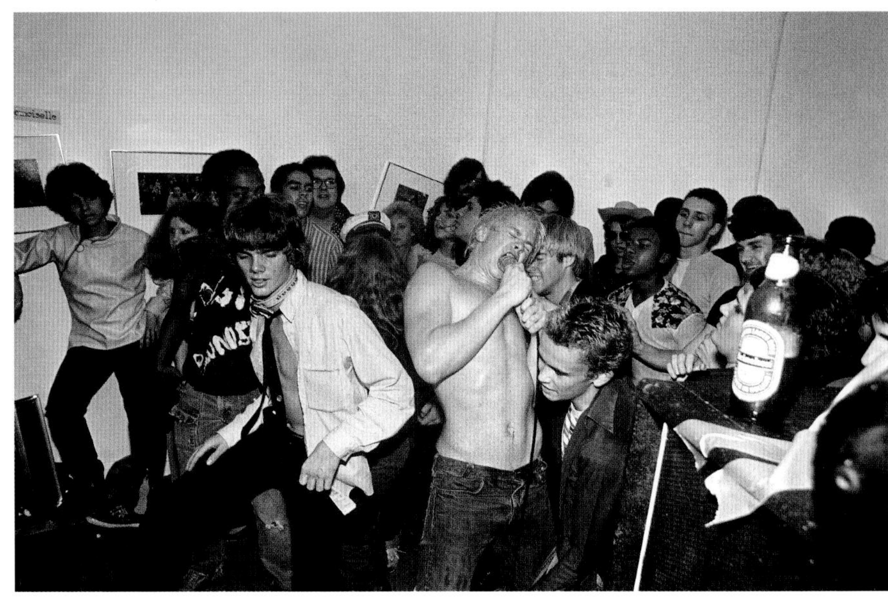

Any attempts at protecting or respecting personal space were abandoned after several songs.

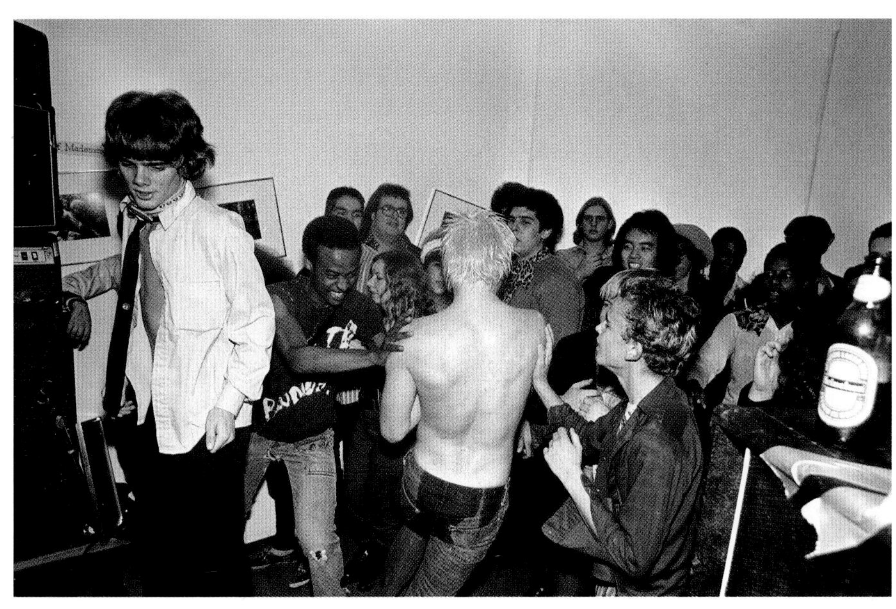

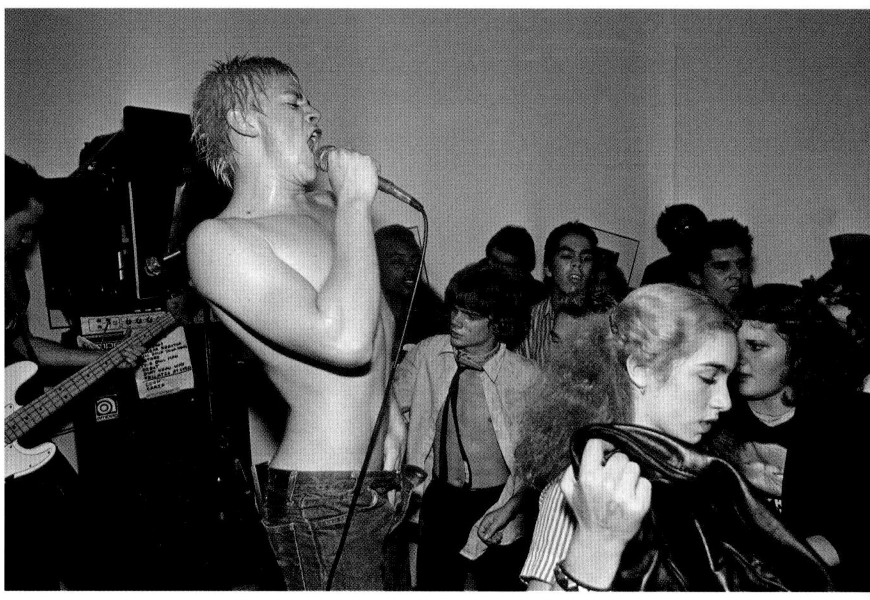

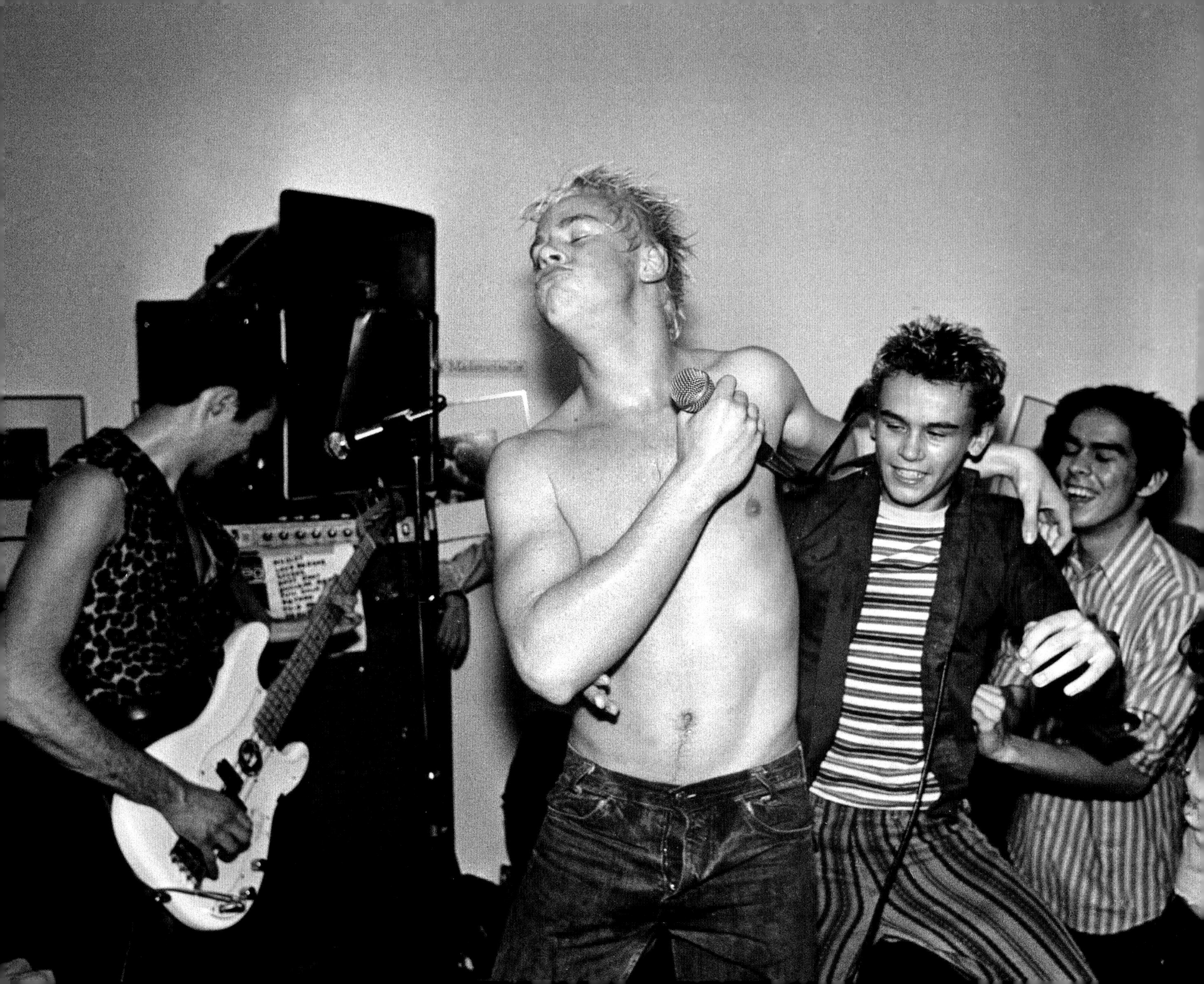

MADAMS ORGAN 1
EARLY STAGES

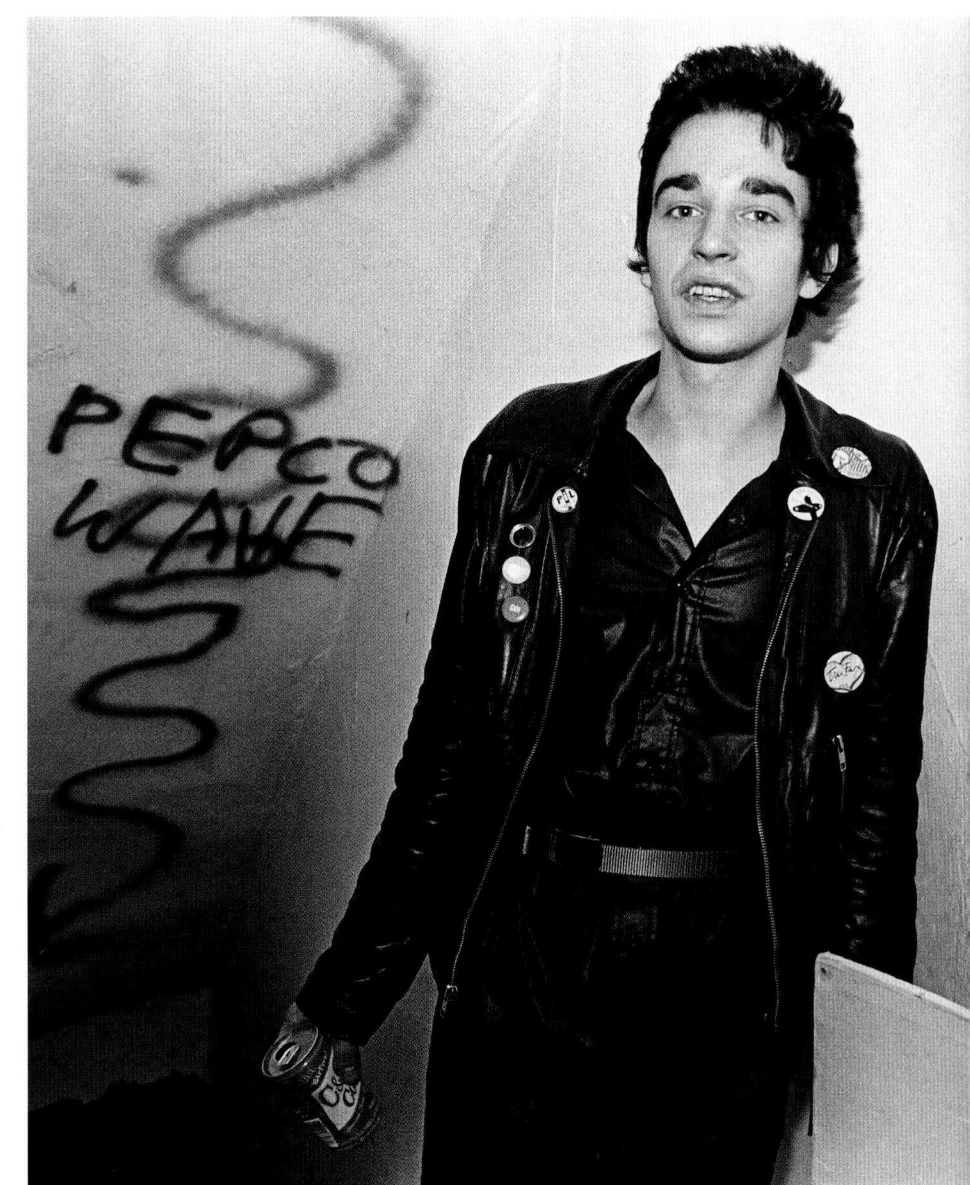

Shirtless and burly, his body is slicked with beer and sweat. His left arm is draped over my shoulder, my right arm around his waist, in a mutually assured embrace. He has just lifted me from the audience and onto the stage, which it turns out was exactly what I wanted him to do.

Not sure how I got there—maybe got a ride from Nathan? I usually rode with Ian or Henry but neither of them were at this show. Three bucks to get in for three bands: locals Tru Fax & the Insaniacs, Trenchmouth, and D.O.A. from Vancouver, British Columbia.

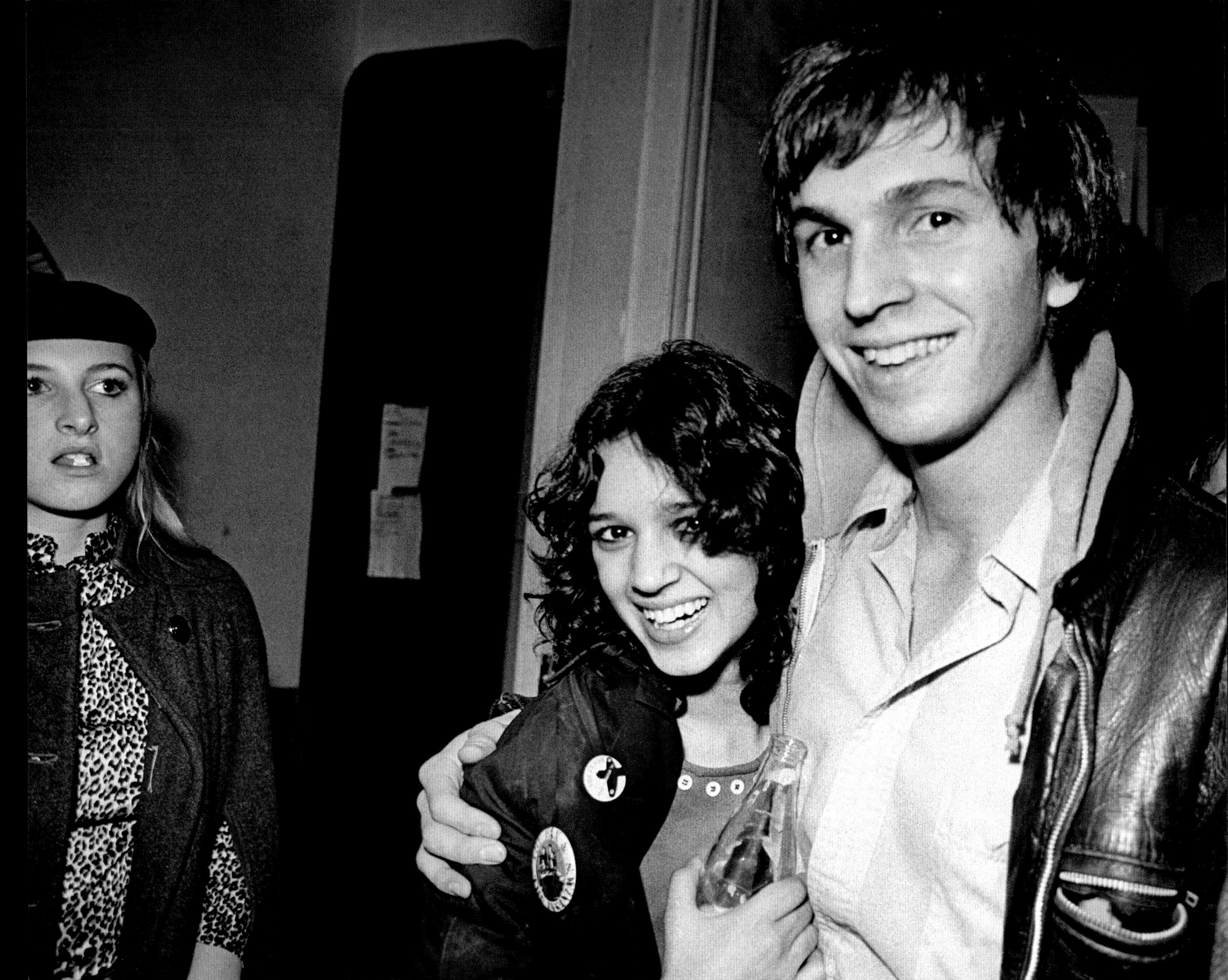

People danced into and with each other, feeling charged by the permissiveness of it all.

It was hot in the windowless room and Charlie Danbury of Trenchmouth had his shirt off as soon as he got onstage. Perhaps even before that. He was a solidly put-together guy. When he stomped his drunken boot, mic stands swayed and dust rose from the boards. He threw himself around and off the stage euphorically.

He knocked me off my feet and we ended up on the floor. I discovered from that angle that the stage was an amateur thing, scavenged lumber held up by liberated milk crates, nails hanging down like stalactites, and crumpled beer cans resting in the dust. Any attempts at protecting or respecting personal space were abandoned after several songs. People danced into and with each other, feeling charged by the permissiveness of it all.

Behind me, Bert is smiling with eyes closed. His face is gleaming and he is pushing me up onto the stage; Charlie's eyes are beatifically closed too, his head flung back and to one side, lips pursing the way people do when satisfied with something. His hair is bleached white and his zipper is down.

I am wearing an absurd arrangement of stripes that warp with my body's movement as I dance. Horizontal lines crawl across my chest, vertical lines pour down my legs. Smiling and shining like Bert, my eyes are open, taking it all in. I am apparently regarding Charlie's torso.

The bassist, Paul Cleary, is wearing his girlfriend's leopard-print vest with nothing underneath and wringing his instrument's neck like he's really trying to hurt it—grimacing with effort.

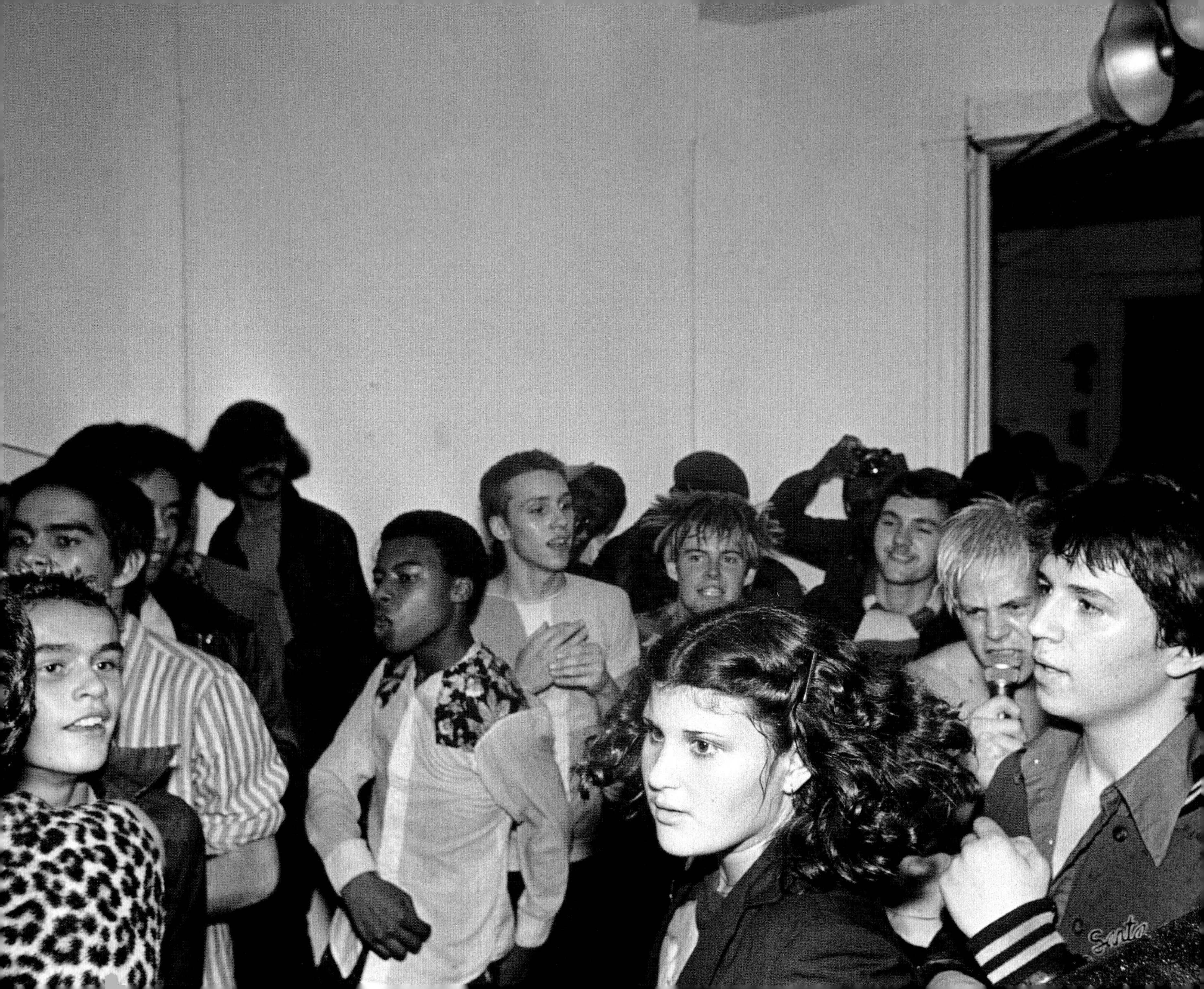
Santa

Art for them had become a concept that reached beyond canvas and paper and even conversation. It was action.

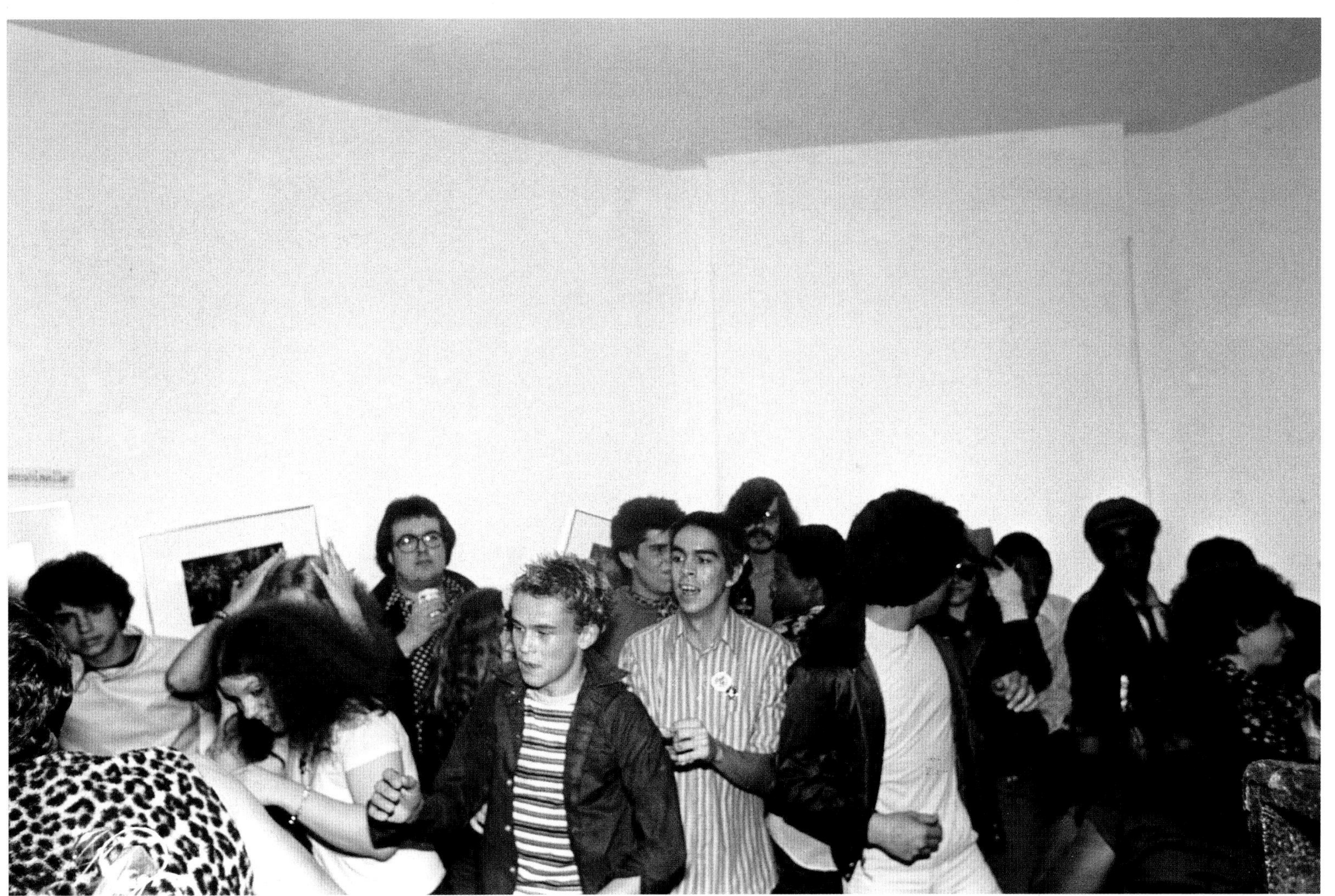

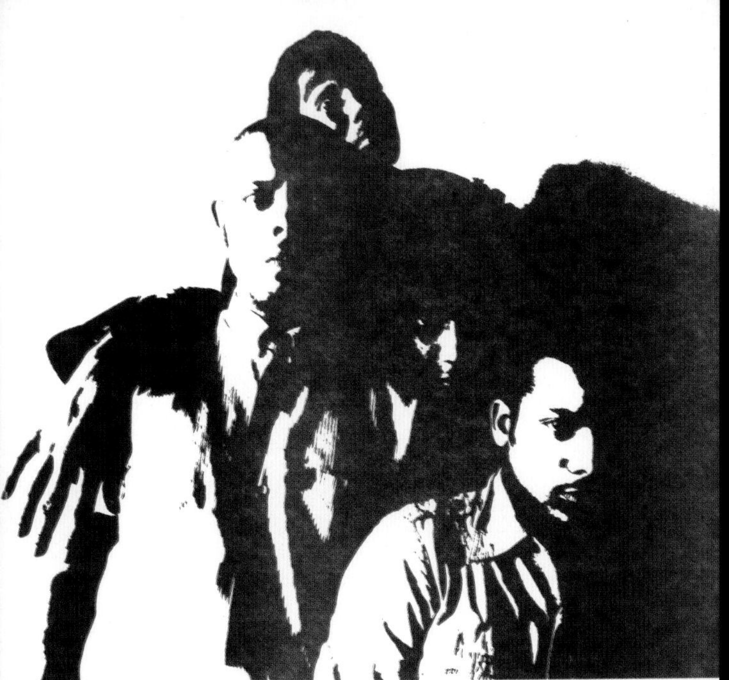

Madams Organ Artist's Cooperative 2

4 2318 18th Street, NW
January 25/26, 1980

Bad Brains with Trenchmouth (Friday)
Bad Brains with The Teen Idles (Saturday)

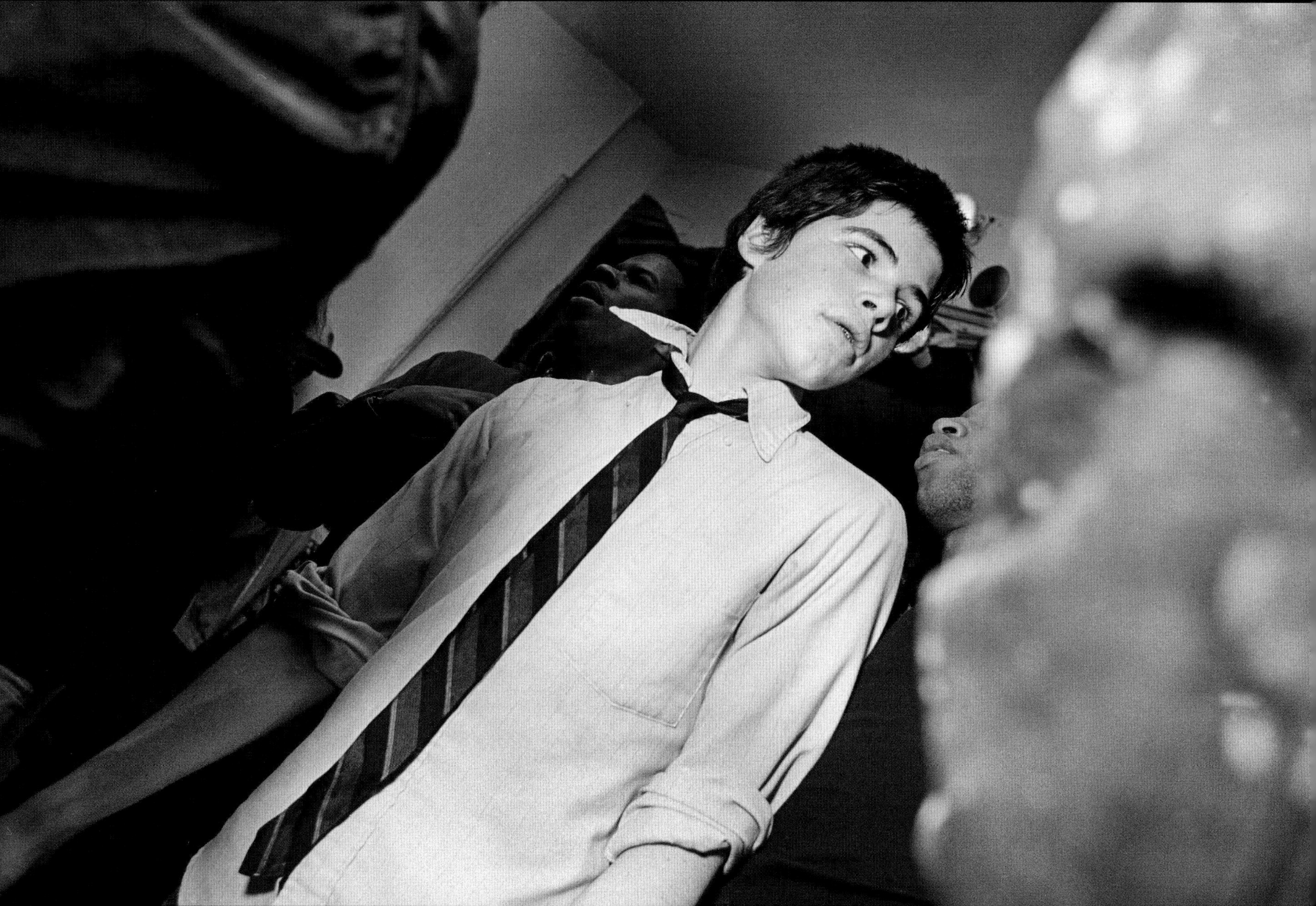

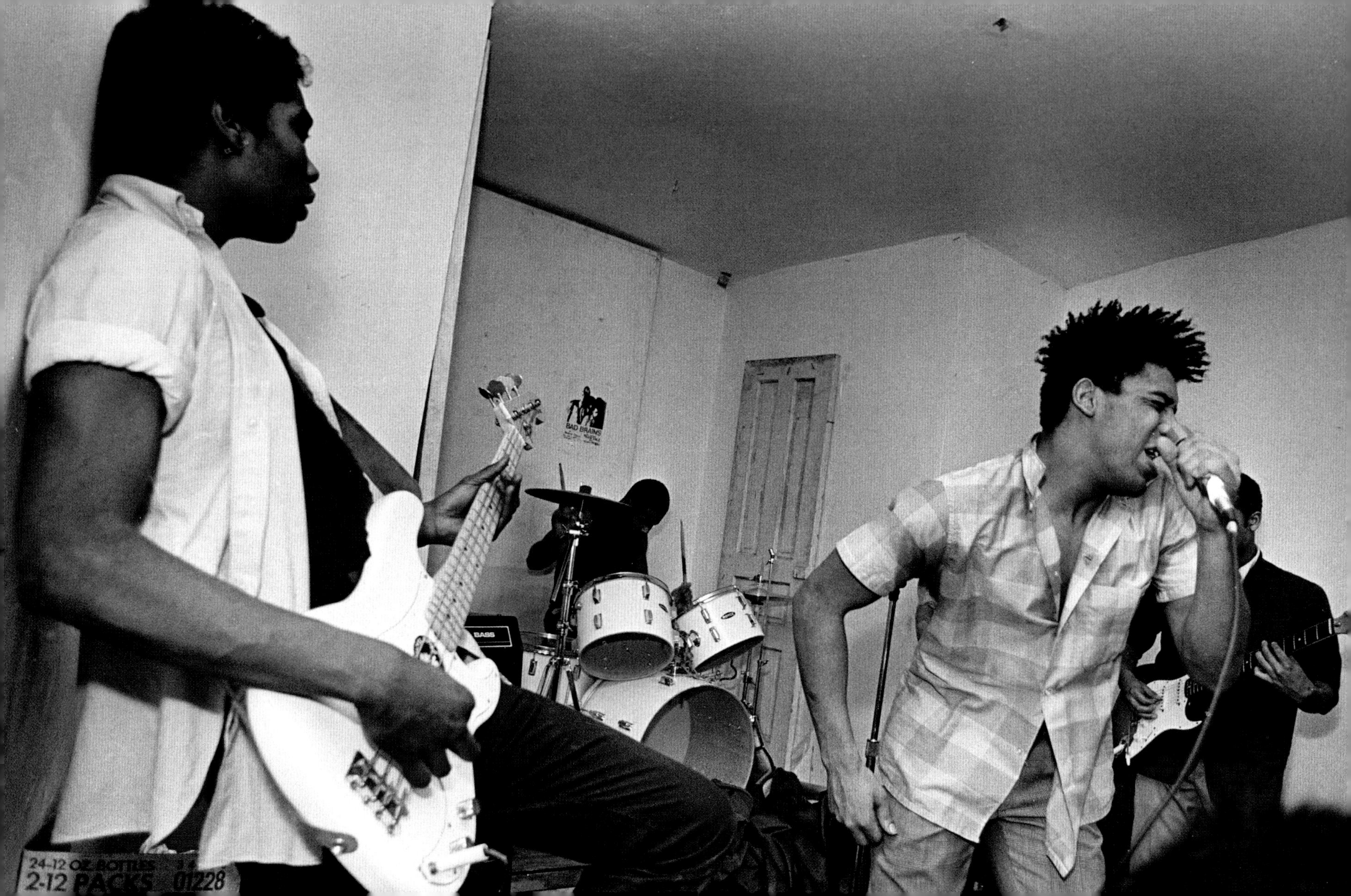
BAD BRAINS
BASS
24-12 OZ. BOTTLES
2-12 PACKS 01228

MADAMS ORGAN 2
FREEDOM & MENACE

Madams Organ was founded on rejection. It started as studios for some Corcoran art students in 1970. Overlooked by curators and teachers for a Corcoran exhibition, they chose to put on their own show. The brochure they put together for it was called *The Madams Organ*, a spoonerism of the neighborhood's name, Adams Morgan.

In the land of the rejected, the field is flattened, open to much opportunity. Here flourish the weeds and nonstandard quality alike. No one aspires, because there is no pinnacle to reach—just be better than whoever is next to you. It is basic, fundamental, and often rude, with bonus points for creative solution. Hardly ever about who you are, but how you do, it's "run what you brung" not Formula 1.

I was fourteen and hated art, especially art-speak and most of all theory. By the time we found it, Madams Organ had run the course of dialogue—from art to philosophy, to political philosophy. It was offering a volatile haven to creative impulse and outburst, as well as fostering revolutionary idea-makers. Marxists in the meetings and armed motorcycles gangs in the kitchen. A place where freedom and menace were served on the same plate. Art for them had become a concept that reached beyond canvas

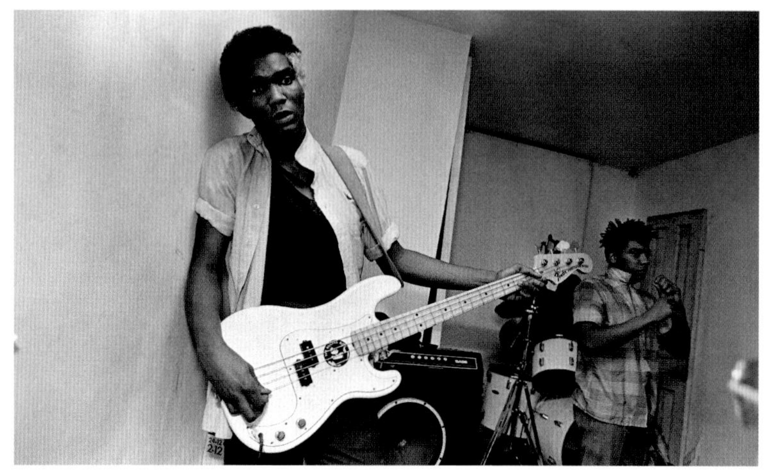

and paper and even conversation. It was action. Action that pushed and pulled at the same time. More than just witness, people were invited and even expected to participate in the rebellion. What was on the other side of the revolution was up for grabs. Punk kicked aside the things that came before because they were in the way. Old-head rebels tried to offer guidance, to make themselves relevant and turn the new wave on to some of the stuff they had been inspired by—and were soundly ignored, in general. Some of them took the rejection kind of hard. Their revolution had become, in spite of itself, an academy. It was measured and dispensed using the metrics of midcentury philosophers.

Punks thought that because they didn't read those books, their ideas were fresh—maybe not, maybe so, but their ideas were coming from a place of emotional honesty, irrepressible in the face of intellectualism.

The property owners tore the concrete steps off the front of the place while the collective-turned-squat was in its last throes, apparently to discourage the unwanted tenants and their activities. The response had been to smash a hole through an exterior wall on the side of the building, steal electricity from the gallery next door, and continue having gigs.

There was originally a small wall that separated the living room from the entry hall. Along the wall to the right was usually the PA board or a table selling something. There was a room in the middle that had been a dining room, but was in my experience a slightly wider, dark place where people stood and smoked and chatted. I usually avoided talking to people, so I would stake out a spot in the living room near the stage and leave it only to go to the bathroom, which meant waiting in the line that extended down the hall and down the stairs. People were

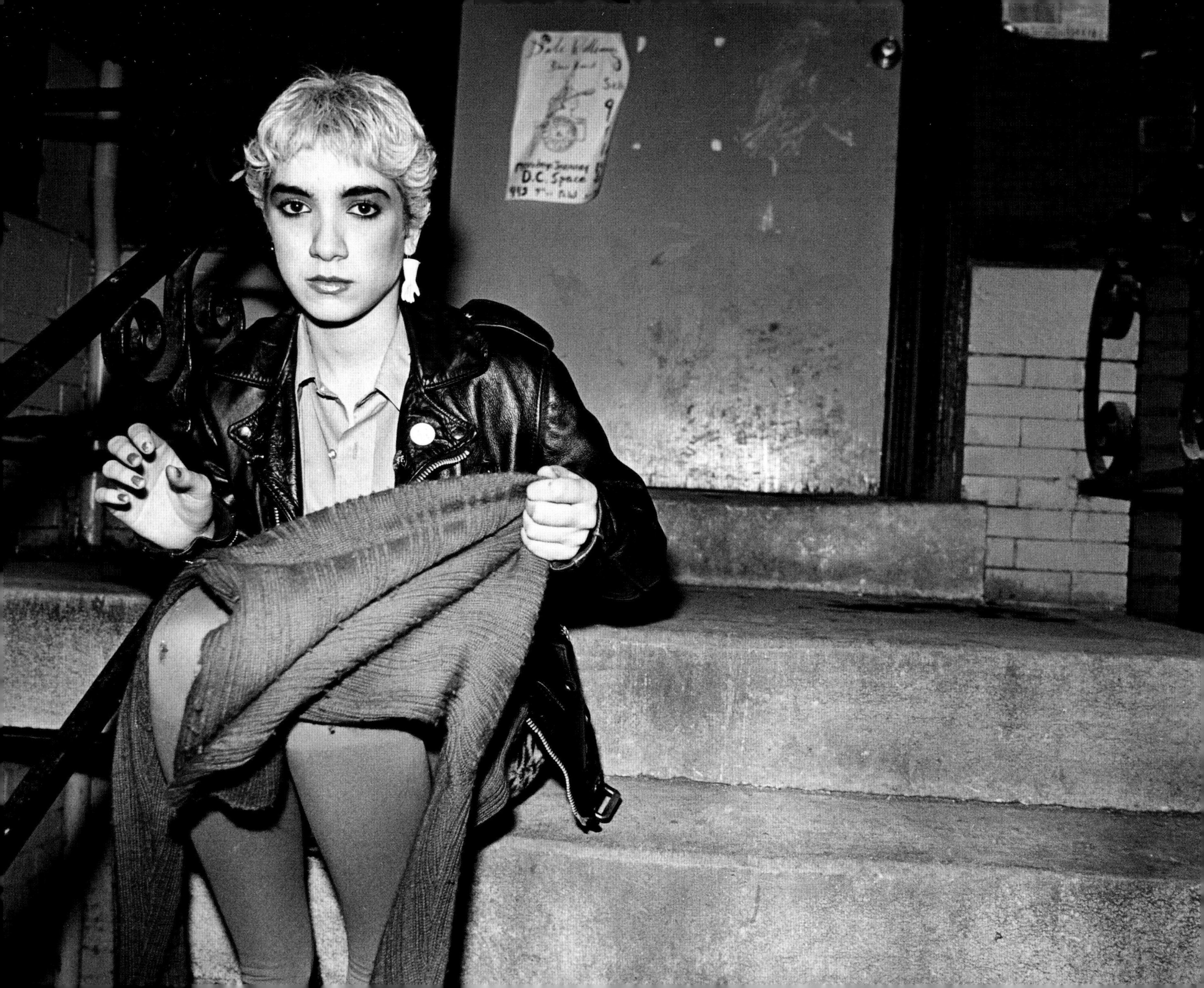
D.C. Space

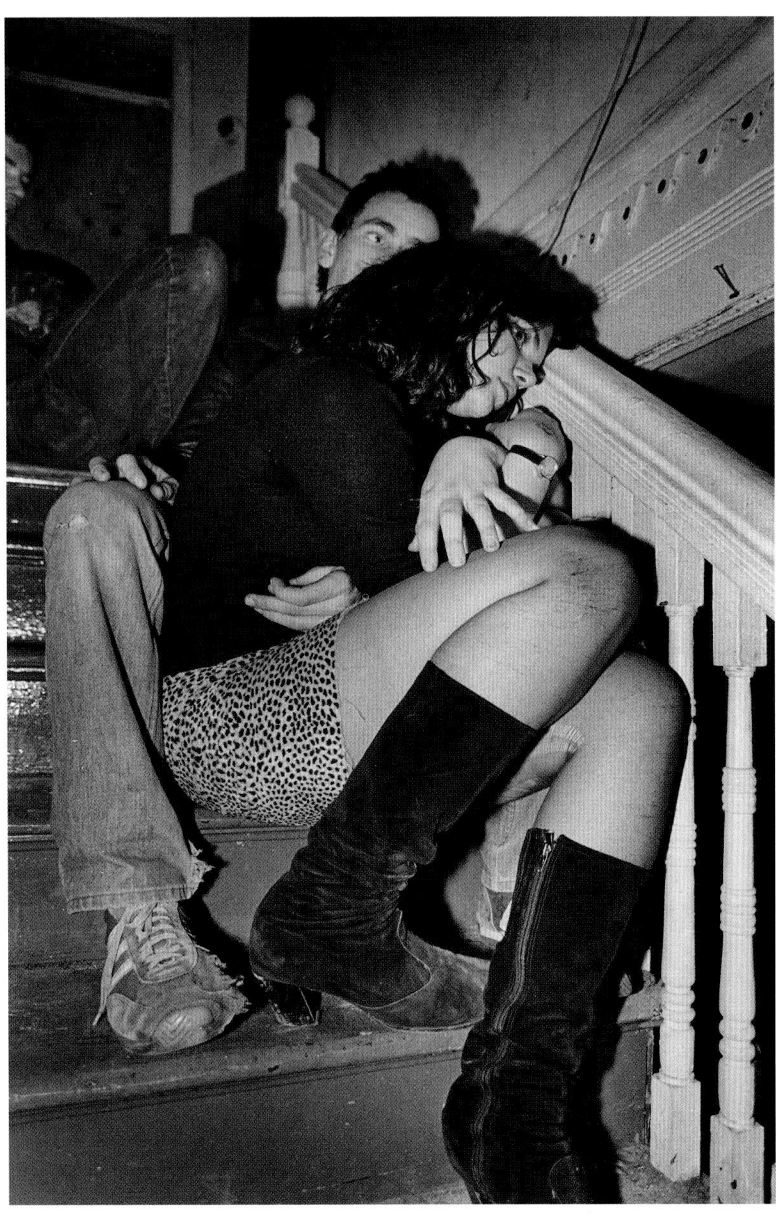

doing everything in the bathroom, occasionally even pissing, so there was frequent yelling when a person or a couple took too long. Eventually, I would get in there, close the door, and try to coax my shy bladder to perform.

Once, my brother Ian and I walked all the way to Madams Organ in a snowstorm to see The Penetrators and The Enzymes. When we arrived, the Pagans Motorcycle Club was in attendance, gathered in the kitchen drinking beer and admiring an Uzi machine gun. Later in the evening, one of the bikers stopped Ian on the stairs, told him he liked his beat-up leather jacket. He asked to try it on, tugged at the bottom edge to adjust the fit around his chest, saying he knew a bunch of his club brothers who would love to have a jacket like it, and started to walk away. Ian asked for his jacket back. The Pagan looked at him with surprise and disgust. After waiting a beat, just long enough to ratchet the tension to ten, he handed the jacket back to Ian, watched as he started to shrug it on, and punched my brother solidly in the solar plexus. The tension and raw danger that those guys brought is the standout memory from that evening.

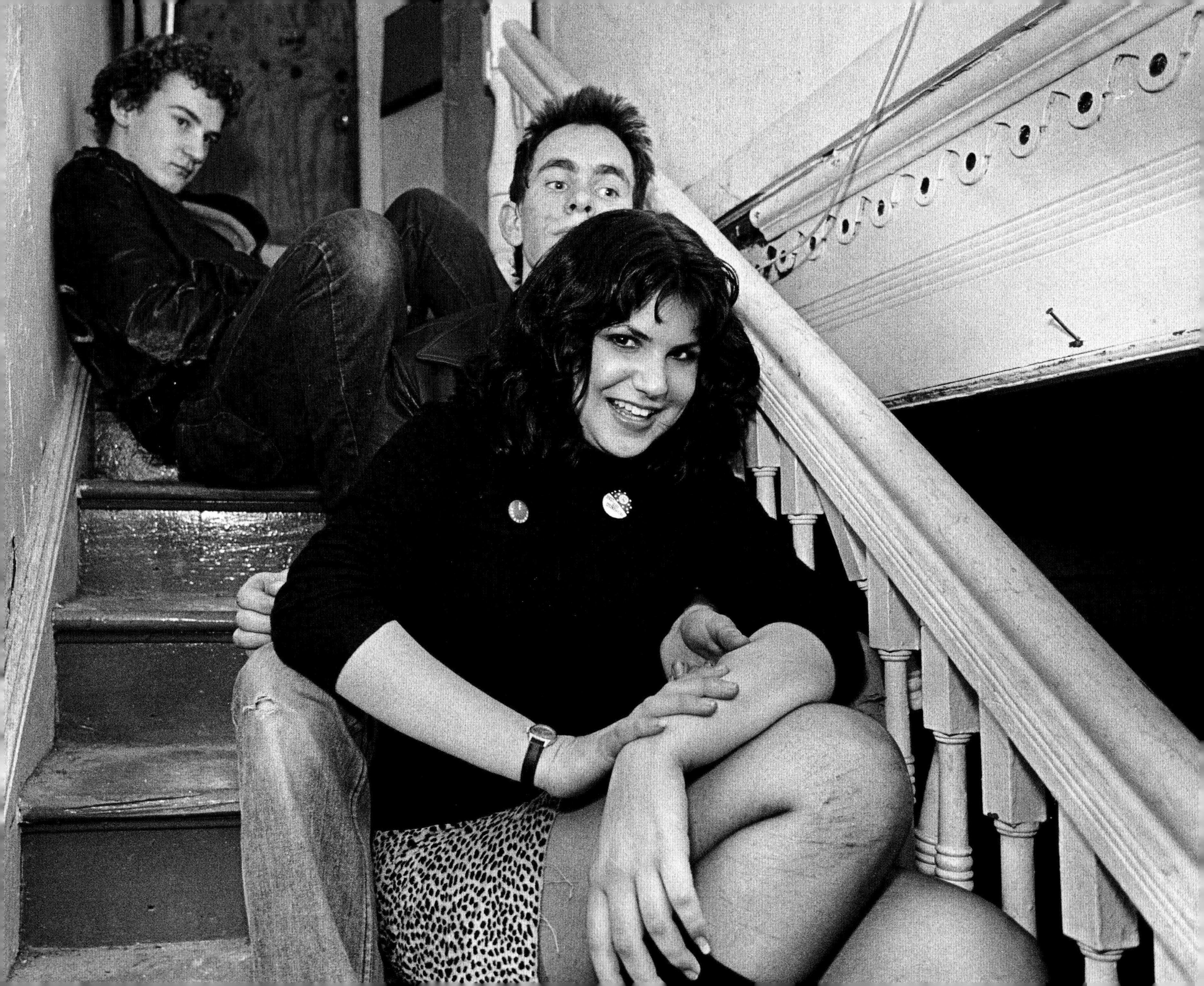

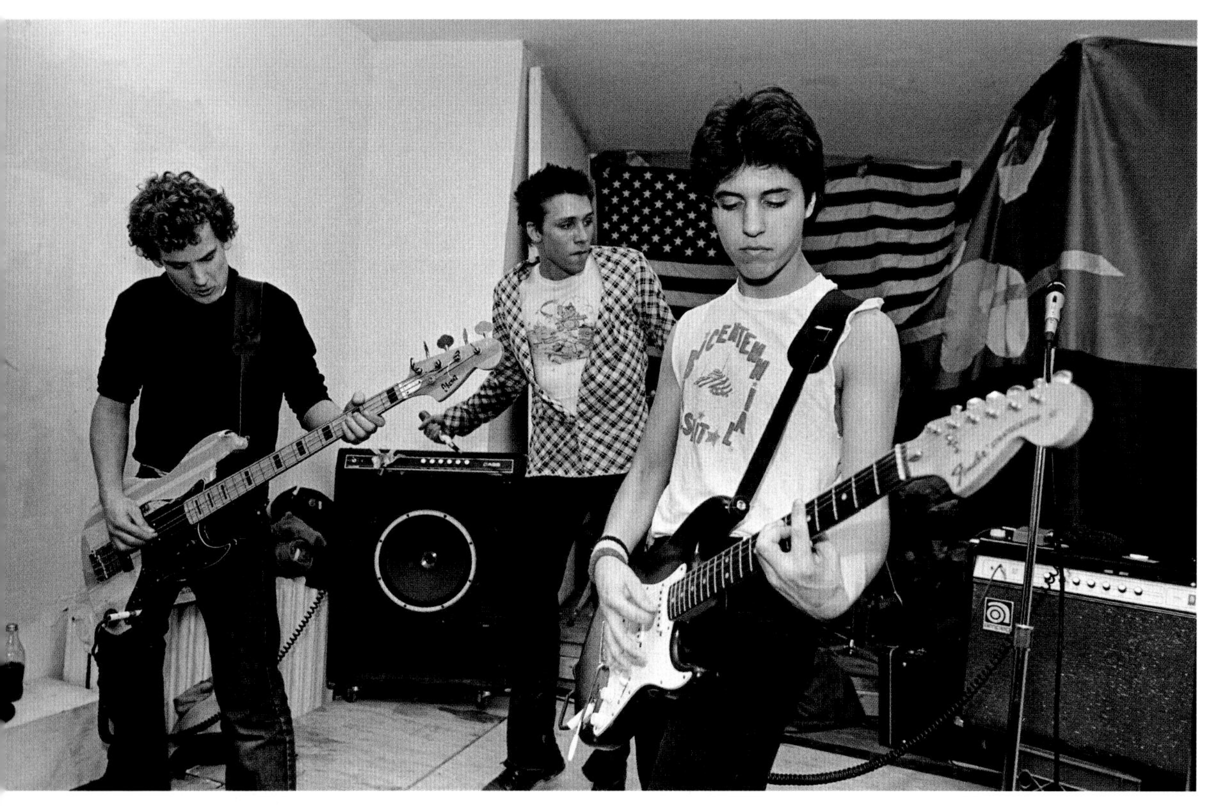

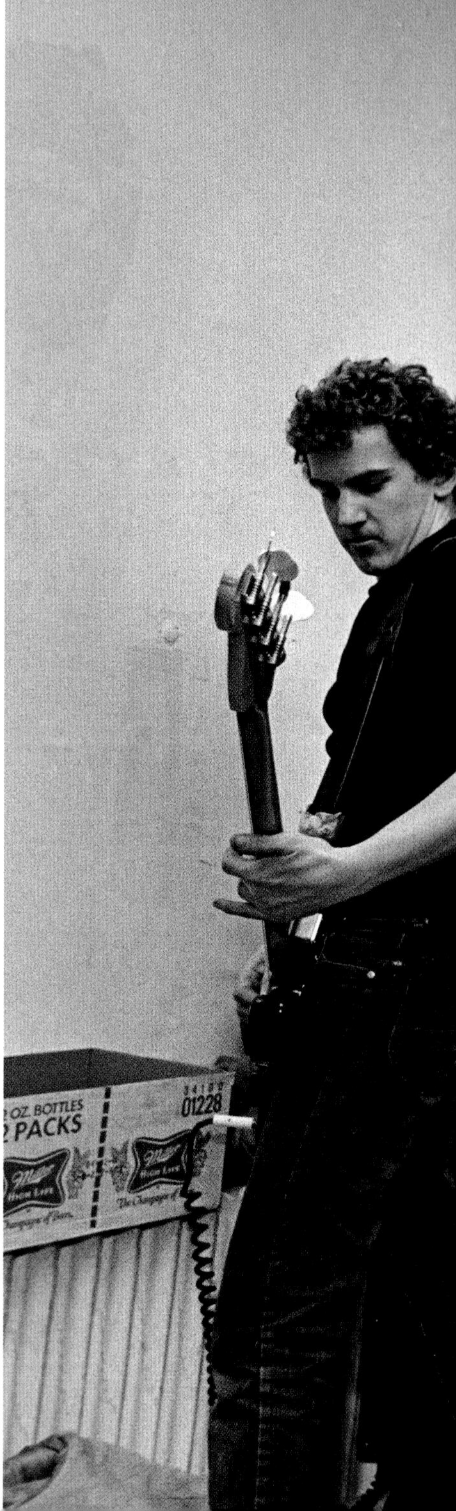
OZ. BOTTLES
PACKS
01228

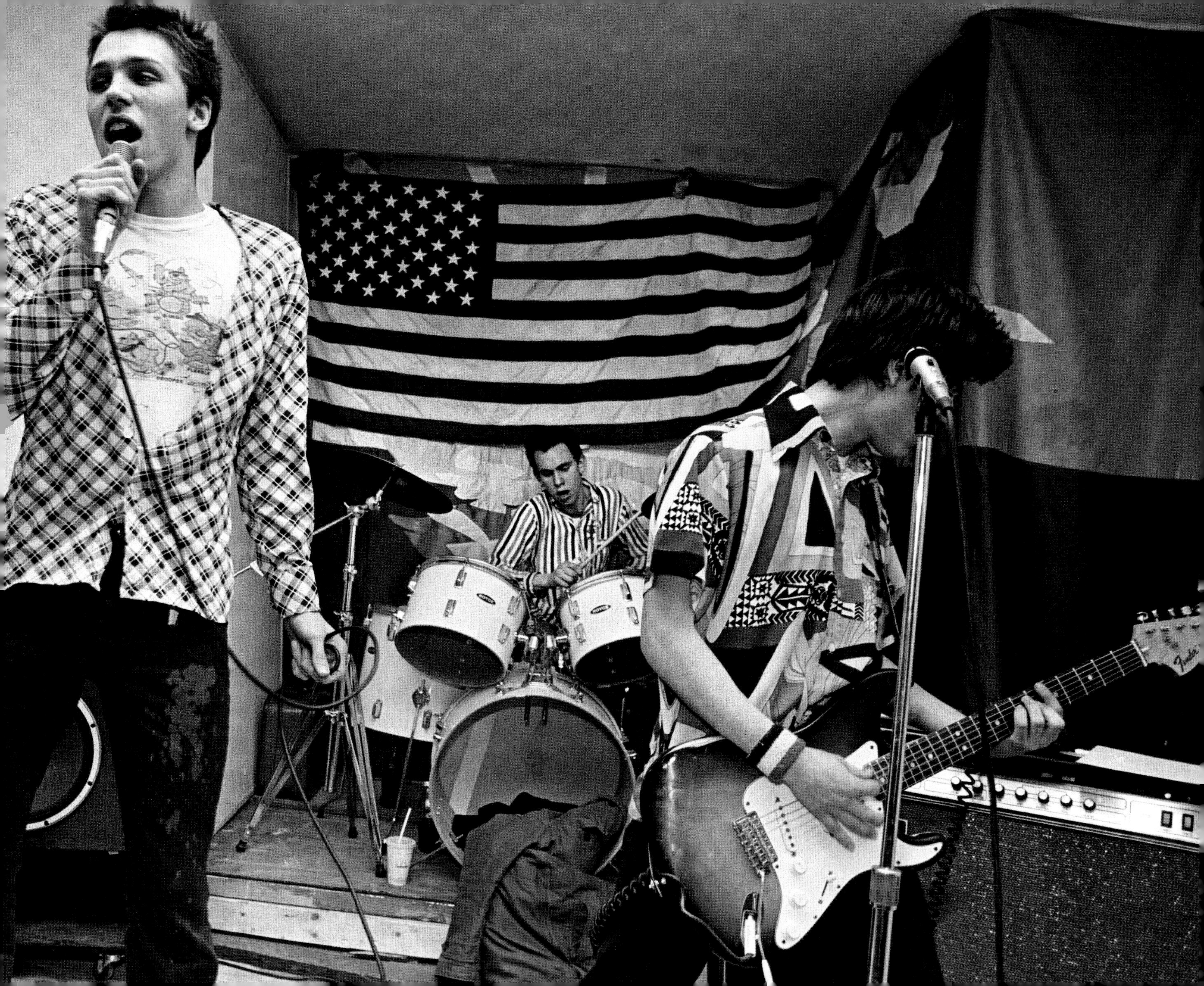

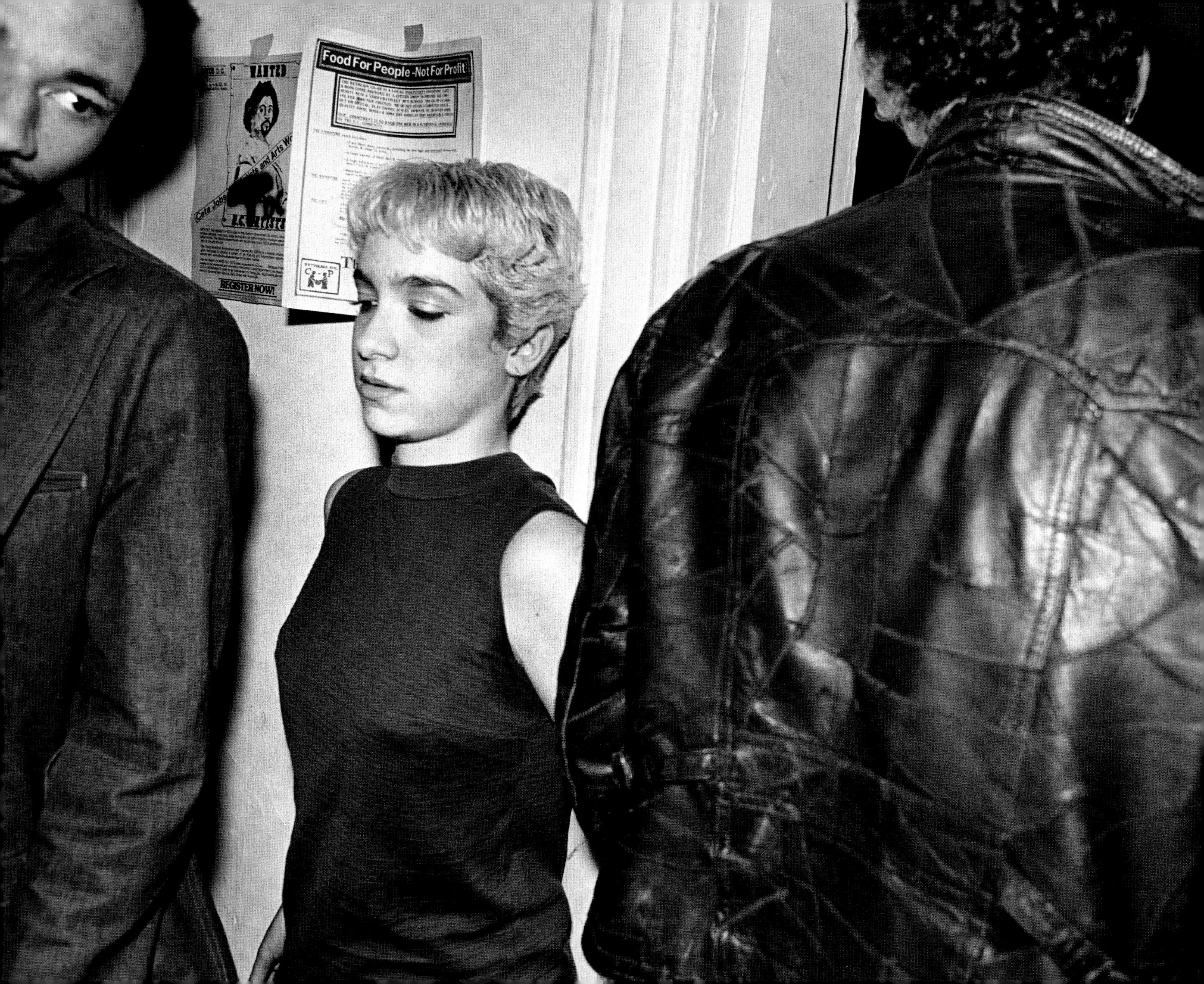

Food For People -Not For Profit
WANTED
REGISTER NOW!

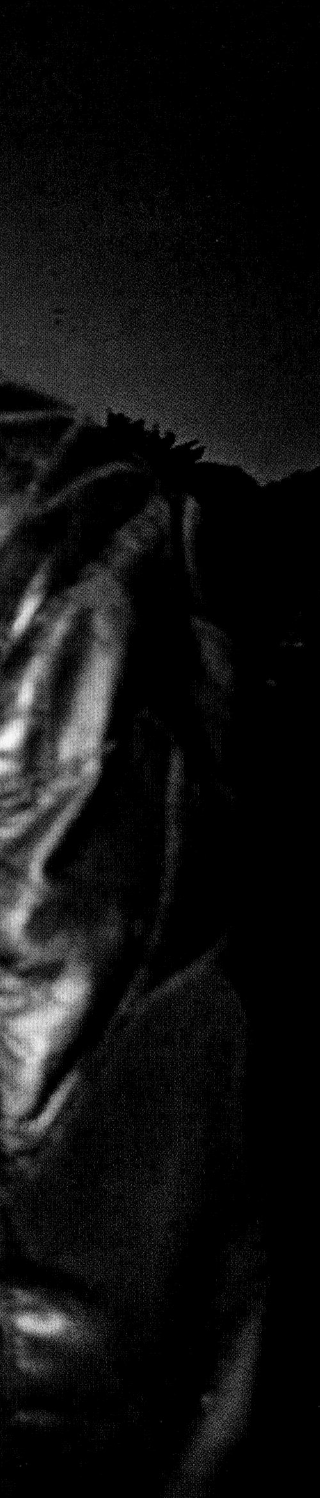

Punk created an uneasy alliance.

There was sometimes friction between hippies and punks at Madams Organ. The radical, political hippies thought we were mindless followers, just the way we thought they were. Punk created an uneasy alliance. The Revolutionary Communist Party used Madams Organ as a meeting spot and thought the punk kids would help their cause—they were constantly trying to bring attention to the trial of their chairman, Bob Avakian, slapping up broadsides all over Adams Morgan with the same picture of him, trying to create a new iconic image. The picture they chose hardly looked like the one of Che Guevara; Bob looked more like a model-train hobbyist advertising something. Nobody I knew was interested in his plight and the RCP's vigorous pursuit of young punk energy started to feel desperate—like vampires in need of fresh blood.

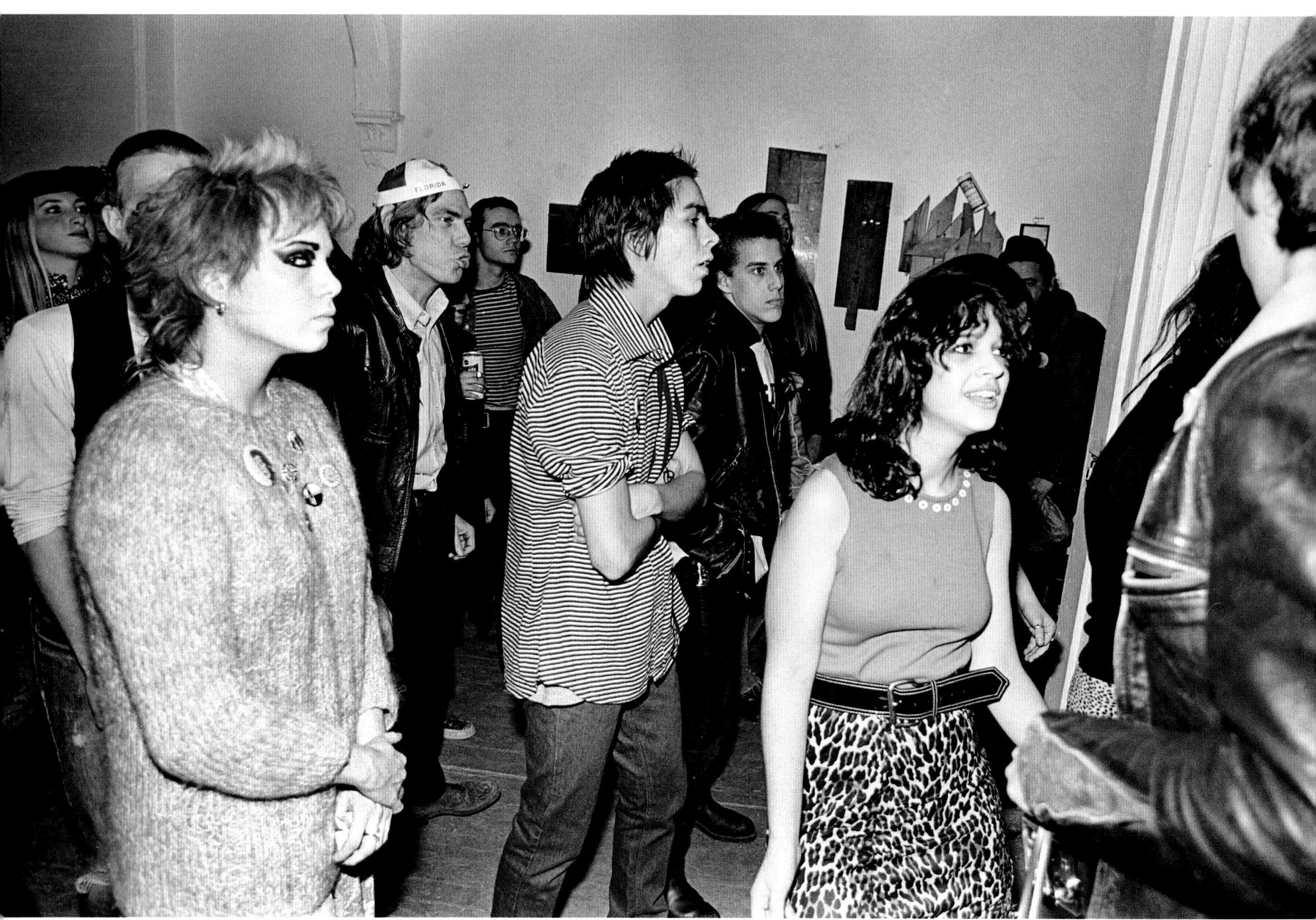
FLORIDA

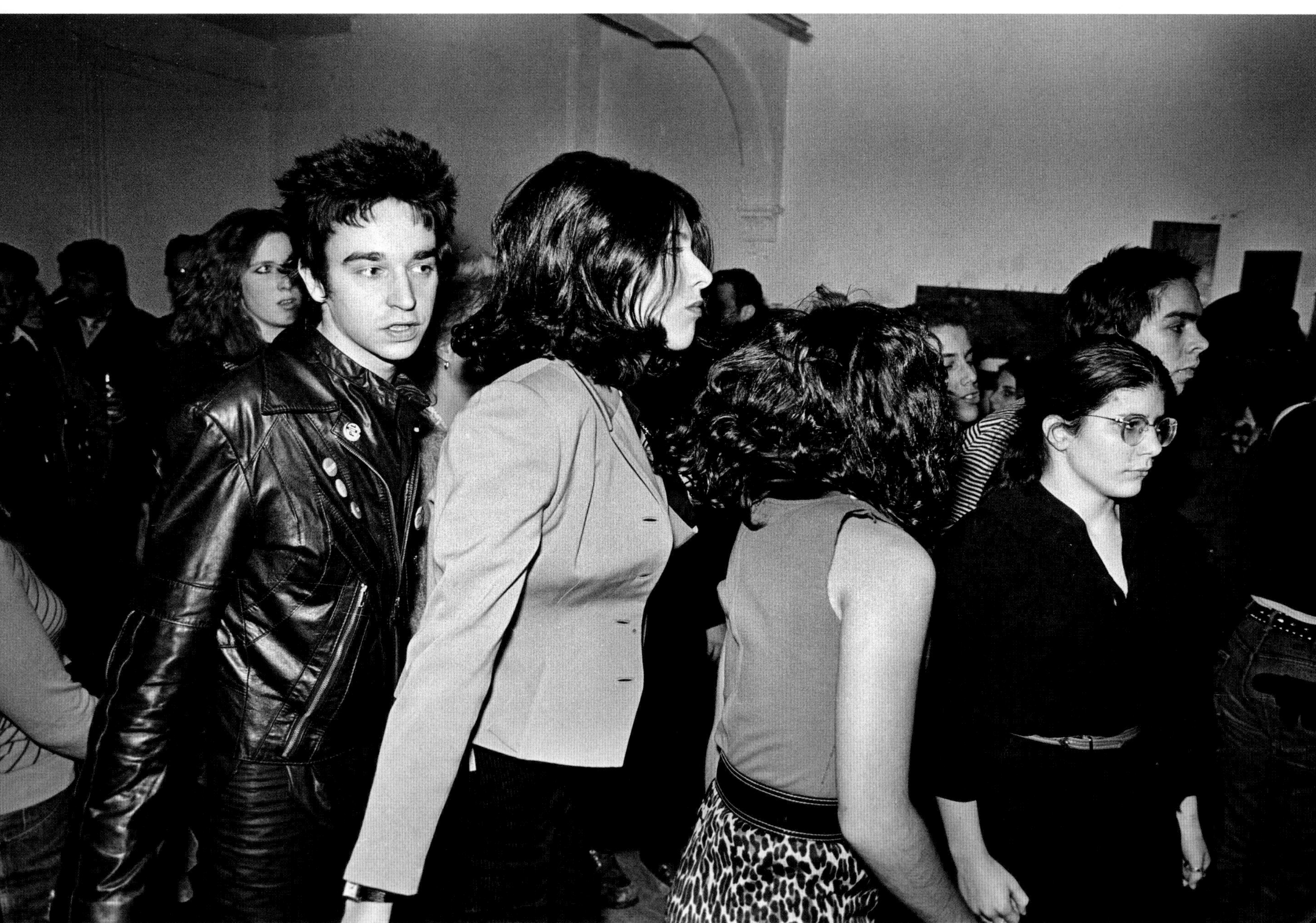

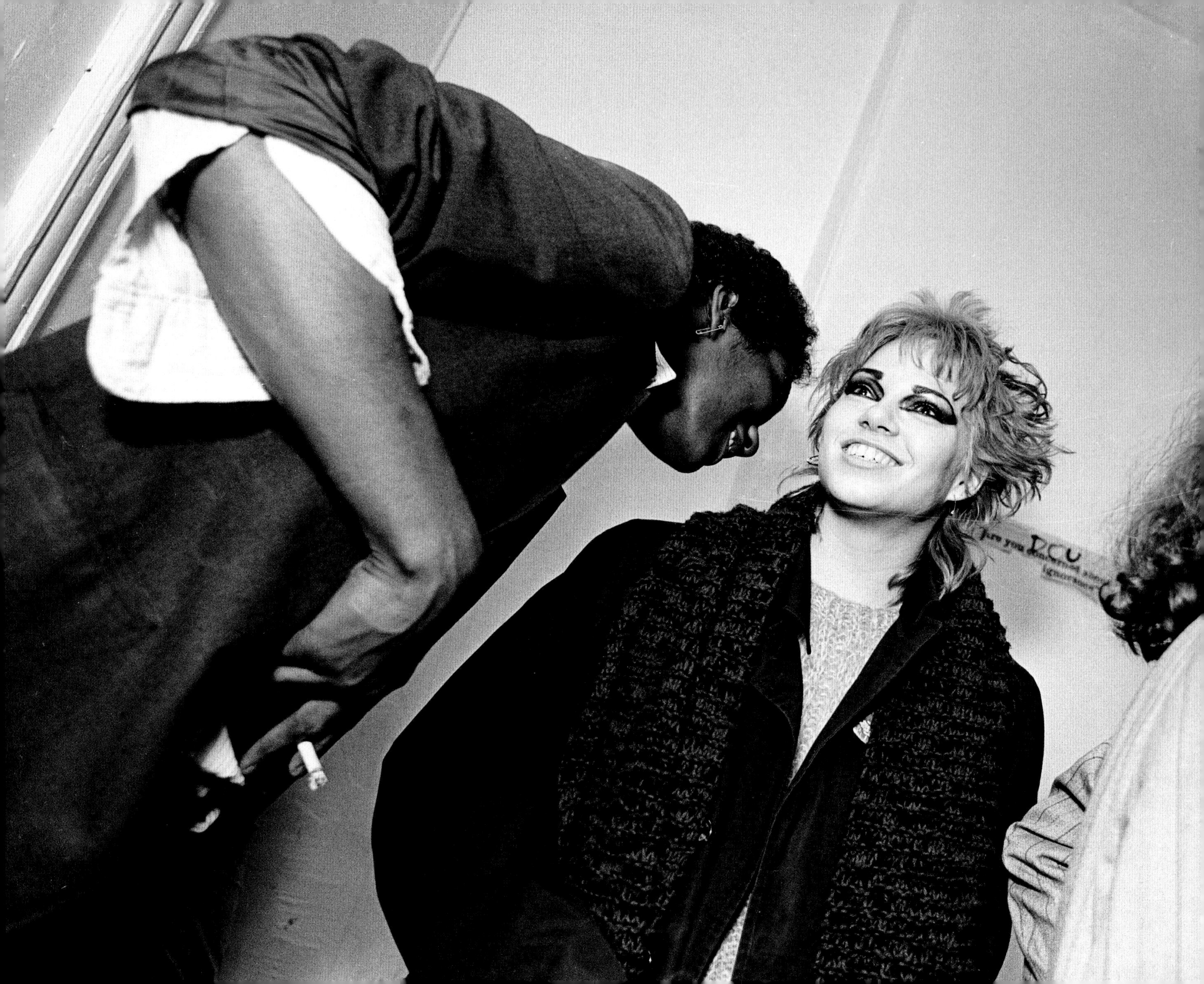

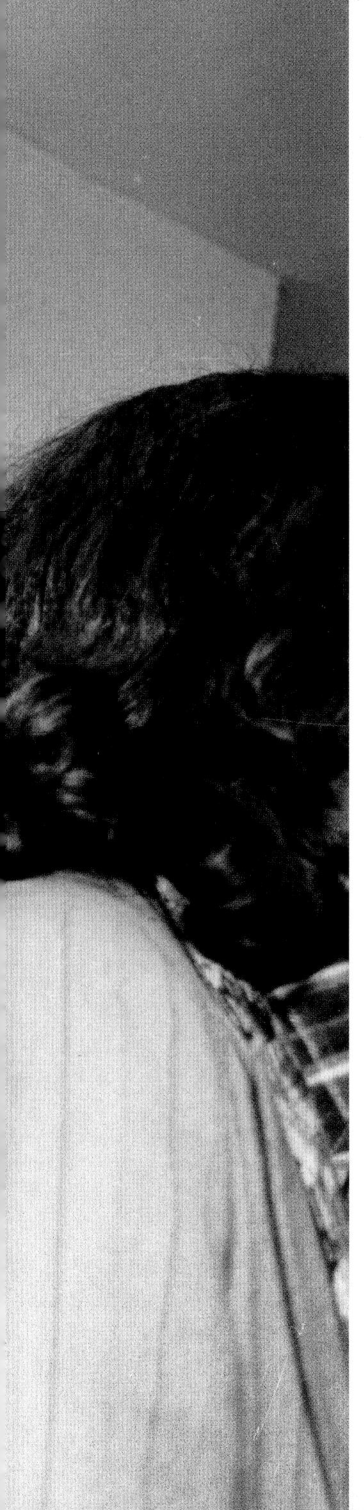

No one aspires, because there is no pinnacle to reach, just be better than whoever is next to you.

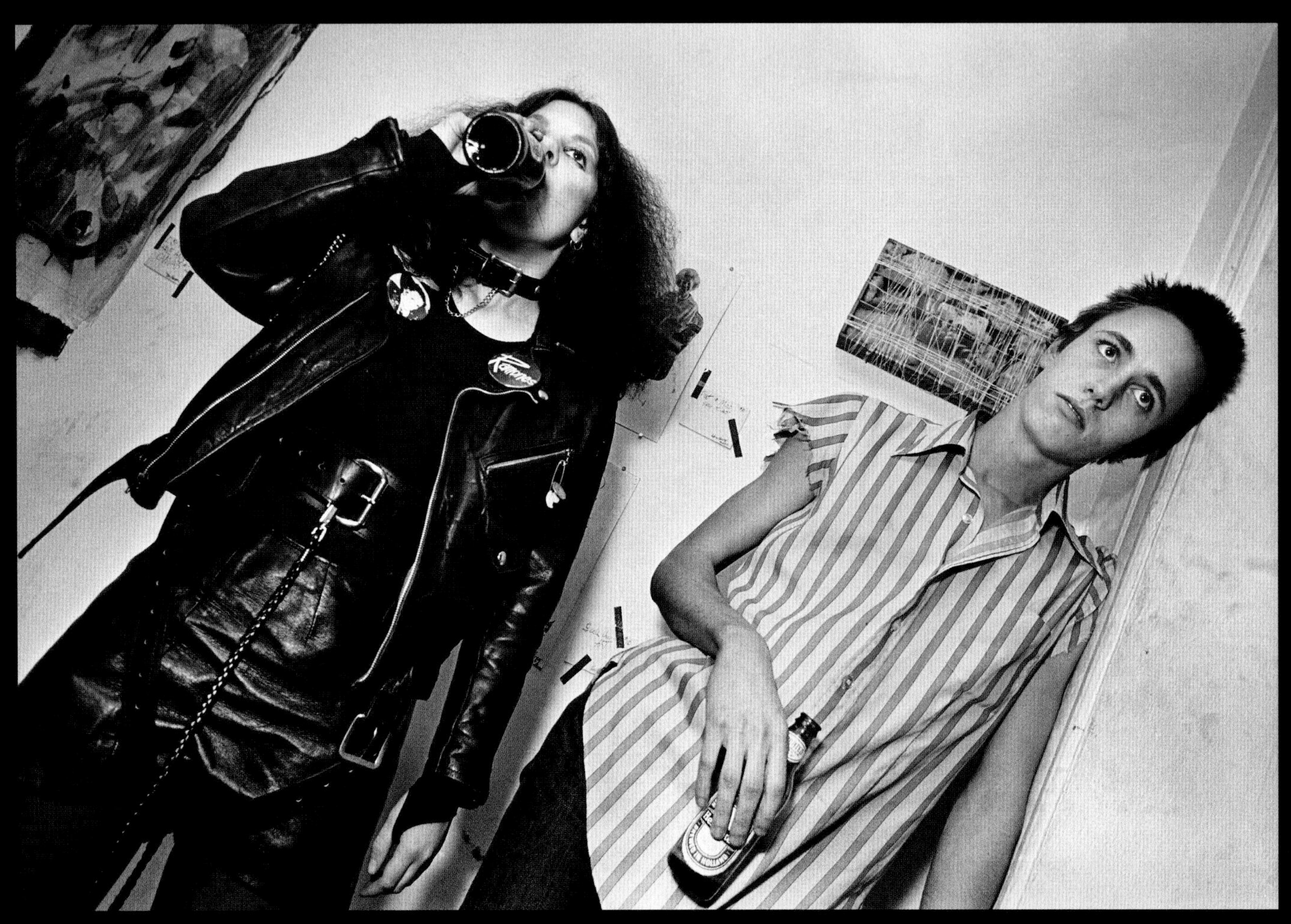

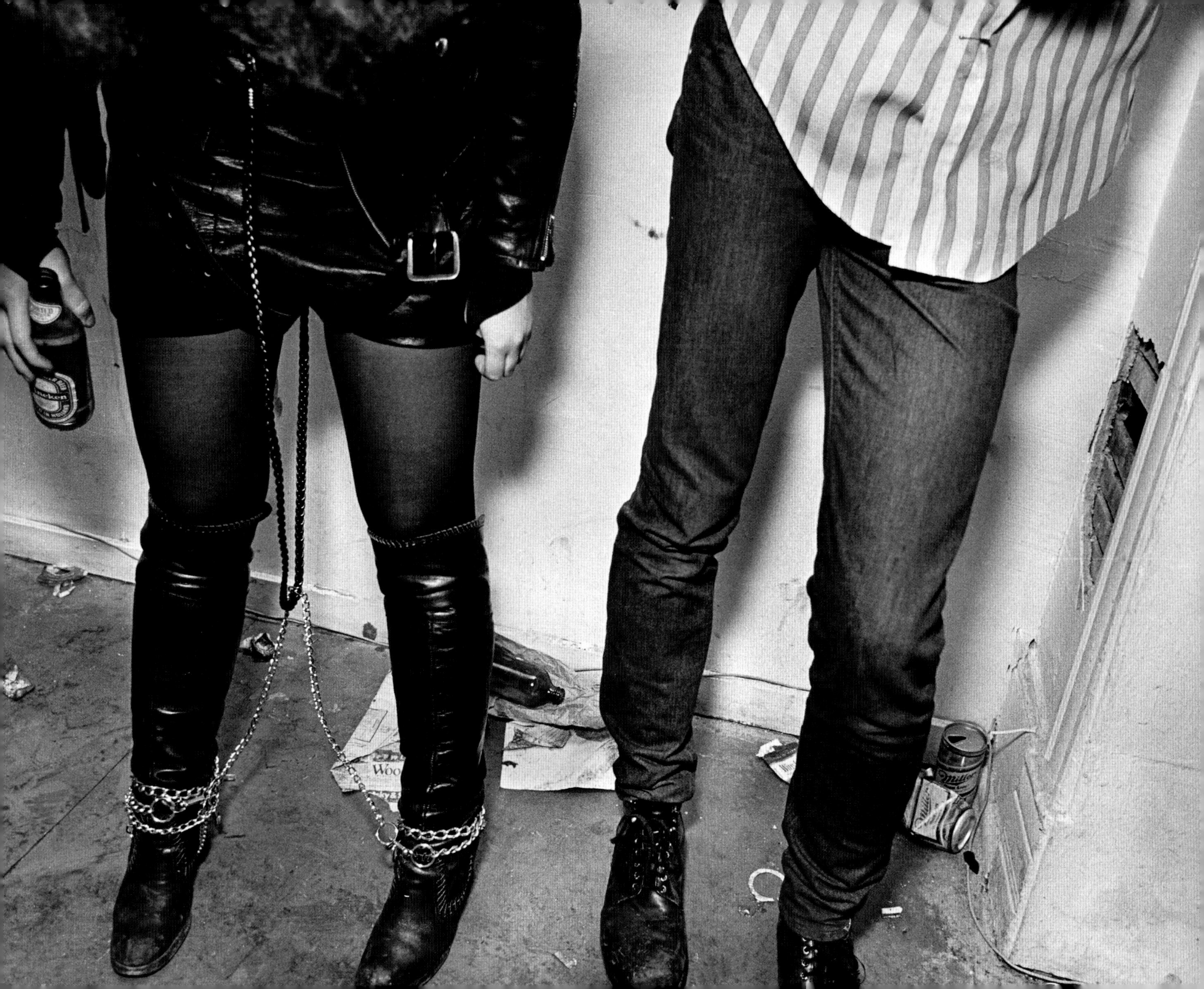
Miller

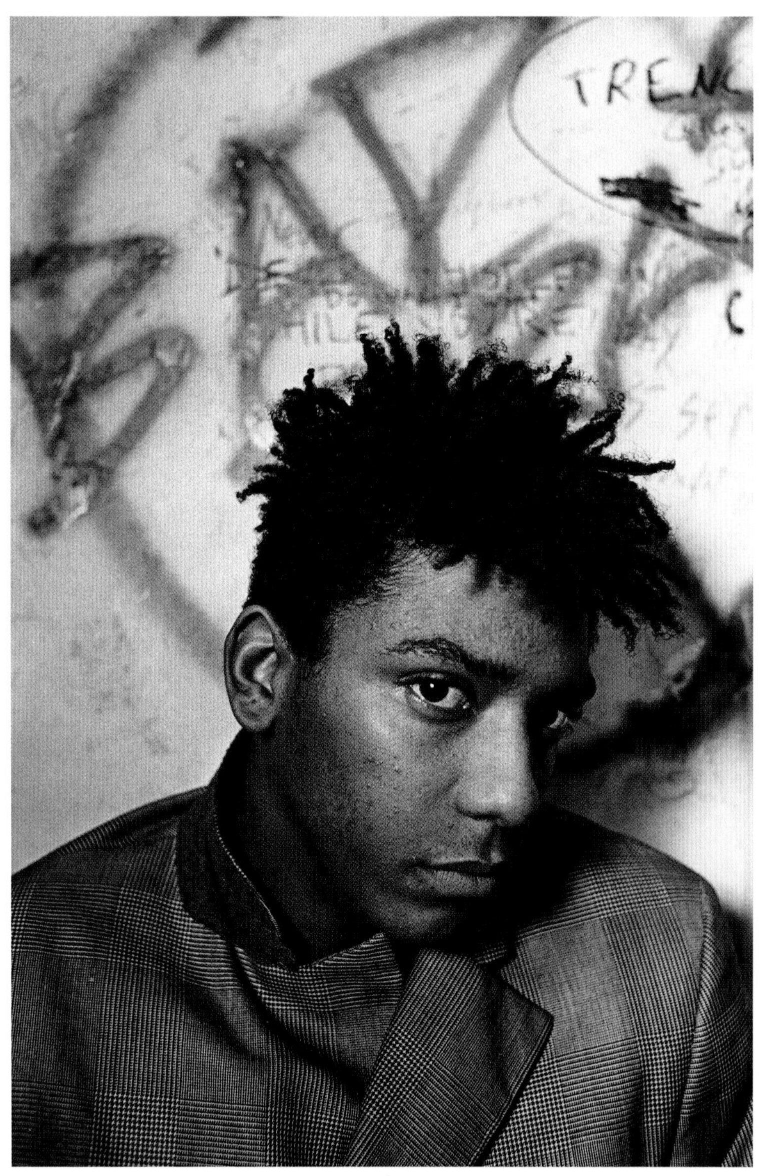

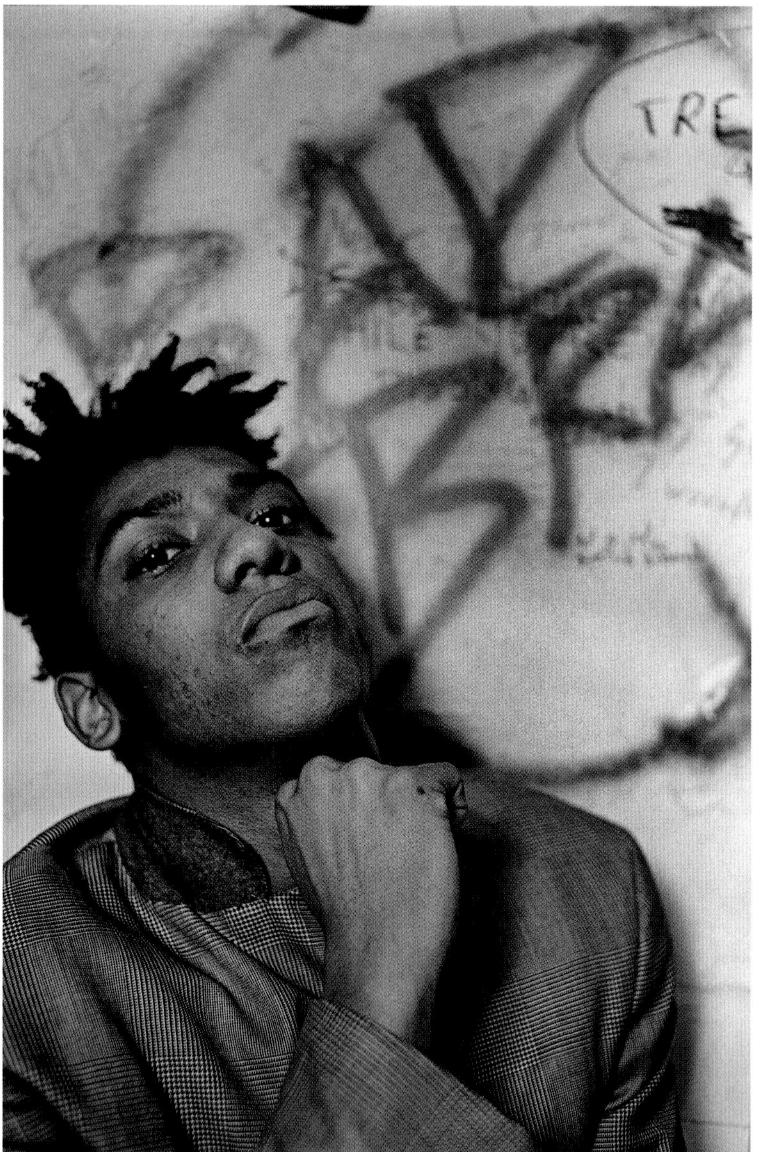

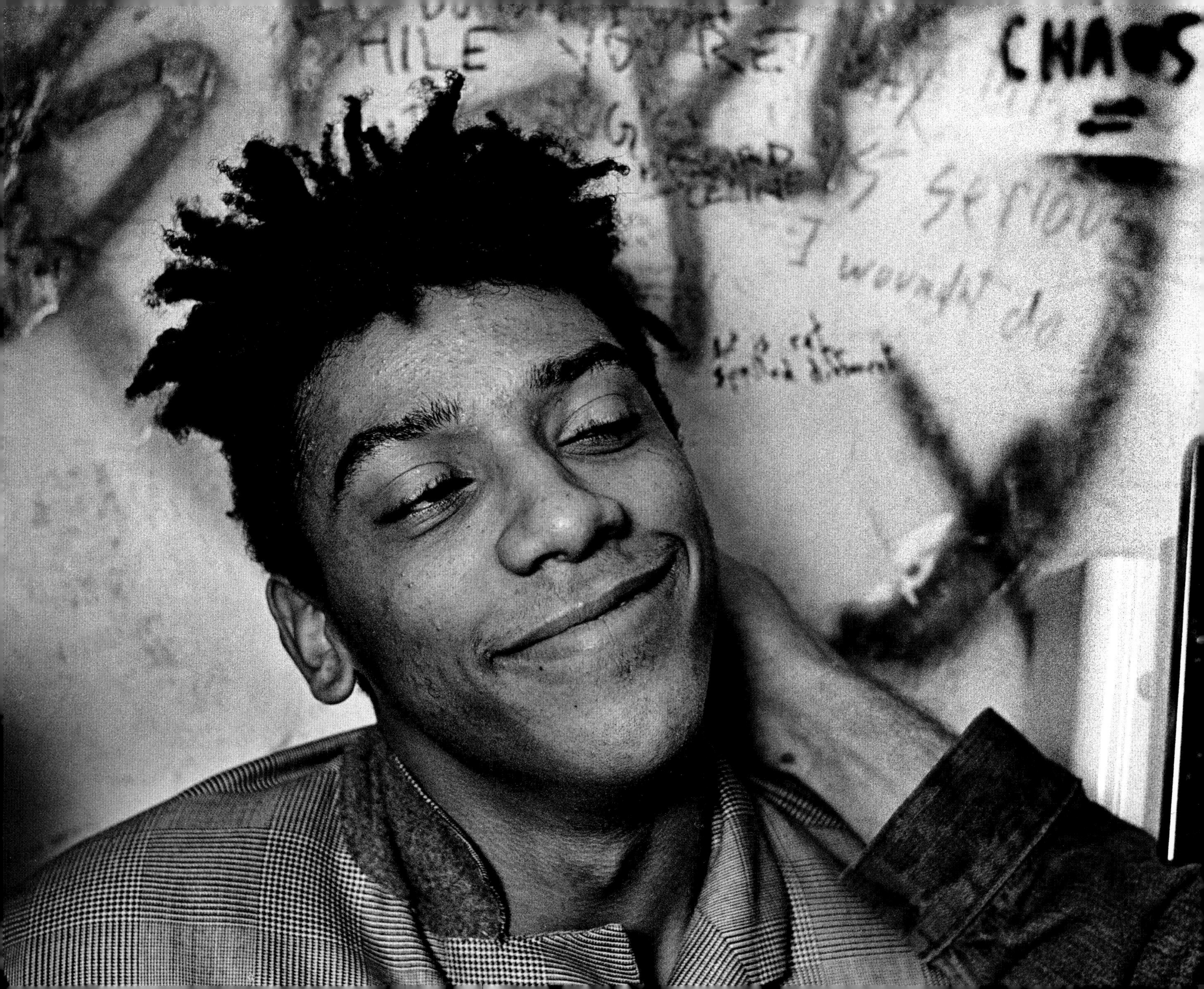

CHAOS

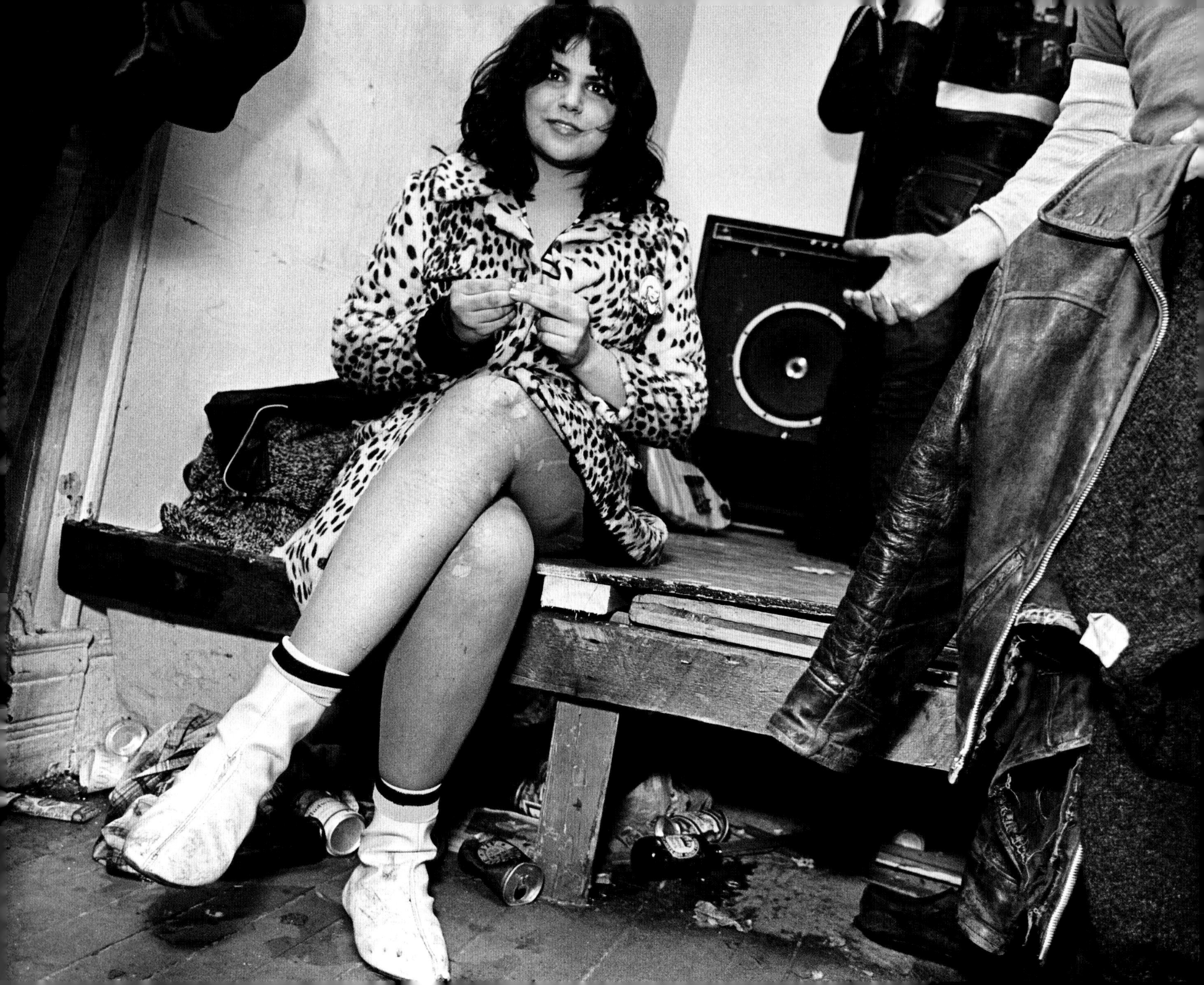

Here flourish the weeds and nonstandard quality alike.

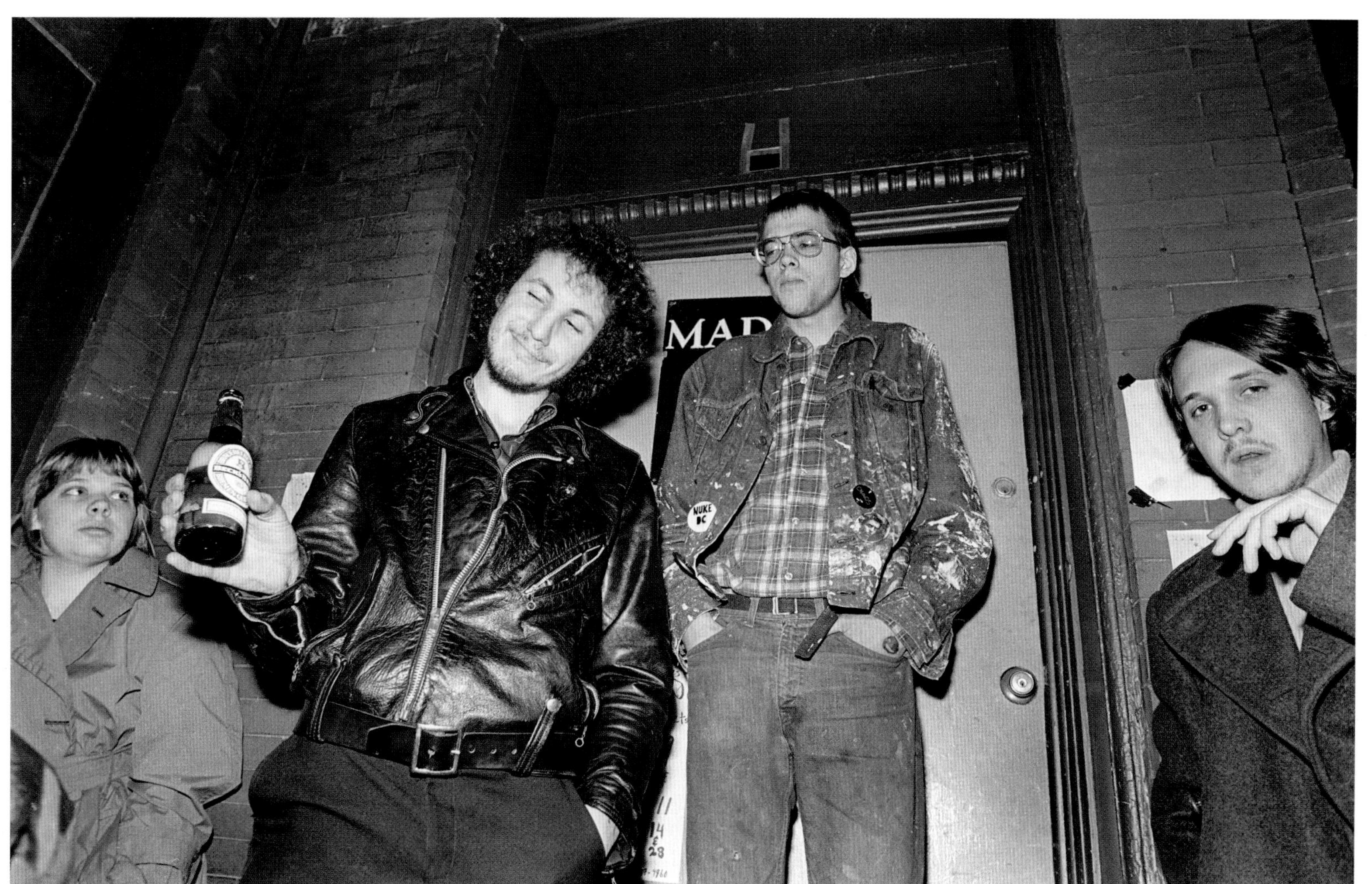

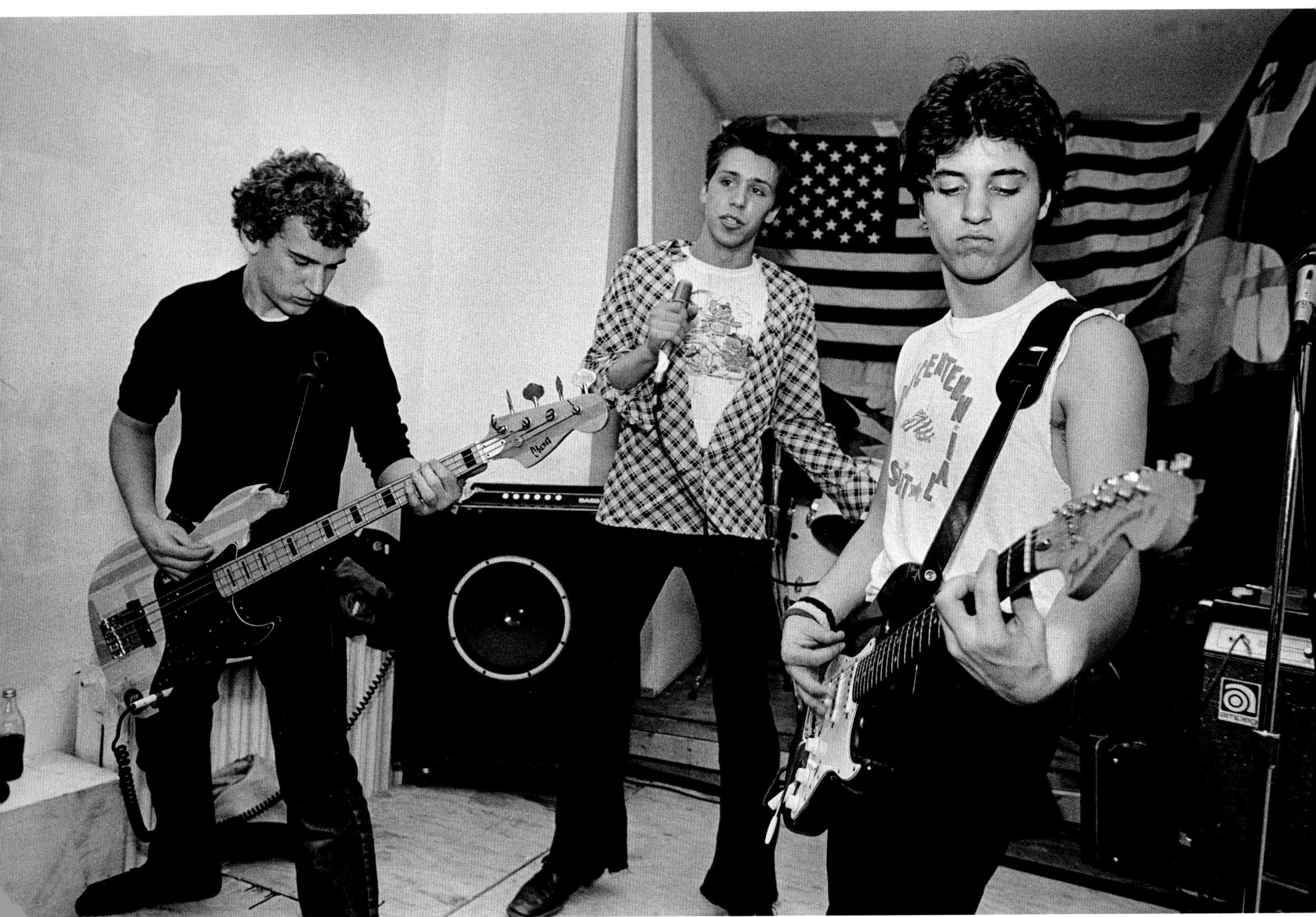

THE TEEN IDLES

Essay by Henry Rollins

The Teen Idles were the right age at the right time in a great city. The local scene was small but growing quickly and The Teen Idles were a big part of all that. As their friend and quasi-roadie, I was there to see a lot of it go down. Their eight-song 7" *Minor Disturbance* EP was Dischord #001, the first release by the soon-to-be-cornerstone independent label Dischord Records.

I grew up with the band's bass player, Ian. When he started playing music, I was there to watch. The other members of the band were Ian's friends from Wilson High School. Practice was usually at Nathan's mother's house, in the basement. I went to every practice I could. I went to almost every show the band ever played, always up at the front.

The band practiced with more intensity and discipline than you would have thought their age and attention span would allow. They were quite committed and played with precision. I sat at the bottom of the basement stairs and watched them rip through their set. It never got boring for me. The songs were simple, the lyrics ironic and sometimes very funny. The members were too smart to fall into sloganeering. I always found their choice of covers interesting: "At the Hop," "Do You Love Me?" "Stepping Stone," all played very fast. I knew every word, kept every flyer. I still have them all. They were more than just a band. It was our one time, one-time-only youth. We didn't go to college. We didn't join the military. We went for something different.

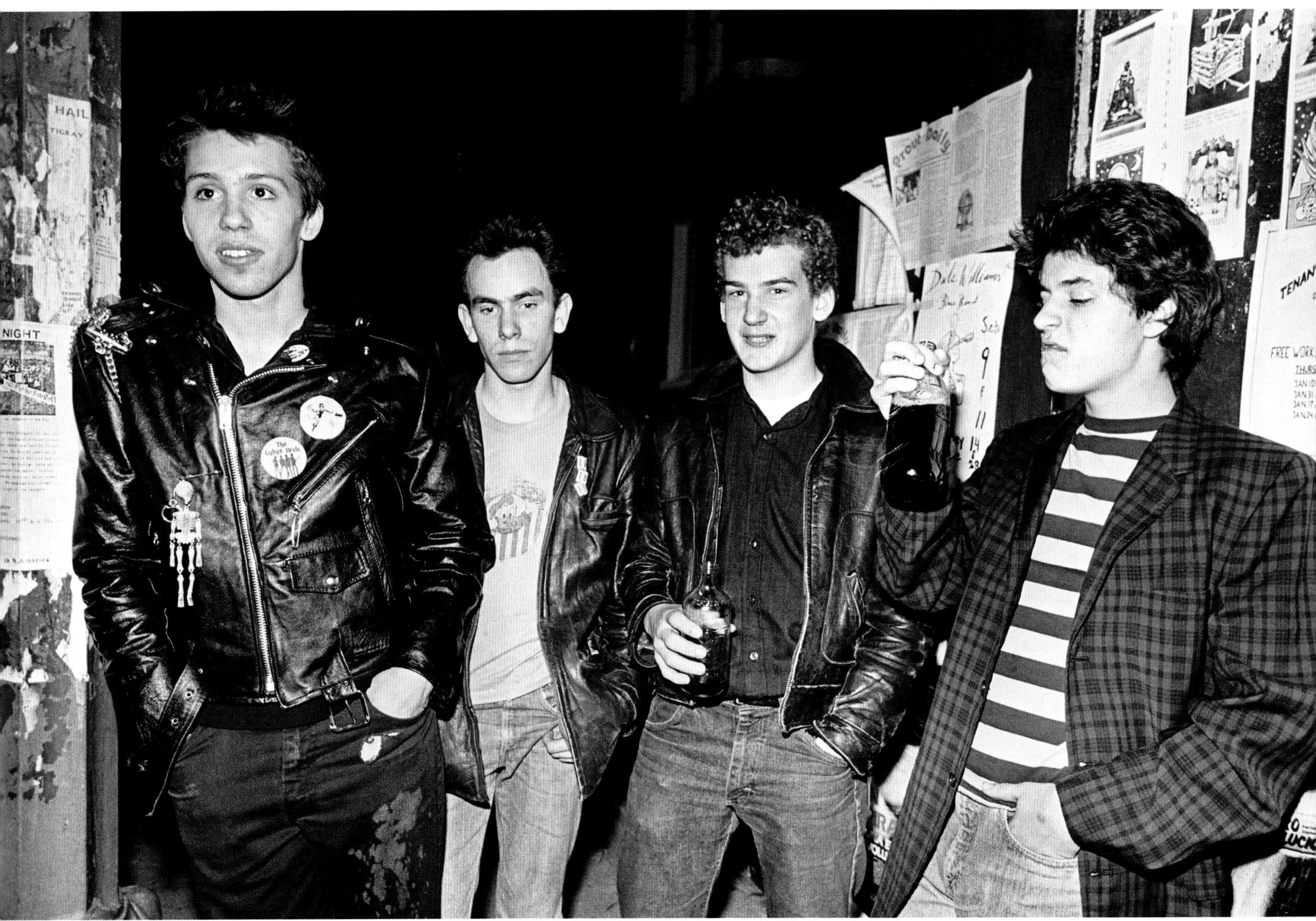
HAIL
TIGRAY
NIGHT
The Cuban Heels
Prout Daily

You can make a record and put it out. You can start a label.

If you want to get a feeling of all that youth and potential, all that road ahead, check out Lucian's portrait of the band. The way Nathan is staring off into the distance and Ian is looking right into the lens. There's so much in that shot. The youth, the beginning of adulthood. I was standing next to Lucian when he took that shot and it's one of my favorite photographs. The Teen Idles played all the time in the DC area, and were one of the bands that really gave that scene much-needed momentum to battle the apathy of the local club owners and small-press music critics, who often thought all these teen bands were just so much youthful howling about nothing.

That's just it though. It wasn't nothing. It was our youth. It was our sweat and raised voices. It was hundreds of amplified hours. The band didn't drink or get high. They did, however, blow the doors off other bands they were on the bill with. All that practice paid off. The Teen Idles showed so many other local bands what was possible. You can make a record and put it out. You can start a label. In those days, this was very new information. They were the first band I ever saw record in a studio. I saw them do their first demo. I was amazed that they were recording. Once they had broken through that barrier, I knew that others would follow and the whole scene was going to open up. It did.

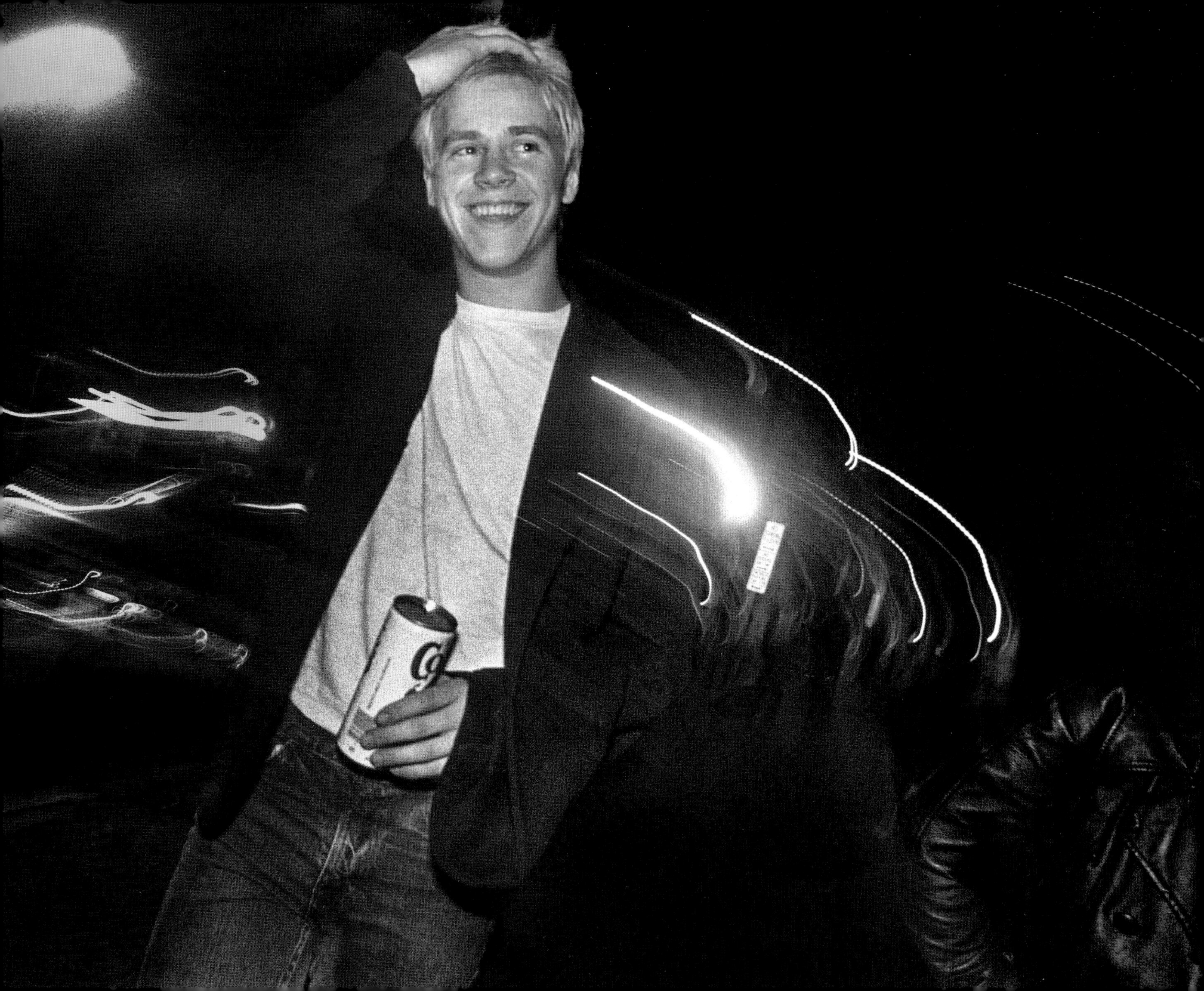

CHARLIE DANBURY, A.K.A. 0110

In the time since this book was first released until now, a number of people in these pictures and from the early punk scene have passed on. Among them was Charlie Danbury, whose ecstatic performance and charismatic everyday persona caught Lucian's eye and lens right away. In his band Trenchmouth, Charlie was probably the performer who first made me want to be in a band, not just watch others doing it. He was one of those types who hit the stage full force from the first note, and then poured it all out without a hint of reservation or self-consciousness.

I didn't really know him well back then. I came to know him better many years later, when he returned to DC from living in various cities around the country. He was now calling himself 0110, the digits used to write binary computer code, which was derived from the *I Ching* (also the last four digits of his mother's telephone number). It seemed like Charlie had been living that full-tilt life every day, and for good or ill he continued in this manner. He didn't seem to know any other way to live. He fed himself fully to the flame, until he had nothing left to burn. I sat with him a few days before he left this world and we talked about Everything for several hours.

The pictures of Charlie capture his early ascent beautifully and precisely. This book is dedicated to him and to the other people from this time who gave of themselves and were committed to their craft, their way of life, and who created the path by walking the path.

BIOGRAPHIES
HARD ART, DC 1979

LUCIAN PERKINS, a two-time Pulitzer Prize winner, worked as a staff photographer for *The Washington Post* for twenty-seven years, until 2007. While at the *Post*, Perkins covered many of the major events of the time, including Russia since 1988, the wars in the former Yugoslavia, the Palestinian uprising in the West Bank, and the wars in Iraq and Afghanistan. He has also chronicled local and national events throughout the United States. Currently, Perkins is an independent photographer and filmmaker concentrating on multimedia projects and documentaries while continuing to pursue his love for the still image. He is also the co-founder of Facing Change: Documenting America, a collective of ten photographers exploring issues facing the United States.

ALEC MacKAYE is a singer and musician best known for his bands The Untouchables, Faith, Ignition, The Warmers, and Hammered Hulls. In more recent years MacKaye has focused on writing.

LELY CONSTANTINOPLE is a photo-based artist from Washington, DC, who has been exhibiting her work nationally and internationally for over twenty years. She is also an archivist for several photographic collections, an editor of photo books, and a teacher.

JAYME McLELLAN has run art spaces in DC for twenty years, including founding Civilian Art Projects where HARD ART was conceived and first exhibited. It has since been on exhibition in New Orleans at the Good Children Gallery, agnes b. headquarters gallery in Paris, and the Center for Documentary Studies at Duke University.

ACKNOWLEDGMENTS

THANK YOU: backers, supporters, confidants, and punks for making HARD ART happen.

SPECIAL THANKS TO: Ian MacKaye for steadfast critical fact-checking and editorial advice from the start; Henry Rollins for his writing and staunch support throughout; Nick Pimentel for his initial work designing the book, brochure, and posters; Lisa Hill for her design and generously agreeing to finish the book; Lizzy Evelyn, Erick Jackson, Sarah Tanguy, and the MacKaye family for early and abiding advice and encouragement; Geoff Dawson for ongoing support; Paul Roth for good counsel; and Amanda Maddox and Chris Murray for their time.

FOR RESEARCH ASSISTANCE: 0110 (Charlie Danbury), Paul Bishow, Matt Davies, Nick English, Dori Hadar, HR, Darryl Jenifer, Trudy Lane, Rogelio Maxwell, Frederick (Toby) Miller, Peter Muise, Sandy Walker, and Scott Wingo. Rest in peace Charley and Edd.

FOR PRODUCTION ASSISTANCE: Bridget Lambert for printing; Noelle Tan for printing the gelatin silver photographs; Cynthia Connolly for advice on venues; Carole Greenwood for food (especially the deviled eggs); the Civilian Art Projects team for their manual labor on the inaugural exhibition in December 2011, including August Conwell, Chanan Delivuk, Jackson Frazier, Rebecca Head, Erin Lingle, Dallas Sheldahl, and Carin Tillman; and Paul Mahon for valuable legal counsel. Last but not least, Johnny Temple and the amazing team at Akashic Books, in manifesting this book into being and carrying it forward.

TO THE PROJECT SUPPORTERS:

Chuck and Jane Alexander
Martin Alexander
Ben Azzara
Colin Bane
Catherine Batza
Catherine Bauer
Carrie Beach
Kim Beatty
Richard Becker
Neal Becton
Robin Bell
Tom Berard
Annie Lou and MJ Berman
Kirsten Bierlein
Andrea Blatchford
Tom Buckley
Jen Buice
Jodi Buonanno
David Byrd
Carmen Calatayud
Colby Caldwell
Liz Calka
Brendan Canty
Tim Castlen
Kim Caviness
Neil Chafin
Ellen Chenoweth
Sharon Cheslow
Cameron Cochran
Michelle Cochran
Anne Constantinople
Nell Constantinople
Nick and Donna Constantinople
Franck Cordes
Bernard Cousineau
Lindsay Cox
Melissa Crafty
Summer Czajak
Thomas Danbury
Ben Davidson
Jay De Lanoy
John DePodesta
Amy Hope Dermont
Franck Dewannieux
Tanya Dhein
Michael Dolfi
Arte Dunning
Gayle Engel
Sarah Feinstein
Dante and Catherine Ferrando
Beatrice Valdes Ferrari
Jodi Ferrier
Peter Fivel
Hilary Flack
Alfredo Flores
Izzy Fraimow
Kristin Freeman
Michael Galluzzo
Sara Gama
Susan Gardinier
LouLou Ghelichkhani
Michael Girard
Julie Gliniany
MaryAnne Golon
Eliza Gonzalez
Jonathan Edward Goodman
Christopher Grady
Pat Graham
Christopher Grant
Joe Halladay
Mark Hampton
Michael Hampton

Peter and Mia Guizzetti Hayes
Marvin Heiferman
Douglas R. Hess
Sam Hiersteiner
Dean Hill
Julie Hill
Alex and Jordan Hoffner
Rachel Holmes
Gary Honig
Philippa Hughes
Elizabeth Hunter
Jeff Huntington
Mike Hurd
Mike Dax Iacovone
Kat Irannejad
Don Irwin
George Jenne
Angela Jerardi
Mike Johnston
Sara Kanach
Darius Kanga
Allyson Kapin
Morris Kasoff
Caroline Kenney
Bart Kibbe
Tyson Kidder
Joseph Kirchner
Eileen Kirschner
Alicia Koundakjian
Justin Kramer
Joseph Lally
Bridget Lambert
Karen Landes
Russell Lebo
Jaime Leclerc
Phil Leitch
Meredith Lesher
Judy Lichtman
Eve Lilley
Erin Lingle
Jason Linkins
Jenifer Lippincott
Caroline Lobaugh
Liz Ludgin
Alexandra Luzzatto
Anne Luzzatto
Benjamin Luzzatto
Robert MacDonald
Kate MacDonnell
Susannah MacKaye
Beth Mailley
Eric Margry
Christine and Seth Martin
Gina Martin
Grisella Martinez
Poet Mase
Benjamin Mason
James Matterlink
Todd McDonald
Mike McDonnell
Leigh McIlvaine
Melissa Hawkins McInerney
Geoff McIntosh
William McKenna
Steven McPherson
Bob Rob Medina
Greg Millar and Gina Matchitt
Anastasia Miller
Charles Moats
Catrin Morris
Stacey Moye
Jeronimo Mazarrasa Muñoz
Jenny Murphy
and Peter Birkenhead
Zachary Myers
Dale Nixon
Kendall Nordin
Johnny North
Chris O'Connor
Asa Osborne
Henry H. Owings
Claire Creaney Packer
Punchy Packer
Cynthia Parfitt
Andy Parker
Julia Parnell
Rob Parrish
Jennifer Patner
Chad Pearson
Carol Pensky
Mark Peterson
Guy Picciotto
Tony Plunkett
Andrea Pollan
Cara Pomponio
Tiffany Pruitt
Bert Queiroz
Karl Reinsch
Bryan Rhodes
Damion Rice
Pat Rice and Mia Esserman
Anna Rodgers
LC Rodriguez
James Rosen
Sara Rosen
Brian Ross
Tony Ross
Paul Roth
Elizabeth Rumsey
Paul W. Ruppert
Corey Rusk
Mark Ryan
Michael Ryan
Maggie Ryner
Jim Saah
Mary Sasser
Mike Saxenian
Emily Shaw
Megan Sheils
Ryan Shepard
Alexandra Silverthorne
Christopher Sims
Casey Smith
Deidra McLellan Smith
Karen Smith
Leslie Smith
Nate "Igor" Smith
Scott Sommers
Abby Stanglin
Elias Stern
Heather Stockslager
Dan Tague
Tanya
Champneys Taylor
Ali and Matt Tennant
Melissa Thaler
Diane Thomas
Nicky Thomas
Jo Tidbury
Mark Tidbury
Federico Tixi
Lucinda Treat
Jessica Trevelyan
Eve-lyn Turmail
Ellis Turner
Gabriel Vogt
W. Bedford Waters
Ellyn Weiss
John Wickstrom
Sean Wiggins
C. Scott Willis
Mary Sherman Willis
William Wiseman
Soung Wiser
Stefan Wood
Aaron Wright
Maura Wright
Amy Glengary Yang
Erin Yanke
Alicia Yates
Joan Yengo
Kevin Young
Ian Youngstrom
Andrea Zuraf

And anyone we may have forgotten.

CAPTIONS

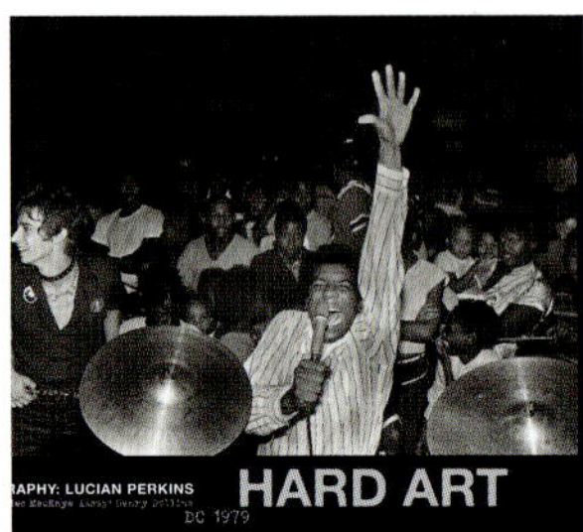

(Cover) HR, Valley Green Housing Complex, 9/9/79

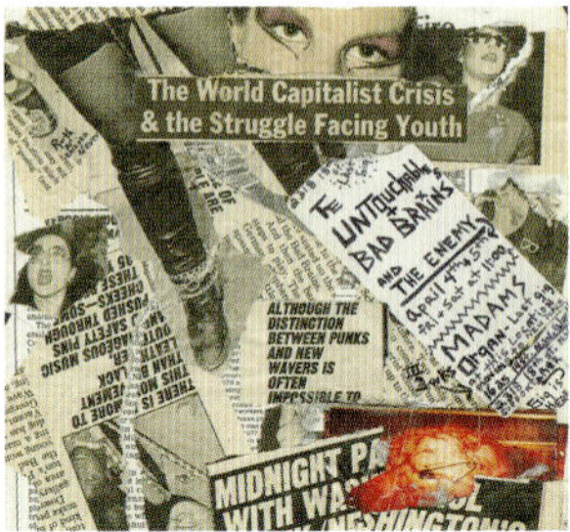

Washington Post article featuring Lucian Perkins' photographs, repurposed by HR

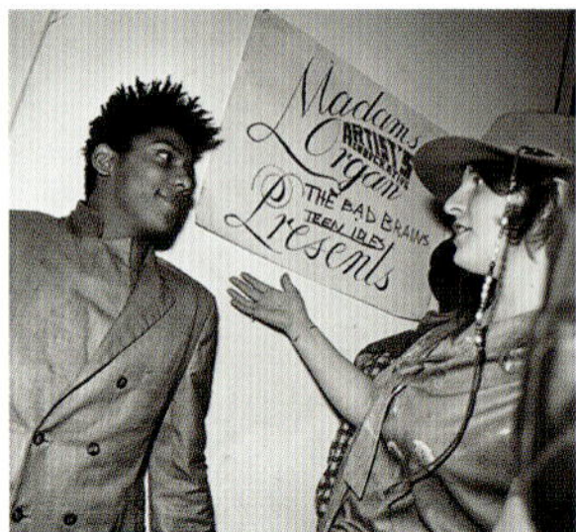

HR, Madams Organ, 1/25-26/80

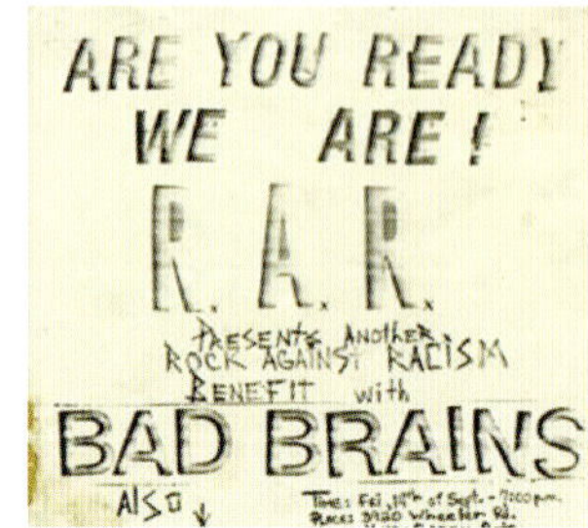

Bad Brains and Trenchmouth, Valley Green Housing Complex, 9/9/79

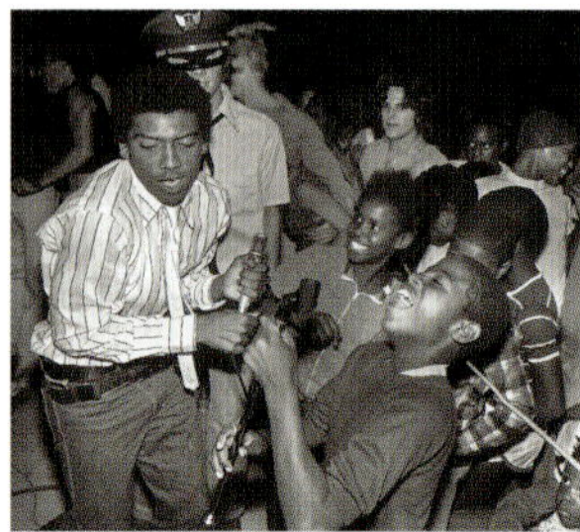

HR, Valley Green Housing Complex, 9/9/79

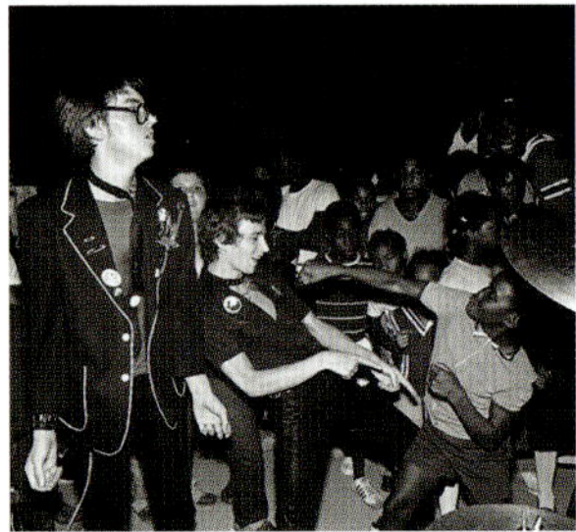

Sab Grey, Tommy Vacant, Tracey, Valley Green Housing Complex, 9/9/79

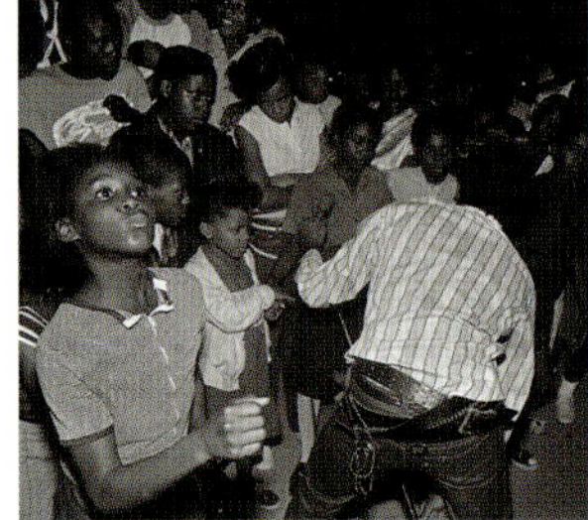

Bad Brains, Valley Green Housing Complex, 9/9/79

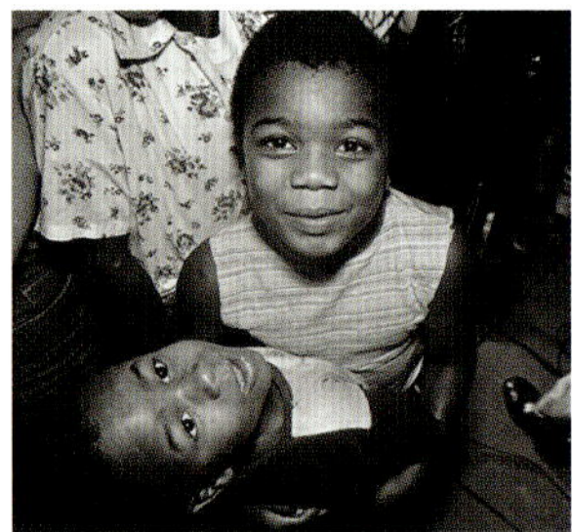

Kids, Valley Green Housing Complex, 9/9/79

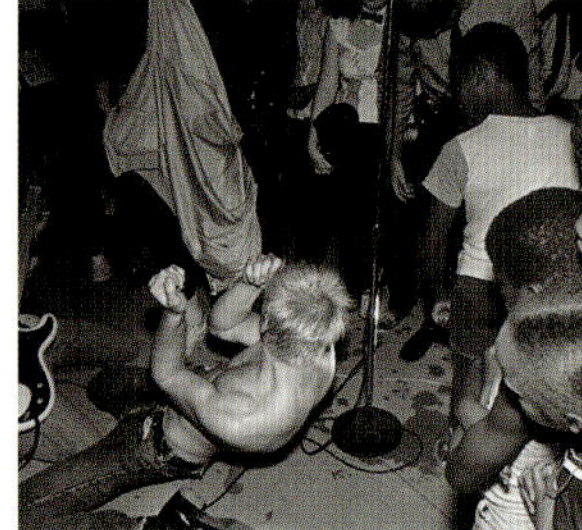

Charlie Danbury, Valley Green Housing Complex, 9/9/79

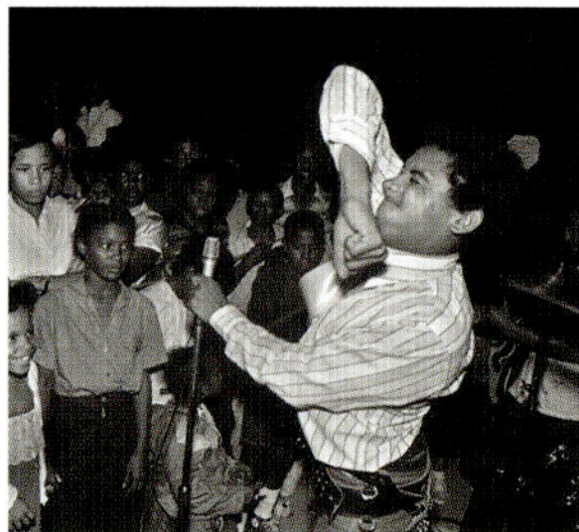

HR, Valley Green Housing Complex, 9/9/79

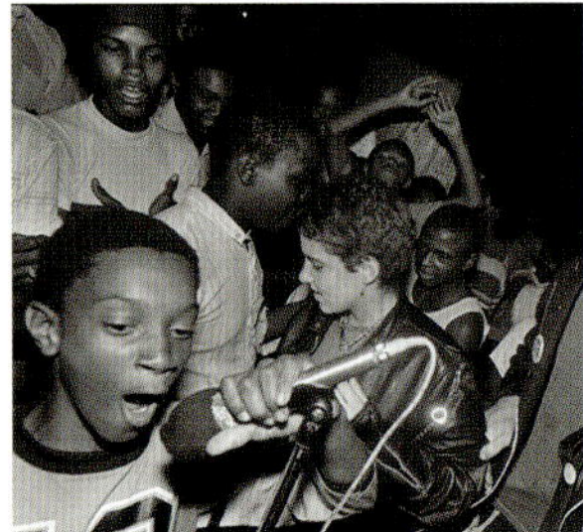

Audience, Valley Green Housing Complex, 9/9/79

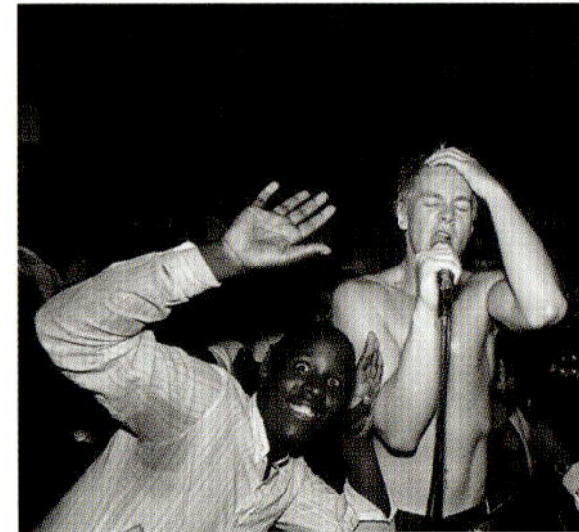

Kid and Charlie Danbury, Valley Green Housing Complex, 9/9/79

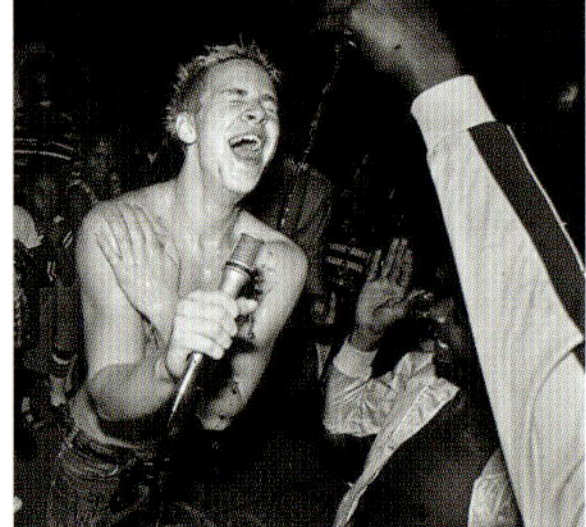

Charlie Danbury, Valley Green Housing Complex, 9/9/79

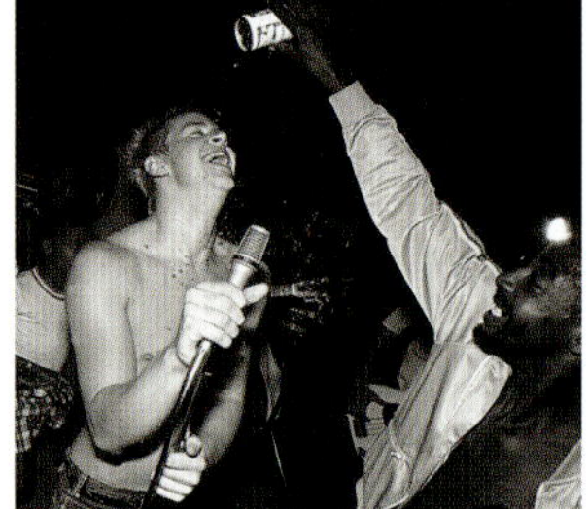

Charlie Danbury and Reds, Valley Green Housing Complex, 9/9/79

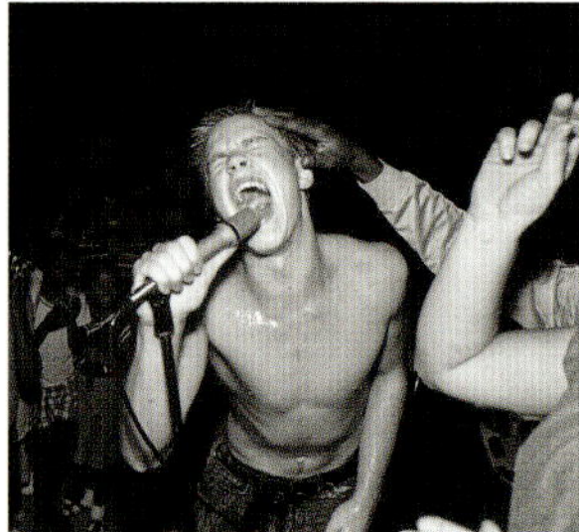

Charlie Danbury, Valley Green Housing Complex, 9/9/79

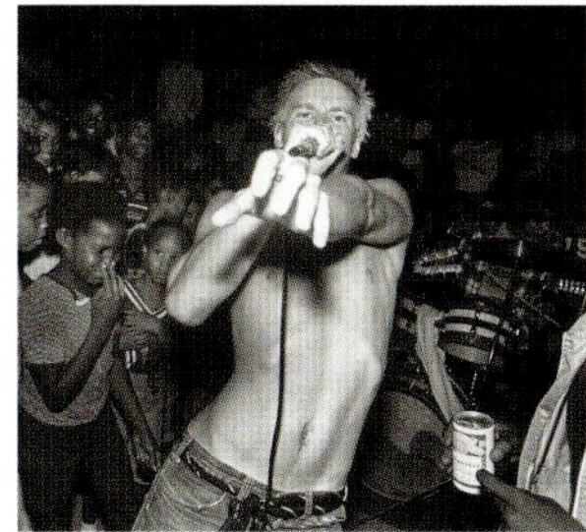
Charlie Danbury, Valley Green Housing Complex, 9/9/79

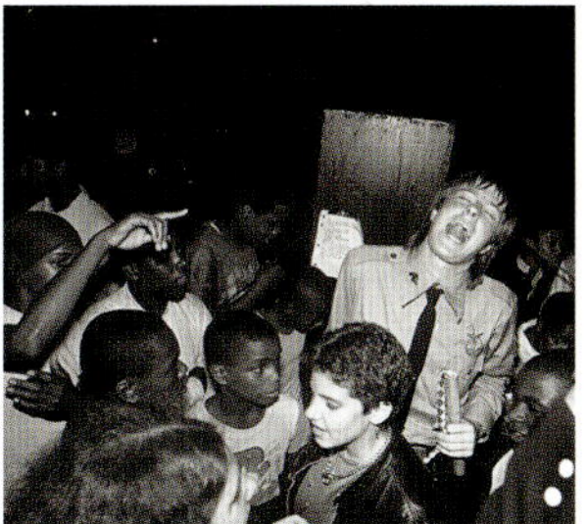
Audience, Valley Green Housing Complex, 9/9/79

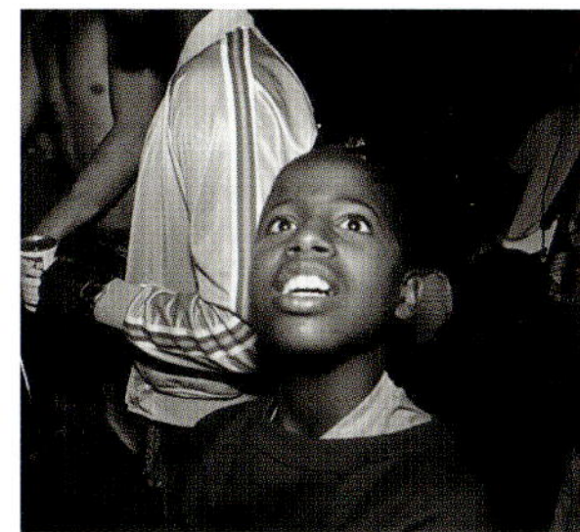
Alonzo, Valley Green Housing Complex, 9/9/79

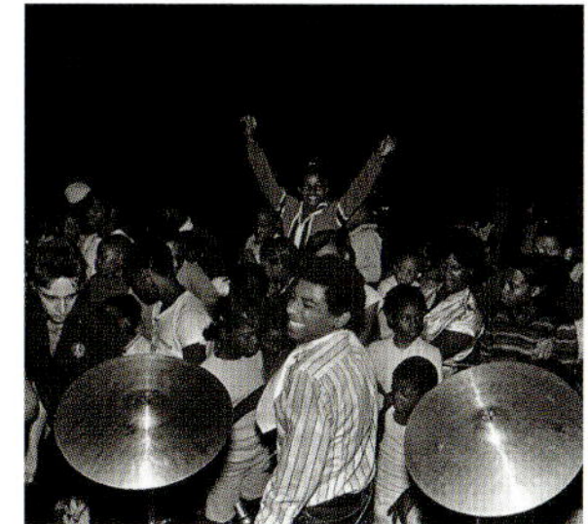
Bad Brains, Valley Green Housing Complex, 9/9/79

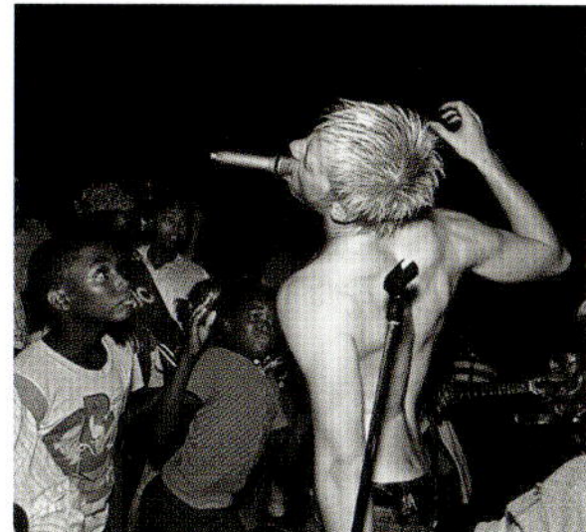
Charlie Danbury, Valley Green Housing Complex, 9/9/79

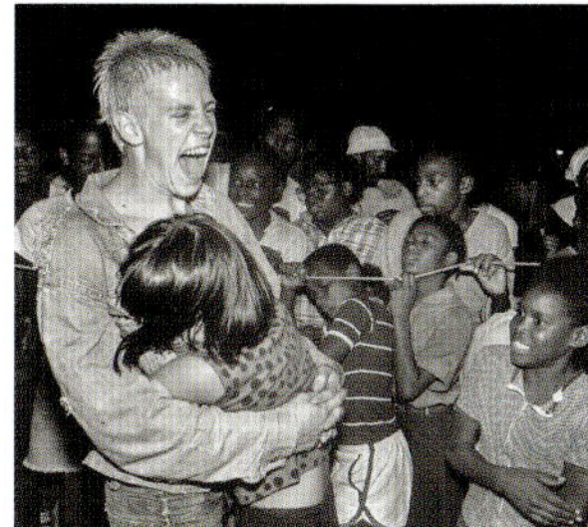
Charlie Danbury, Arlette, Tracey, Valley Green Housing Complex, 9/9/79

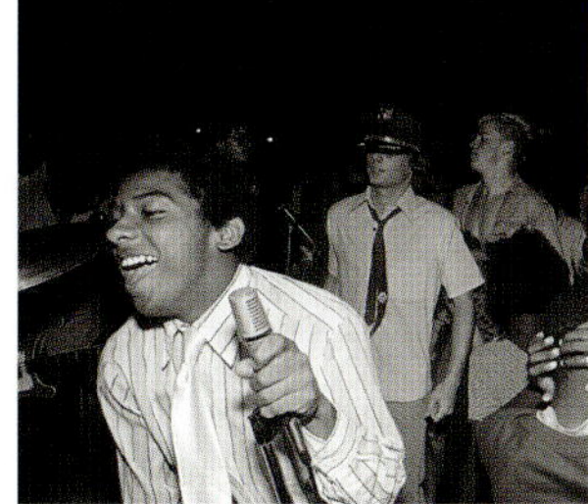
HR, Andy Hayes, Charlie Danbury, Valley Green Housing Complex, 9/9/79

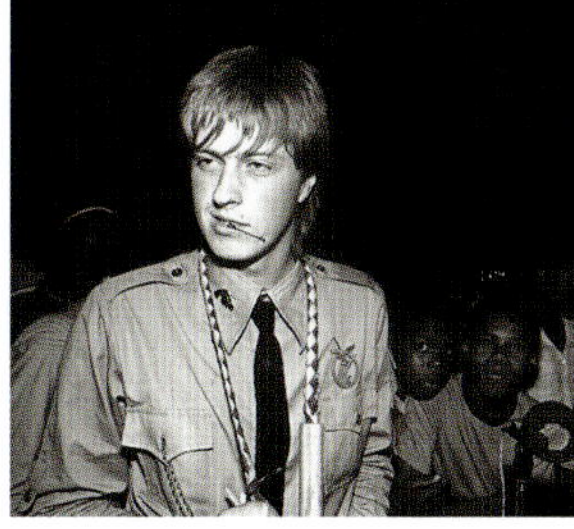
Punk rocker, Valley Green Housing Complex, 9/9/79

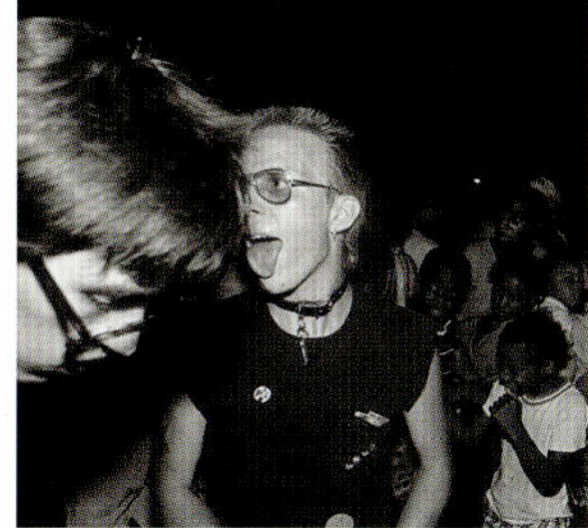
Sab Grey and Edd Jacobs, Valley Green Housing Complex, 9/9/79

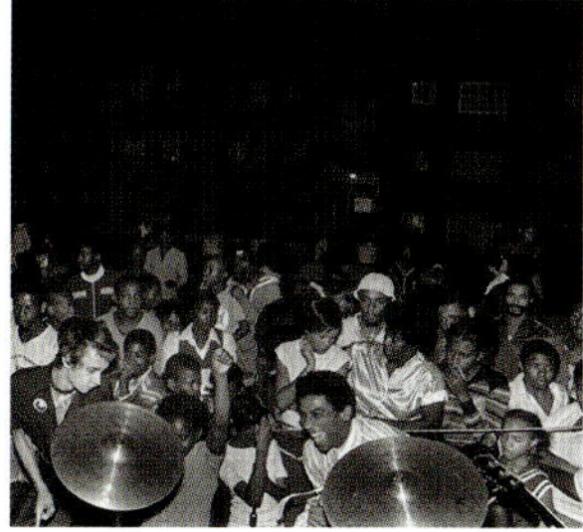
Bad Brains, Valley Green Housing Complex, 9/9/79

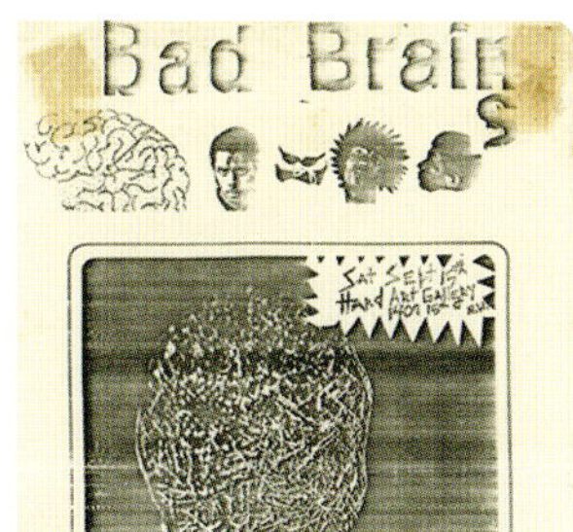

Bad Brains, The Slickee Boys, Hard Art Gallery, 9/15/79

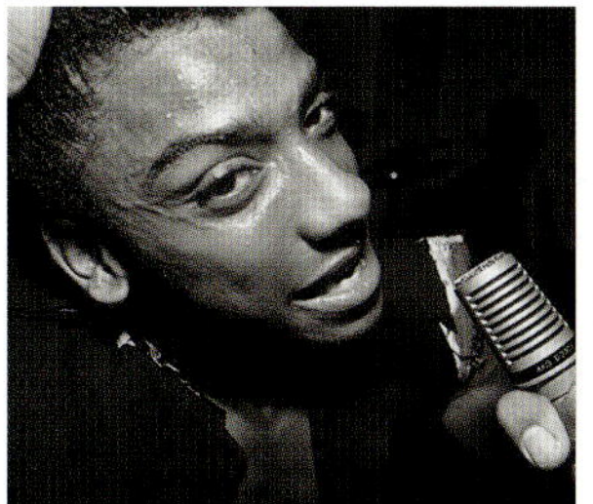
HR, Hard Art Gallery, 9/15/79

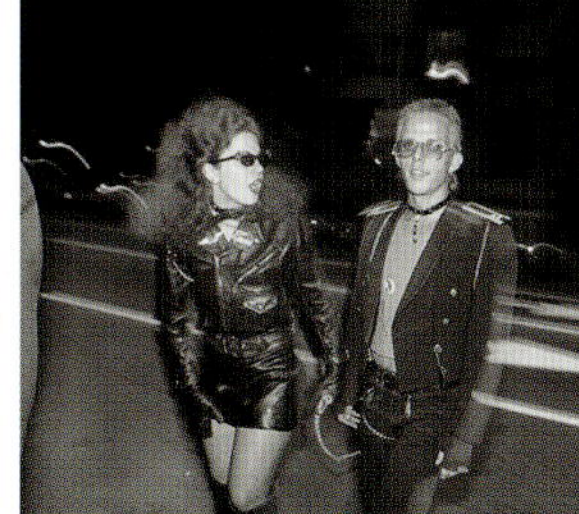
Ruth Gutekunst and Edd Jacobs, 15th and P Streets, 9/15/79

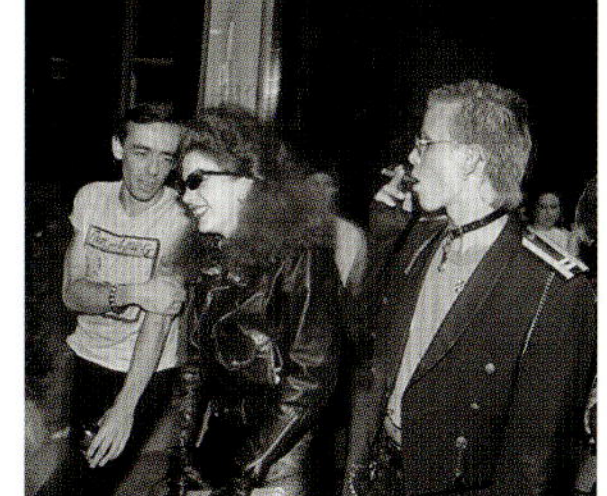
Nick English, Ruth Gutekunst, Edd Jacobs, 15th and P Streets, 9/15/79

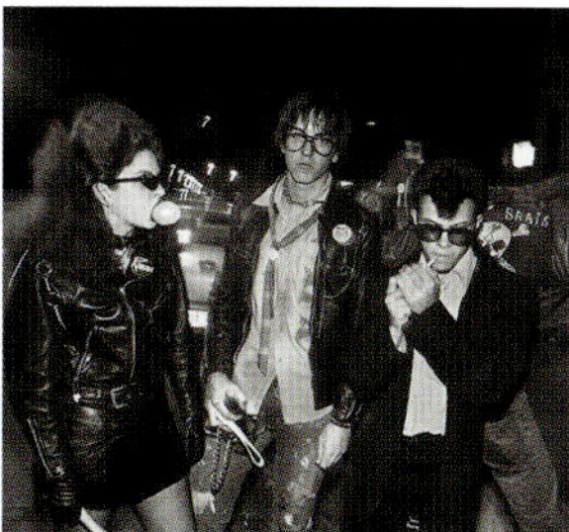
Ruth Gutekunst, Sab Grey, Scott Brown, Earl Hudson, 9/15/79

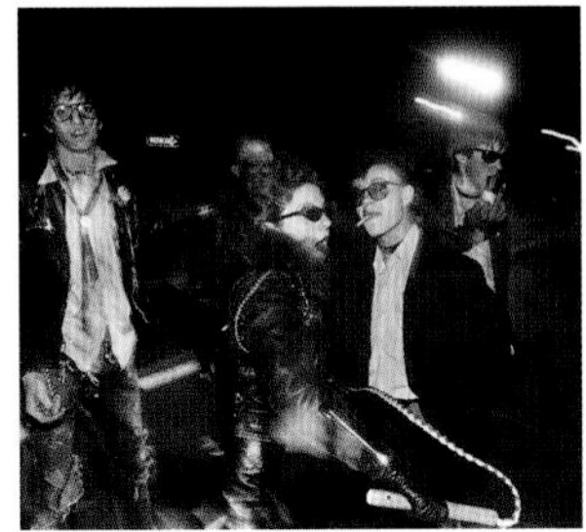

Ruth Gutekunst, Sab Grey, Scott Brown, Earl Hudson, 9/15/79

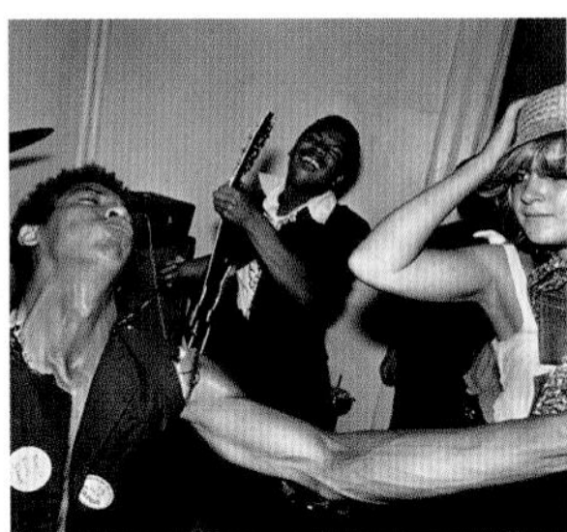

Bad Brains, Hard Art Gallery, 9/15/79

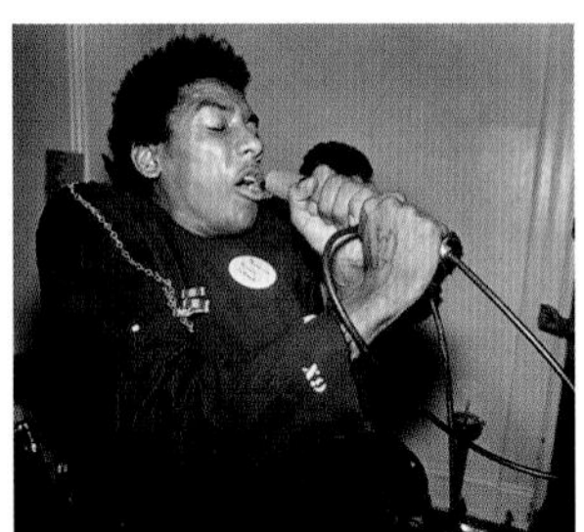

HR, Hard Art Gallery, 9/15/79

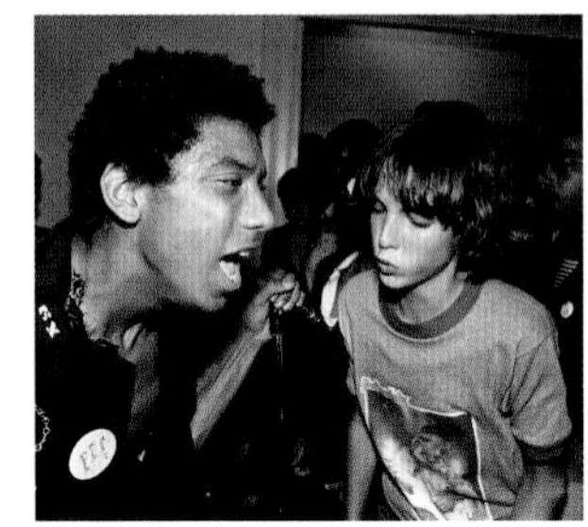

HR and Charley Davis, Hard Art Gallery, 9/15/79

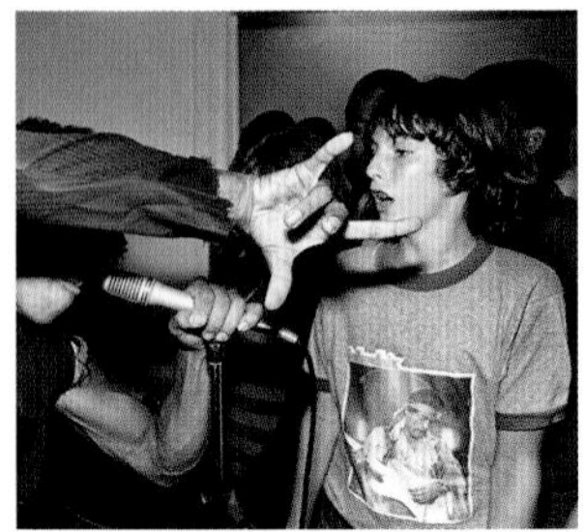

HR and Charley Davis, Hard Art Gallery, 9/15/79

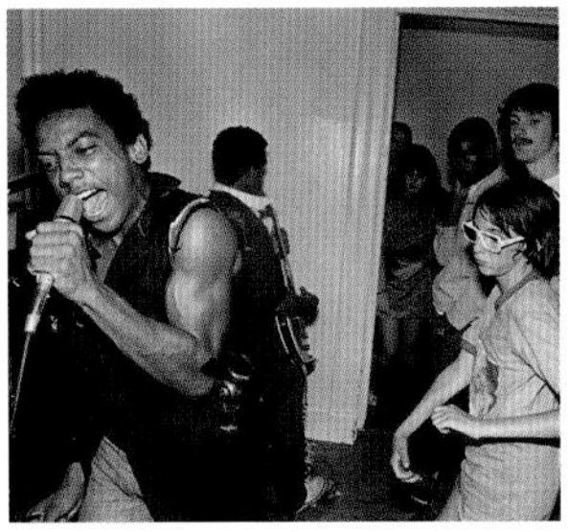

HR and Charley Davis, Hard Art Gallery, 9/15/79

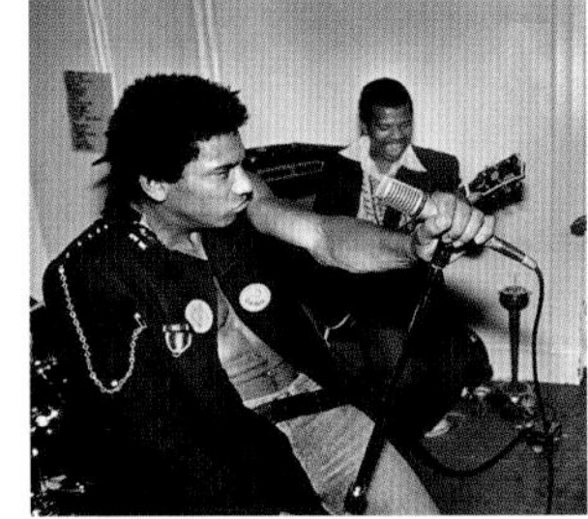

HR and Dr. Know, Hard Art Gallery, 9/15/79

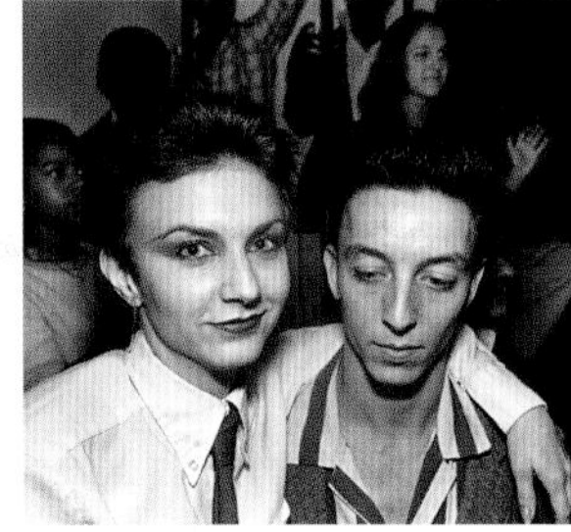

Deena and John Blessing, Hard Art Gallery, 9/15/79

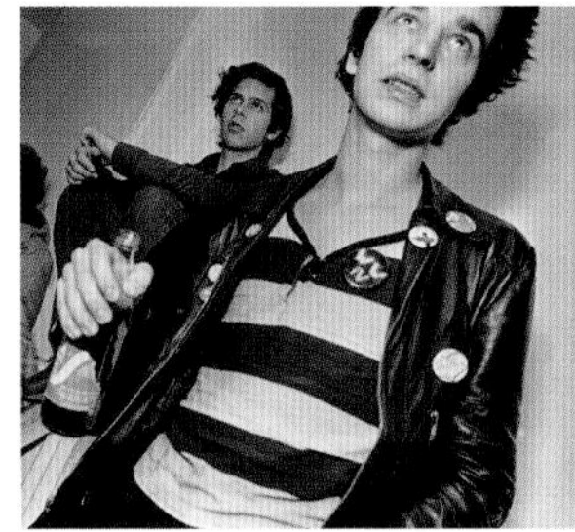

Tommy Vacant, Hard Art Gallery, 9/15/79

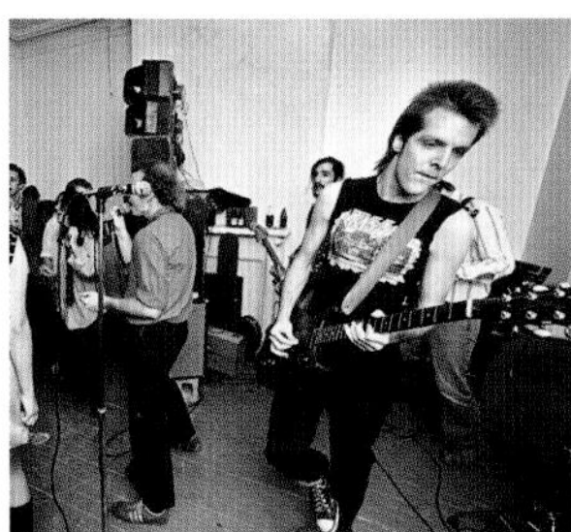

The Slickee Boys, Hard Art Gallery, 9/15/79

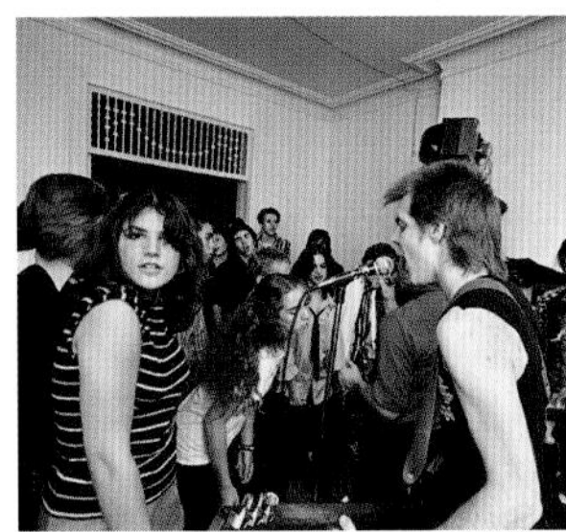

Anne Bonafede and Marshall Keith, Hard Art Gallery, 9/15/79

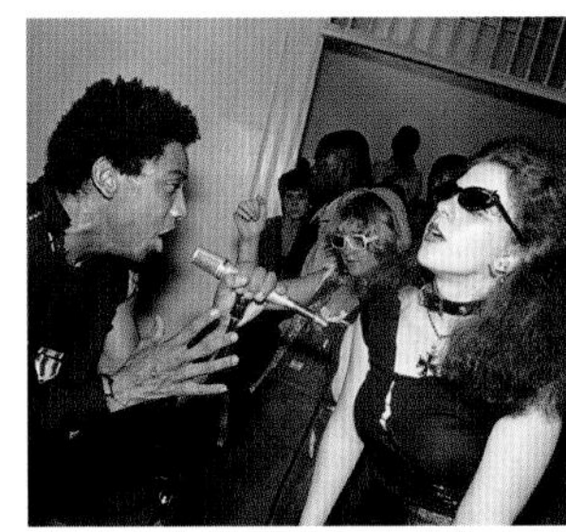

HR and Ruth Gutekunst, Hard Art Gallery, 9/15/79

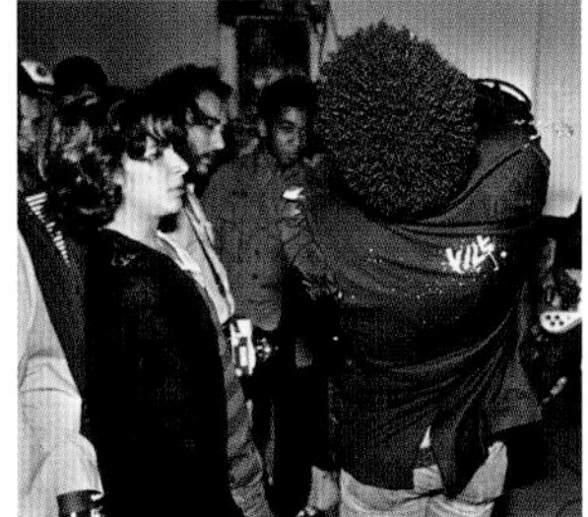

HR, Hard Art Gallery, 9/15/79

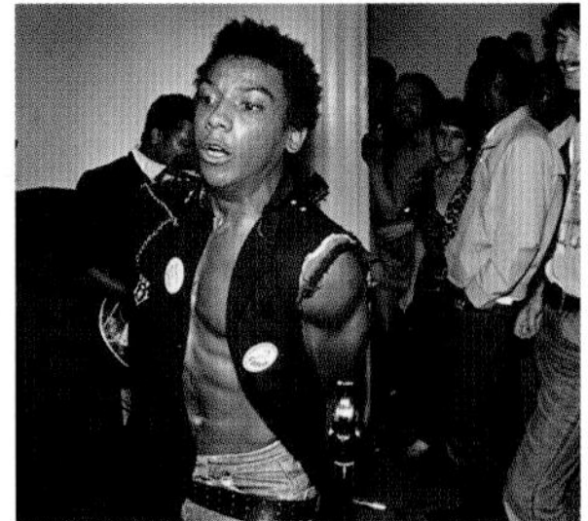

HR, Hard Art Gallery, 9/15/79

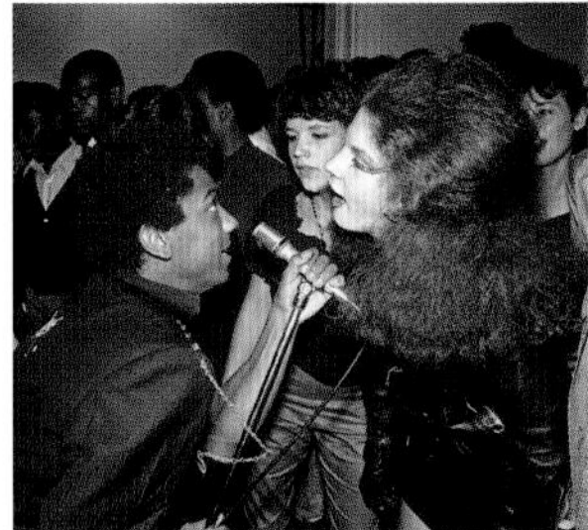

HR and Ruth Gutekunst, Hard Art Gallery, 9/15/79

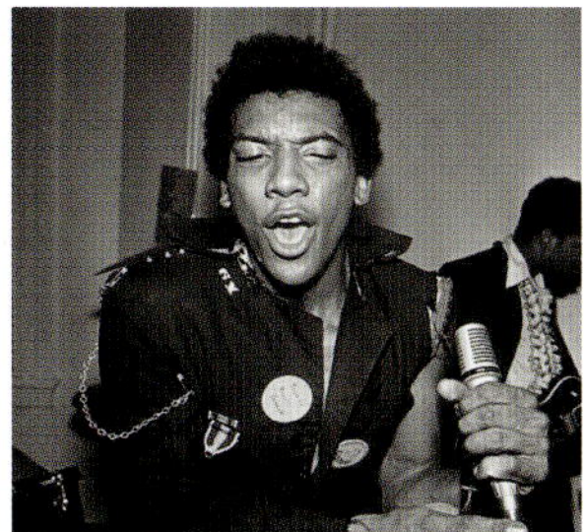

HR, Hard Art Gallery, 9/15/79

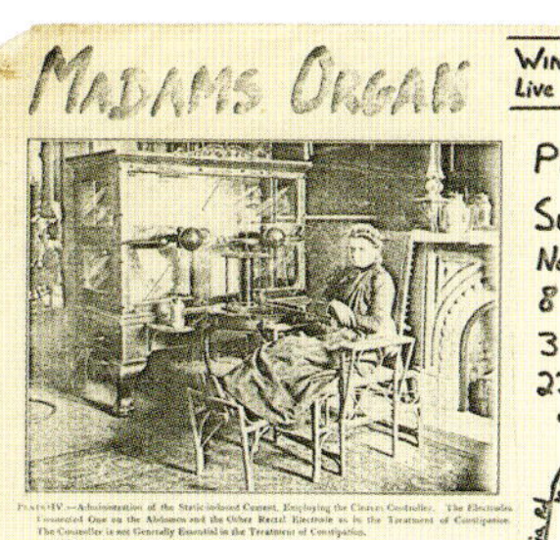

D.O.A., Trenchmouth, Tru Fax & the Insaniacs, Madams Organ, 11/11/79

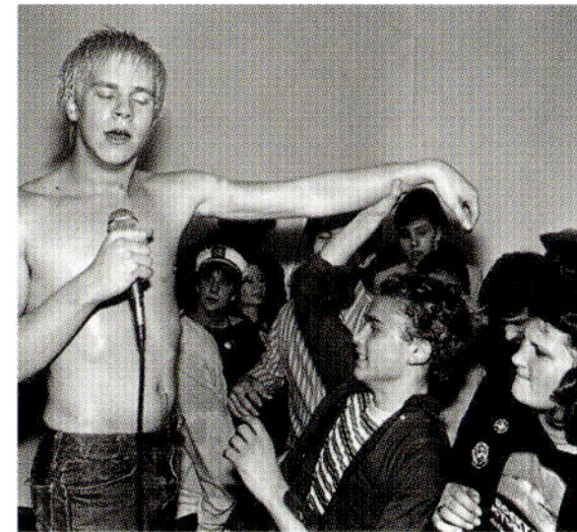

Charlie Danbury and Alec MacKaye, Madams Organ, 11/11/79

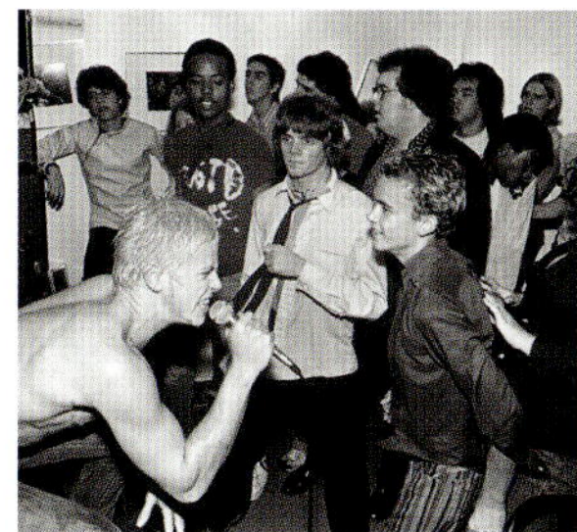

Charlie Danbury, Madams Organ, 11/11/79 (series of four photos)

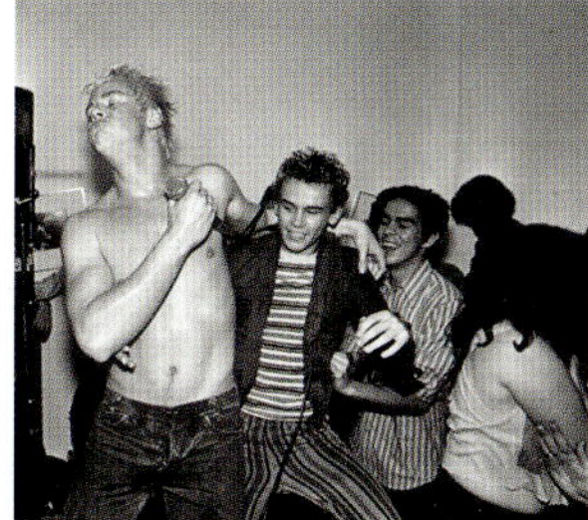

Charlie Danbury and Alec MacKaye, Madams Organ, 11/11/79

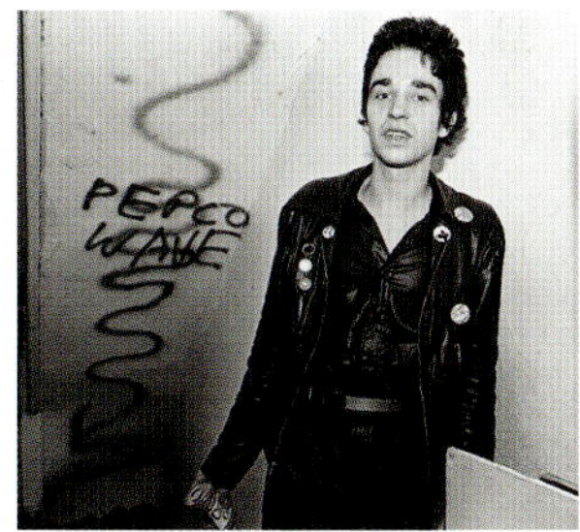

Tommy Vacant, Madams Organ, 11/11/79

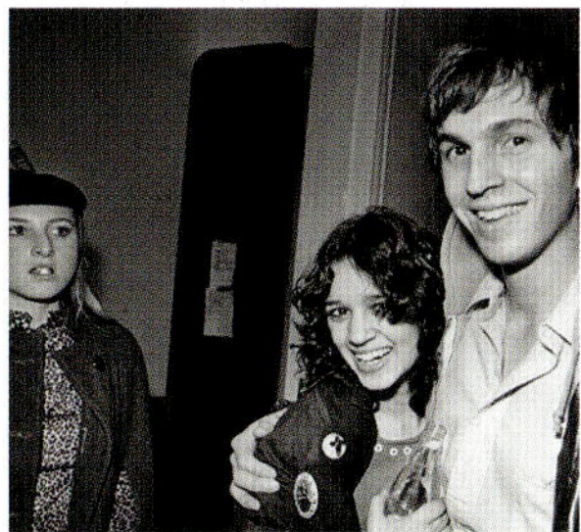

Kari Winter and Steve Carr, Madams Organ, 11/11/79

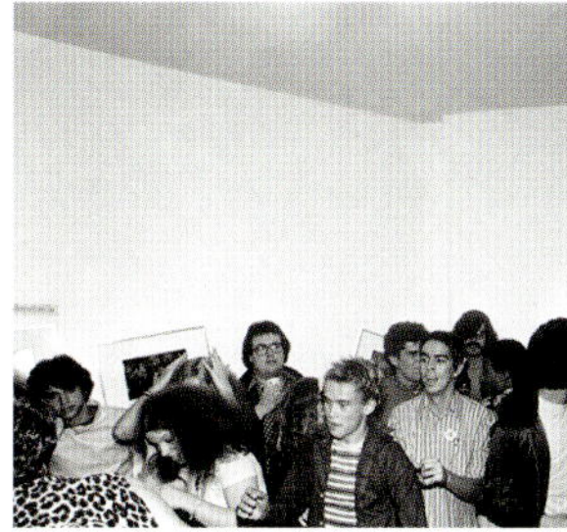

Trenchmouth crowd, Madams Organ, 11/11/79

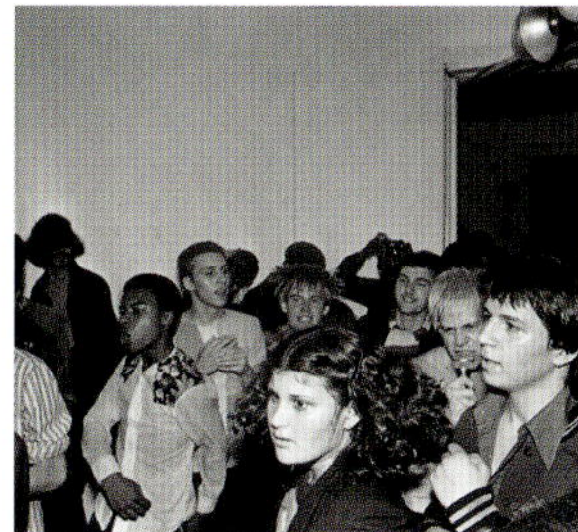

Trenchmouth crowd, Madams Organ, 11/11/79

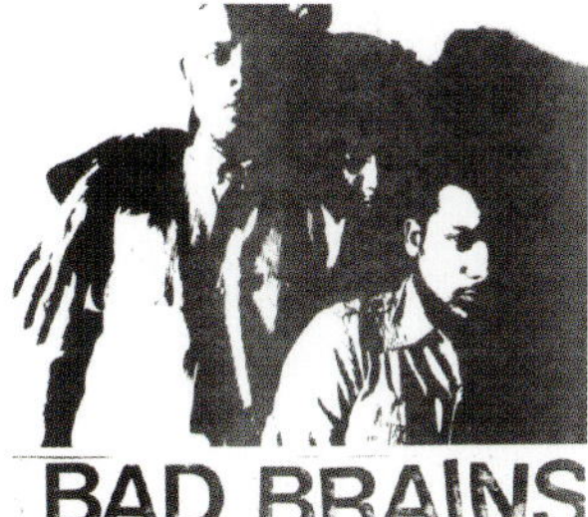

Bad Brains and The Teen Idles, Madams Organ, 1/25-26/80

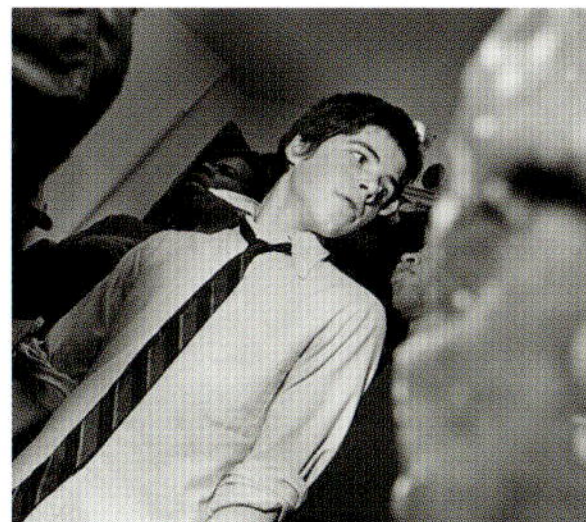

Eddie Janney, Madams Organ, 1/25-26/80

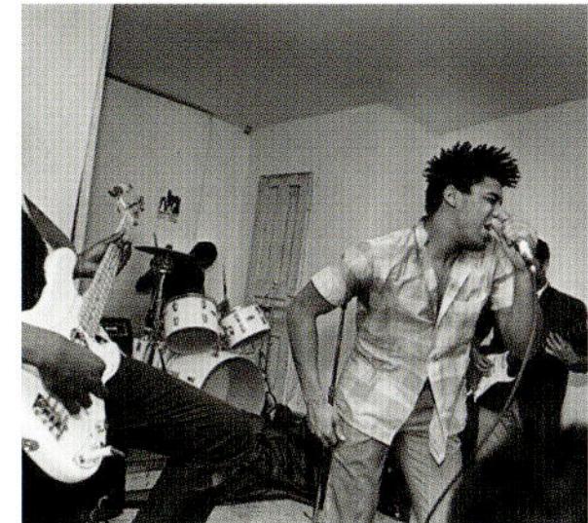

Bad Brains, Madams Organ, 1/25-26/80

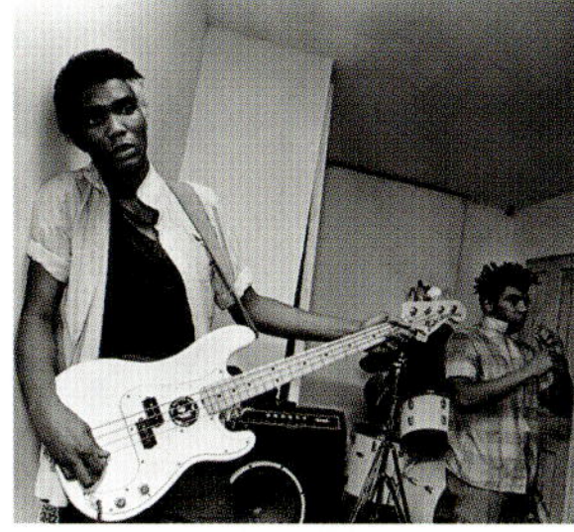

Darryl Jenifer, Madams Organ, 1/25-26/80

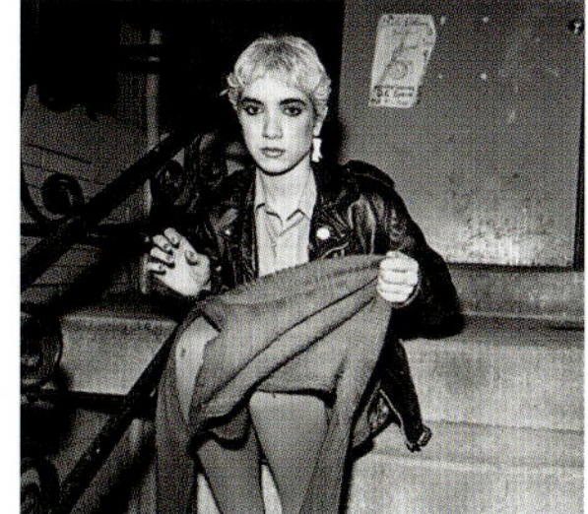

Vivien Greene, Madams Organ, 1/25-26/80

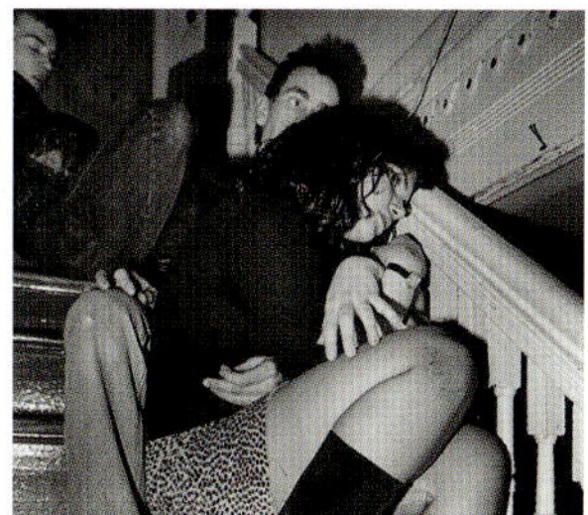

Ian MacKaye, Jeff Nelson, Anne Bonafede, Madams Organ, 1/25-26/80

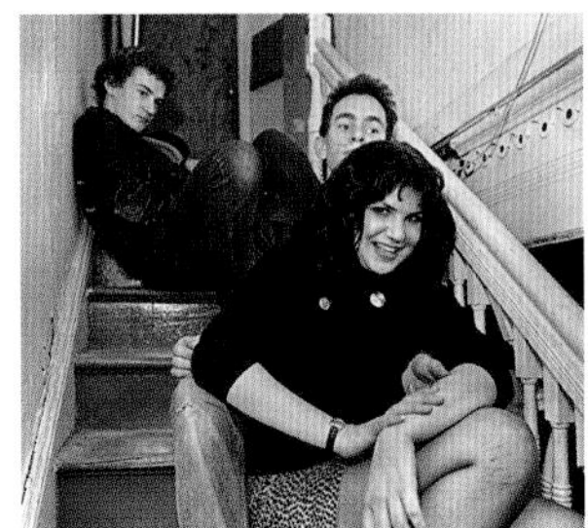
Ian MacKaye, Jeff Nelson, Anne Bonafede, Madams Organ, 1/25-26/80

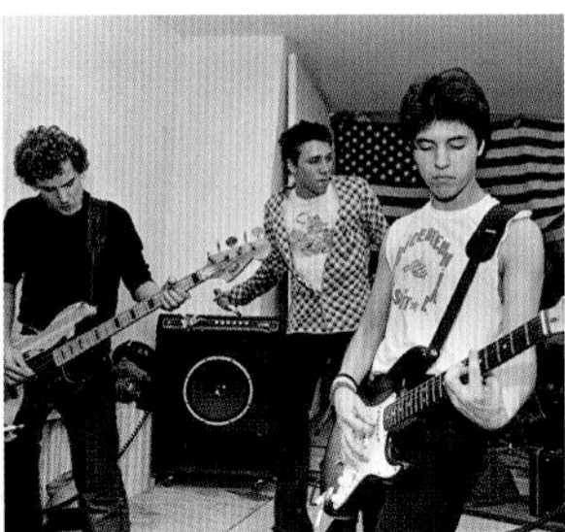
The Teen Idles, Madams Organ, 1/25-26/80

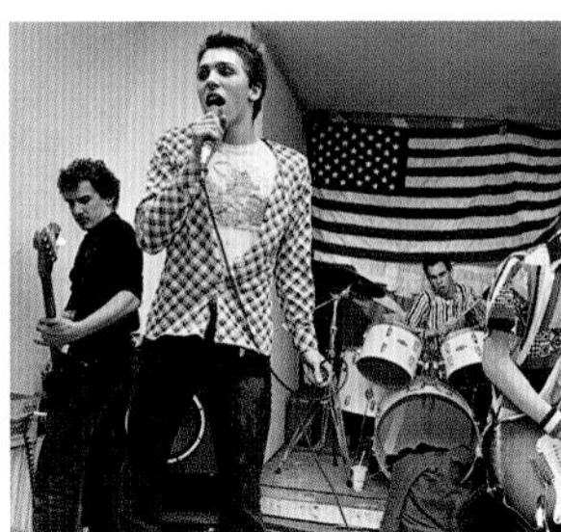
The Teen Idles, Madams Organ, 1/25-26/80

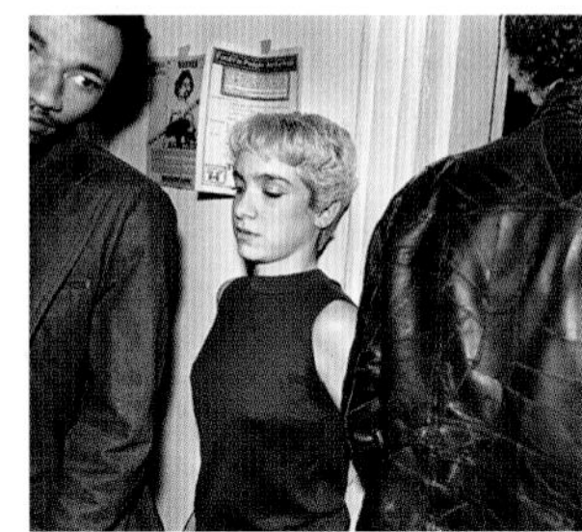
Vivien Greene, Madams Organ, 1/25-26/80

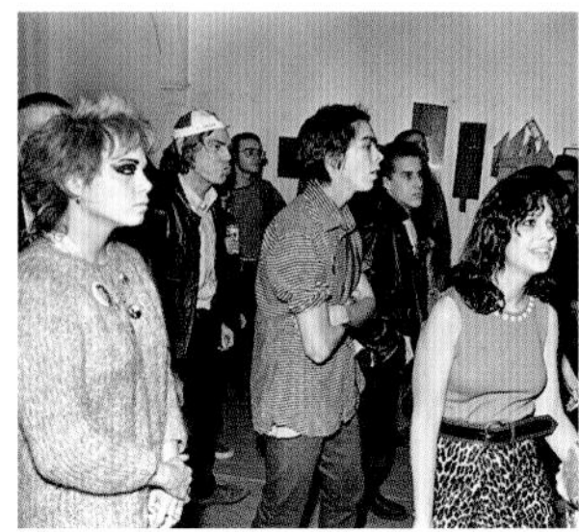
Ann Aptaker, Bert Queiroz, Mark Sullivan, Kari Winter, Madams Organ, 1/25-26/80

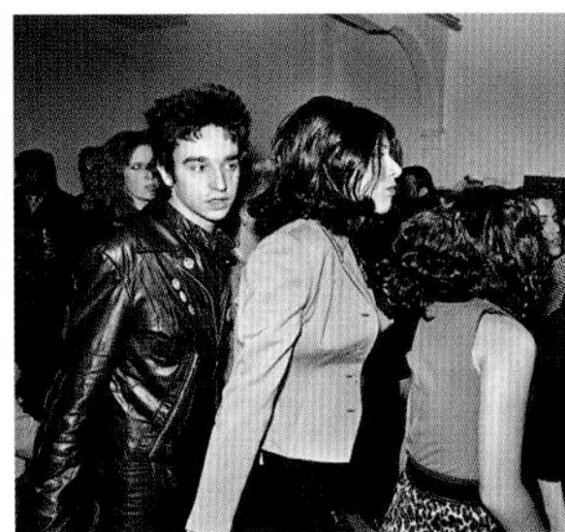
Tommy Vacant, Andrea Rashish, Kari Winter, Madams Organ, 1/25-26/80

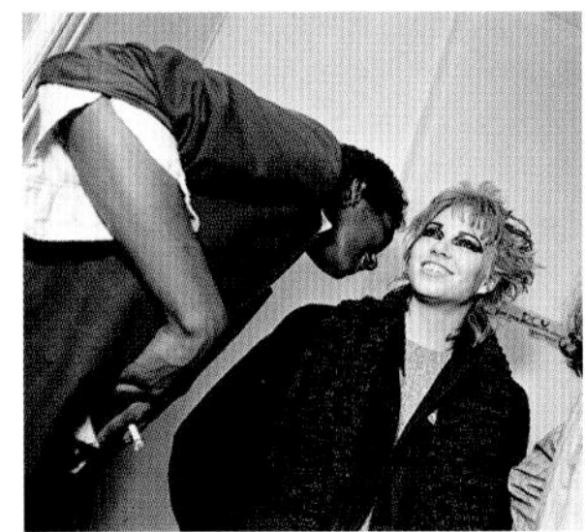
Darryl Jenifer, Ann Aptaker, Madams Organ, 1/25-26/80

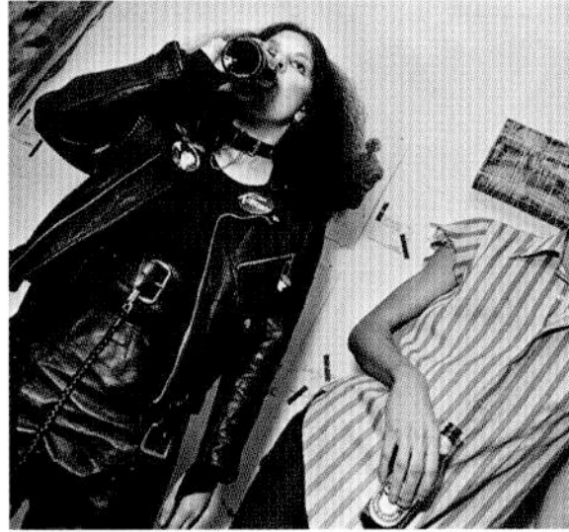
Ruth Gutekunst and Bruce Buelken, Madams Organ, 1/25-26/80

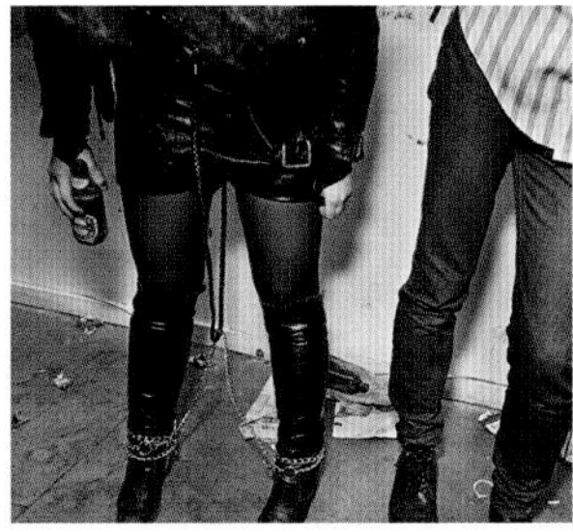
Ruth Gutekunst and Bruce Buelken, Madams Organ, 1/25-26/80

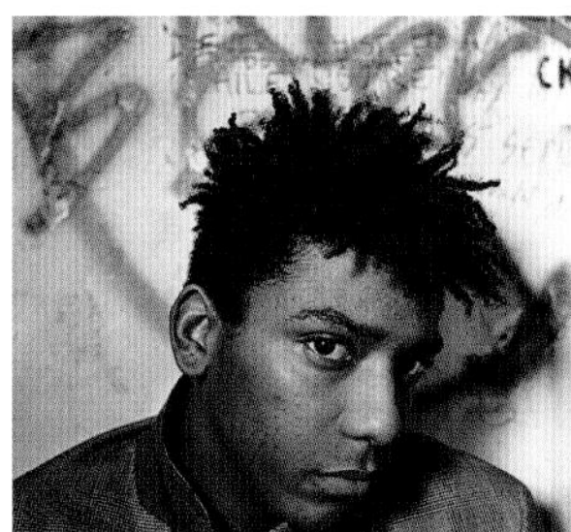
HR, Madams Organ, 1/25-26/80 (series of three photos)

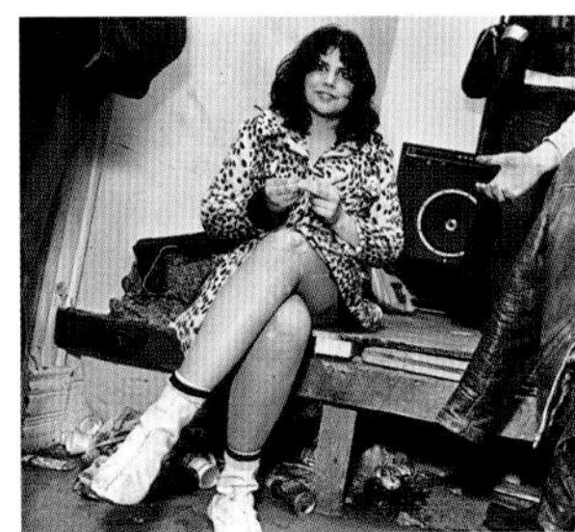
Anne Bonafede, Madams Organ, 1/25-26/80

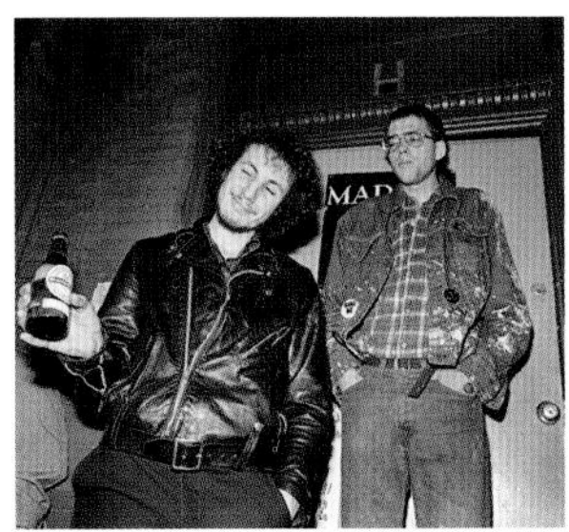
Russell Braen (back right), Madams Organ, 1/25-26/80

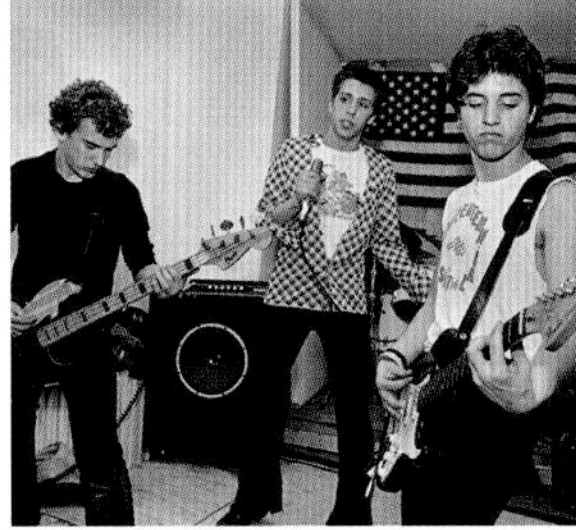
The Teen Idles, Madams Organ, 1/25-26/80

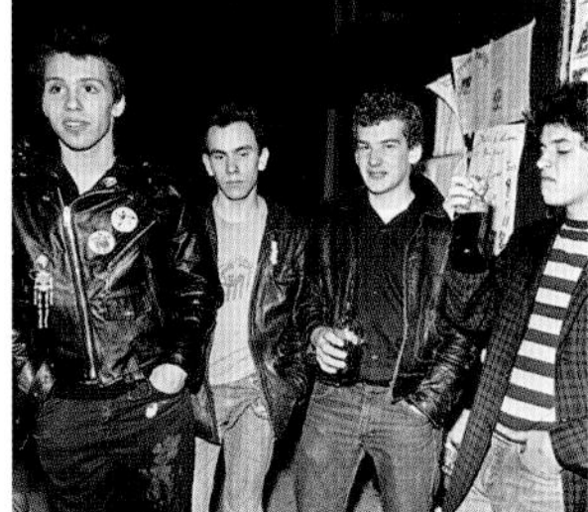
The Teen Idles l-r: Nathan Strejcek, Jeff Nelson, Ian MacKaye, Geordie Grindle 18th Street, Adams Morgan, 1/25-26/80

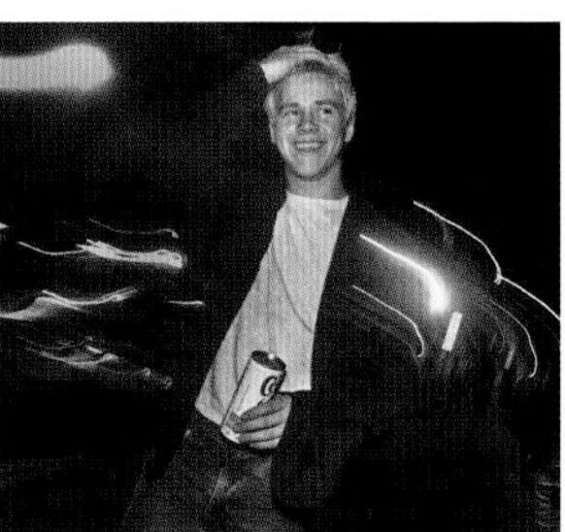
Charlie Danbury, outside of Ontario Theatre, 1979

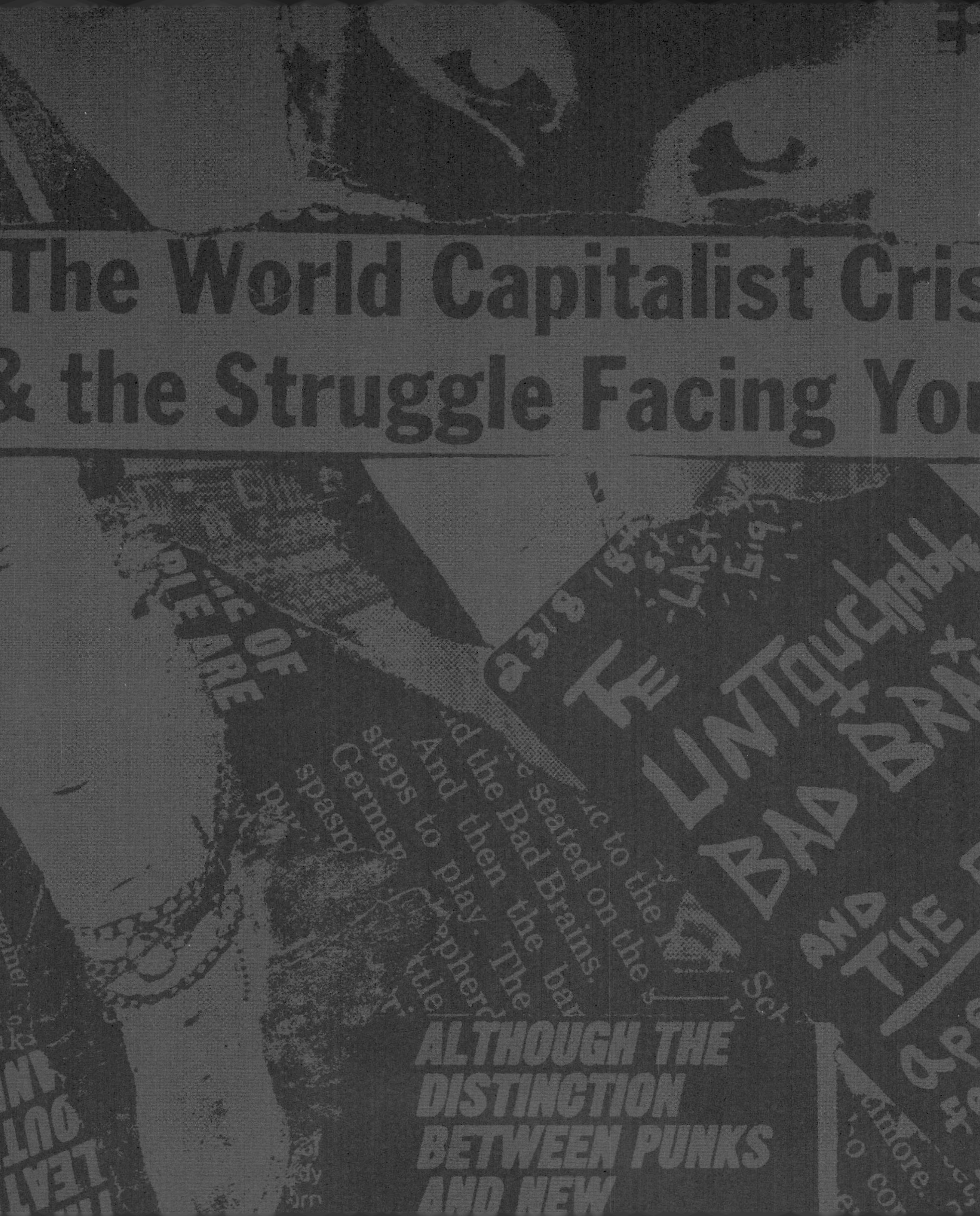
The World Capitalist Cris
& the Struggle Facing You
The Untouchables & Bad Brains
and the Bad Brains.
And then the ban
steps to play. The
ALTHOUGH THE
DISTINCTION
BETWEEN PUNKS
AND NEW